INDIGENOUS ECONOMICS

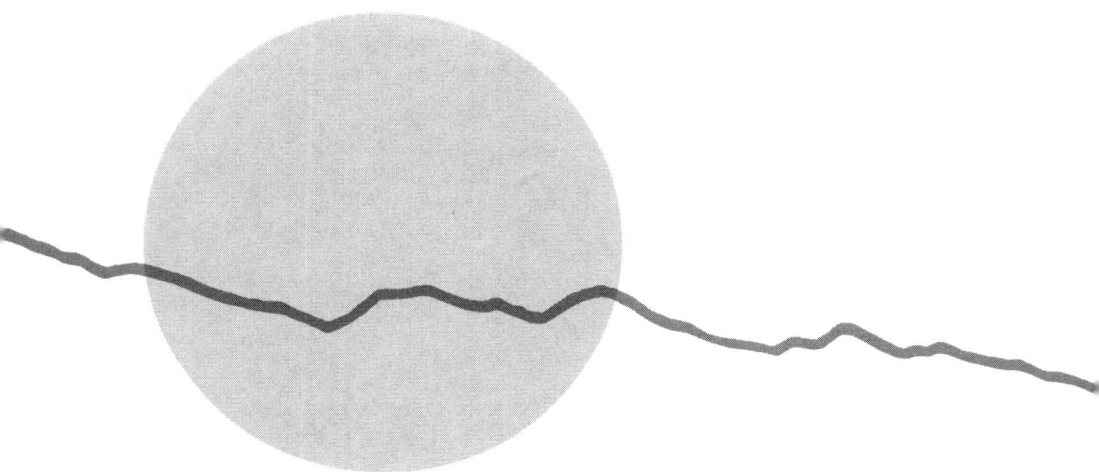

INDIGENOUS
ECONOMICS

Sustaining Peoples and Their Lands

RONALD L. TROSPER

THE UNIVERSITY OF
ARIZONA PRESS

TUCSON

The University of Arizona Press
www.uapress.arizona.edu

We respectfully acknowledge the University of Arizona is on the land and territories of Indigenous peoples. Today, Arizona is home to twenty-two federally recognized tribes, with Tucson being home to the O'odham and the Yaqui. Committed to diversity and inclusion, the University strives to build sustainable relationships with sovereign Native Nations and Indigenous communities through education offerings, partnerships, and community service.

ISBN-13: 978-0-8165-4661-9 (hardcover)
ISBN-13: 978-0-8165-3345-9 (paperback)
ISBN-13: 978-0-8165-4662-6 (ebook)

Cover design by Leigh McDonald
Typeset by Sara Thaxton in 10/14 Warnock Pro with Politica and Eurostile LT Std

Publication of this book is made possible in part by the Alfred P. Sloan Foundation Program in Public Understanding of Science.

Library of Congress Cataloging-in-Publication Data
Names: Trosper, Ronald L., author.
Title: Indigenous economics : sustaining peoples and their lands / Ronald L. Trosper.
Description: Tucson : University of Arizona Press, 2022. | Includes bibliographical references and index.
Identifiers: LCCN 2021060217 (print) | LCCN 2021060218 (ebook) | ISBN 9780816546619 (hardcover) | ISBN 9780816533459 (paperback) | ISBN 9780816546626 (ebook)
Subjects: LCSH: Economics—Sociological aspects. | Indigenous peoples—Economic conditions. | Ethnoecology. | Sustainability. | Sustainable development.
Classification: LCC HM548 .T758 2022 (print) | LCC HM548 (ebook) | DDC 305.8—dc23/eng/20211230
LC record available at https://lccn.loc.gov/2021060217
LC ebook record available at https://lccn.loc.gov/2021060218

Printed in the United States of America
♾ This paper meets the requirements of ANSI/NISO Z39.48-1992 (Permanence of Paper).

Dedicated to
Alexander Vernon
Stephen Hocker

In Memory of
David D. Trosper
1951–2015
Dorothy M. Trosper
1920–2013
Thurman H. Trosper
1917–2007
Henrietta Blueye
1947–1982

CONTENTS

PREFACE AND ACKNOWLEDGMENTS

This book explores the implications of relationality for economic analysis. For Indigenous people, relationality applies in a world in which all beings are conscious, implying equality among humans, nonhumans, and more-than-humans. The search for a unifying theme or fundamental principles for Indigenous economics was difficult, a journey I would like to briefly describe here.

Of course, the answer is obvious within the field of Indigenous studies. Leanna Betasamosake Simpson (2017) centers her analysis on relationality, as do many others (S. Wilson 2008; McGregor 2014; Whyte et al. 2017). The answer is not obvious for a person trained in economics, even one such as myself who recognizes the importance of reciprocity motivated by generosity. The field of economics developed in a culture that praised individualism as an antidote to the domination of people by monarchs and religion in Europe. From my awareness of Indigenous culture, I knew that both generosity and individual autonomy are highly valued. Respecting individual autonomy is evident historically, especially in the prominence of the variety of sexual orientations reported during the early colonial period and subsequently (Roscoe 1988, 1998; Jacobs, Thomas, and Lang 1997; Driskill et al. 2011; Morgensen 2011). I eventually learned that individual autonomy also was a characteristic of relational societies.

When I set out to write what in this work is chapter 5, I wanted to emphasize the use of generosity and reciprocity to solve common pool dilemmas. I found explaining two issues to be difficult: Why would people be generous, and why would people set up systems that required reciprocity such as that

I had studied on the Northwest Coast? I decided to examine relationality to see if that known characteristic of Indigenous society could help. Indeed, it could. I had been reading Margaret Archer's work and used it in an article that described how the idea of emergence was shared between many ecological models and her sociological ones (Trosper 2005). I had also liked her four volumes on persons and agency (Archer 2000a, 2003, 2007, 2012). After I had submitted my book proposal, she and Pieropolo Donati published *The Relational Subject* (Donati and Archer 2015). The two authors, by combining their work, emphasized the importance of relational goods. By using that analysis, I could place relationality at the core of the analysis. Another helpful source was the short chapter by Hoyt L. Edge (1998), cited by Marina J. Apgar et al. (2015), which explained why relational societies more strongly support individualism than do the societies that produced standard economic theory.

Once I had reorganized the book to put relationality first, chapter 5 became easier to write. I was able to provide an answer to a similar problem that had bedeviled Elinor Ostrom in explaining why the operators of a common pool resource adopted the principles that she identified with her comparative method. Chapter 6, on leadership, and chapter 7, on entrepreneurship, both benefited from using the relational approach. Even with these improvements, the first draft of the book did not fully use the relational viewpoint. Three reviewers of the first draft each in their own way noted the weaknesses, and one of them suggested a major reorganization of the book, which proved very helpful. I thank Paul Boyer for giving me the opportunity to summarize the key ideas of this book in *Native Science Report* (Trosper 2019a).

My original attention to reciprocity had resulted from my previous writing, which in turn had developed as I pursued my career. My Harvard PhD dissertation was about the impact of settler colonialism on income on my reservation, the Confederated Salish and Kootenai Tribes of the Flathead Indian Reservation, Montana. The application of the allotment policy in 1910 had serious impacts on per capita income in 1970 because the settlers had taken so much wealth in land. When I started to teach courses on American Indian economic development in my first job as an assistant professor, at the University of Washington in 1974, the literature was very thin, written primarily by social scientists other than economists. The small band of young economists who wrote dissertations on economic topics about the time I wrote my dissertation moved on to other fields. Partly out of frustration about the lack of data and the paucity of the literature in economics, in 1982

I left university employment to work for the Council of Energy Resource Tribes and then my own tribe. I hoped that I would both learn much more about Indigenous economic issues as well as be able to return to academics. Working for my tribe was particularly useful and provided me understanding of contemporary governance challenges on reservations.

I took some time to start submitting papers again. Fortunately, the School of Forestry at Northern Arizona University was interested in my work. I joined that faculty in 1989. I studied forestry economics from an Indigenous viewpoint. I began to learn a great deal about ecology and forest ecology from my forestry colleagues. I experienced working in a truly interdisciplinary college at a university that valued Indigenous knowledge. I also learned from the tribes with whom we worked, primarily San Carlos Apache, Navajo, White Mountain Apache, Menominee, and the Pueblos of northern New Mexico. Graduates of the program came back to help current undergraduates learn that to speak up in class was not being aggressive. The National Science Foundation, the Ford Foundation, and the Department of Agriculture funded programs to support the students in many ways.

While I worked for my tribe, I learned why the elders objected to the construction of Kerr Dam on the site of a large waterfall at the mouth of Flathead Lake: the waterfall was a living being that deserved respect. There could have been other objections, such as blocking the migration of fish in and out of the lake. As we argued with the Montana Power Company about how the dam was operated, the ecological impacts of the dam were very important. The Tribal Council of the Confederated Salish and Kootenai Tribes easily decided that the 10 percent of income from the dam due to using it as a peaking facility was not worth the ecological damage on the seventy-two miles of river below the dam, and council members voted for a baseload operation. Restoring the rapids to life was no longer possible.

After this experience, and the subsequent forestry studies at Northern Arizona University, I decided to write the article "Traditional American Indian Economic Policy" to explain why American Indians treat their lands differently when they have the power to do so (Trosper 1995). Shortly after writing that article, I realized than the potlatch system on the Northwest Coast was an obvious and simple solution to the fishermen's dilemma resulting from unregulated access to a common pool resource. This led to a successful application for a Pew Fellowship in Conservation and the Environment and a series of papers. The Pew funding allowed me to investigate further during a sabbatical, with visits to people in British Columbia, especially the Nisga'a, who were able to teach me a great deal about how they cared for salmon and themselves. This led to *Resilience, Reciprocity and Ecological Economics: Northwest Coast Sustainability* (Trosper 2009). The title was designed to have the book show up with keyword searches, but it still hasn't been a best seller. The book argues that reciprocity can solve social dilemmas such as those that exist with common pool resources. It explains how social institutions supported sharing the wealth generated by the salmon fishery. I very much appreciated the invitation from the Canadian Society for Ecological Economics; Nicolas Kosoy and the student organizers invited me to be a keynote speaker at their conference Engaging Economics of Change in 2019.

The 1995 article had stressed culture and values as important for understanding American Indian economic policy. Although I was aware of Marshall Sahlins's work on the primacy of culture, particularly his *Culture and Practical Reason* (1976), I still was not fully satisfied with reconciling the influence of culture with the influence of material matters. Wandering through the library stacks at Northern Arizona University, I came across Archer's *Culture and Agency* (1996). That intriguing title meant I had to check it out. Here was an integrated view of culture, structure, and agency that I found satisfying. I began to read her work and those of other critical realists such as Douglas Porpora (2015). Archer recommends a recursive approach to the dynamic analysis that would be the next step in analysis of relational systems.

Throughout this journey, many people have helped me. Since this is my capstone book, I am thanking all the people who made studying Indigenous people and thought so interesting, fascinating, enjoyable, and productive.

I first want to thank my husbands, Alexander Vernon and Stephen Hocker. They have supported my work even as it seemed I ignored them when so focused on this book they had to yell to get my attention.

My two PhD advisors, Kenneth Arrow and Albert Hirschman, were excellent role models. I had a heavy dose of skepticism about economics while in graduate school from Samuel Bowles and Stephen Marglin, whose subsequent work has been very helpful. I learned about the importance of respect from Joanne Bigcrane and Thompson Smith while studying the impact of a hydroelectric dam on my reservation, a position reinforced by the White Mountain Apache Tribe when they objected to disrespectful treatment of trees that were cut down, measured, but not taken to the mill in the process of research on tree growth.

Once I started studying the potlatch system, a great many people helped. First was support and annual meetings of the Pew Fellows in Conservation and the Environment funded by the Pew Charitable Trusts. I met and learned from other scholars, such as Mac Chapin, Marcus Colchester, Carl Folke, Robert Johannes, Gary Nabhan, and Bernard Nietschman. With support from Pew, I was able to spend time at the Newberry Library and use its fabulous library on American Indians. Many people taught me about Indigenous people on the Northwest Coast: Keith Atkinson, Beverly Bird, Russell Collier, Kii7iljuus (Barbara J. Wilson), Charles Menzies, Gary Merkel, Debbie Miller, Antonia Mills, Deanna Nyce, Evelyn Pinkerton, Gordon Prest, Teresa Ryan, Anne Marie Sam, Terry Teegee, Nancy Turner, and Martin Weinstein.

I have been active in the Traditional Ecological Section of the Ecological Society of America, where I appreciated the contributions of Jesse Ford, Robin Wall Kimmerer, Frank Lake, Mimi Lam, Dennis Martinez, Teresa Newberry, Raymond Pierotti, Enrique Salmón, and Michelle Stevens.

I enjoyed my time teaching in the Faculty of Forestry at the University of British Columbia (UBC), where I met and learned from Gary Bull, George Hoberg, John Innes, Bruce Larson, Paul Lawson, John Lewis, Thomas Maness, Harry Nelson, John Nelson, William Nikolakis. Pamela Perrault, David Tindall, and Paul Wood.

I also learned from students at UBC, whether I chaired or served on their committees: Lisa Ambus, Justin Barnes, Janice Barry, Kyle Bateson, Jeremy Boyd, Ajith Chandran, Jason Forsyth, Tom Green, Angeline Gough, Garth Greskiw, Nigel Haggan, Andrea Holly Kennedy, In Ae Kim, Edison Lee-Johnson, Andrea Lyall, Nancy MacPherson, Jessica Rogers, Monika Singh, Lori Sparrow, Sinclair Tedder, Joleen Timko, and Sarah Weber. The Social Sciences and Humanities Research Council funded Kyle Bateson's work with the Missanabie Cree. Our advisory committee helped greatly in designing the Q survey of the people in the First Nation, who have finally acquired some land as promised.

My students and I had research projects with the Adams Lake Indian Band, Carrier-Sekani Tribal Council, Esketemc First Nation, Katzie First Nation, Nisga'a Nation, Sliammon First Nation, Stellat'en First Nation, Sts'ailes First Nation, and Ulkatcho First Nation.

I was on a committee of the National Research Council to study the Community Development Quota Program for providing Alaska Natives access to a share of the Bering Sea fishery. I particularly liked meeting Marshall Sahlins and Steve Langdon, who taught me much about Inuit and other Alaskan Natives.

The Canadian Sustainable Forest Management Network (SFMN) provided funding and introduction to the many people who taught me about Indigenous peoples in Canada: Fikret Berkes, Luc Bouthillier, Iain Davidson-Hunt, Peter Duinker, Shaski Kant, Henry Lickers, David Natcher, Peggy Smith, Marc Stevenson, Adrian Tanner, and Stephen Wyatt.

The SFMN provided me a stipend that funded travel when John Parrotta organized a task force on Traditional Forest Related Knowledge for the International Union of Forest Research Organizations that exposed me to traditional thought around the world. He invited me to help edit the book we produced (Parrotta and Trosper 2012). The final chapter of the book answers the question, "How can traditional knowledge change and still remain traditional?" The answer, provided by a consensus of the authors of the chapters in the book, is that those who maintain their traditional knowledge do so in the midst of change by limiting market exchange and by maintaining the goal of sustainability, their relationships to land, their systems of reciprocity, and their identity. I have used that answer throughout this book, while placing relationality at the core of explaining why those features are maintained.

After I returned to Arizona to join the Department of American Indian Studies at the University of Arizona (UA), I had many great visitors to my two classes, Principles of Indigenous Economics and Traditional Ecological Knowledge: Rick Colbourne, Marie-Eve Druin Gagne, Kelsey John, Michael Kotutwa Johnson, Kiera Ladner, Jason Mika, Kepa Morgan, Joseph Pugliese, Chellie Spiller, Richard Stoffle, Kyle Whyte, and Ofelia Zepeda. The people from Aotearoa / New Zealand and Canada arrived funded by Fulbright awards, thus assisting international friendships.

Once at UA, I renewed friendships and discussions with the Native Nations Institute and Harvard Project on American Indian Economic Development: Randall Akee, Manley Begay, Stephen Cornell, Miriam Jorgensen, and Joseph Kalt. They led in creating the new Association for Economic Research of Indigenous Peoples; I presented at their brown-bag seminar in 2020.

The University of Arizona faculty also were very supportive and helpful: Stephanie Carroll, Karletta Chief, Benedict Colombi, Dan Ferguson, Amy Fatzinger, Mary Jo Fox, Francine Gachupin, Matthews Sakiestewa Gilbert, Patrisia Gonzales, Robert Hershey, Joe Hiller, Tom Holm, James Hopkins,

Keith James, John Paul Jones, Tsianina Lomawaima, Andrea McComb Sanchez, Len Necefer, Sheilah Nicholas, Tristan Reader, Melissa Tatum, Rebecca Tsosie, Aresta Tsosie-Paddock, and Robert Williams.

Matthew David Schwoebel and Peter DuBois helped me with research tasks. Sarah Abney kindly read the whole draft and helped me clarify many parts. Sheila McMahon helped greatly by editing the manuscript.

I also want to thank my students Derwin Begay, Jonathan Byrn, PennEyls Droz, Peter DuBois, Elizabeth Eklund, Ian Ellasante, Juanita Francis, Gavin Healey, Michael Kotutwa Johnson, Tommy Jones, Alexis Kopkowski, Larea Lewis, Hyealim Lim, Tammy Morago, Sean O'Meara, Lisa Palacios, Lynn Rae, Jacelle Ramon-Sauberon, Seafha Ramos, Sarah Renkert, Gina Richard, Matthew Schwoebel, Caitlyn Shoulder, Elizabeth Shulterbrant, Rachel Starks, and Matthew Tafoya.

I thank the Alfred P. Sloan Foundation Program in Public Understanding of Science for support for the costs of publication.

INDIGENOUS ECONOMICS

CHAPTER 1

Living Well by Developing Relationships

What does "development" mean for Indigenous peoples? This book argues that development means enhancing relationships, with the result of "living well through relationships." "Living well" is the English translation of *buen vivir* or *vivir bien* in the Andean countries, where Indigenous languages use *sumac kawsay*, *allin kawsay*, *suma quamaña*, and other terms for similar ideas. Although *well-being* could also be a synonym, it is most often assumed to mean individual well-being (Atkinson 2013; White 2017). Living well means supporting and enhancing relationships that include the natural world as well as humans.

Indigenous peoples have resisted the kinds of economic development pursued by the industrializing states for a long time. Their objections have been heard but not considered, and many may believe that Indigenous ideas about the proper organization of economies are out of date, a feature of the past that can no longer be considered relevant. To set the stage for the rest of the book, this chapter presents five examples of Indigenous peoples using relationality to pursue new relationships in contemporary times. Partly because economic development has caused dramatic environmental problems in the twenty-first century, Indigenous ideas are making a comeback despite the weak positions Indigenous peoples have all over the world. The United Nations has adopted a nonbinding Declaration of the Rights of Indigenous Peoples. Although that declaration does not have the force of international law, it does have moral influence in advocating treating Indigenous peoples fairly, on their own terms. These five examples all show that Indigenous peoples are able to use their relational view of the world to promote new relationships following their own desires.

In 1997 Gilbert Rist surveyed the promotion of "development" that began after World War II, to determine what powers such as the United States meant by the term (Rist 1997, 2002). The World Bank, International Monetary Fund, and units of the United Nations all set out to encourage the Global South to pursue development of their economies. As an empirical sociologist, Rist wanted to identify observable things that would signal the presence of development. He proposed that one could identify development as designed by the international organizations by observing three features of the encouraged practices: (1) the transformation of the natural environment, (2) the transformation of social relations, and (3) an increase in the production of commodities. He proposed that these measures are the ones that would be observed in the Global South, the so-called underdeveloped countries, if they pursued development. That social relations and the environment have been disrupted in the North, in Europe and North America, was not the focus of his attention. Other authors have argued that there is a decline in community for everyone as a result of increases in market relations in the North (Marglin 2008). This book is about ideas and ways of life that the expansion of European powers pushed aside as they conquered other parts of the world, particularly the Americas, Australia, and New Zealand.

Living Well Is the Opposite of Development

The articulation of alternatives such as *sumac kawsay* and *buen vivir* explicitly dismisses all three features of development. The destruction of nature and social relations is not what Indigenous peoples desire and does not encompass living well for *all* beings. While an increase in material standard of living as measured by commodities may be seen as good, it is worth having only if all beings flourish as a result.

Good living through the development of relations provides an alternative to the international promotion of development that Rist describes. The practice of trying to change the meaning of development by modifying it with descriptive adjectives, as in the case of "sustainable development," creates a concept that is internally and necessarily contradictory, an oxymoron. "Sustainable development" contains the idea of limits with "sustainable" and the idea of indefinite growth with "development." One does not want to perpetuate the pattern of oxymoron creation by using a term such as "relational development"; an improvement of relations among all beings does not occur when some are harmed by development.

An English translation of *buen vivir* provides a good alternative. This book's proposed definition of *living well* reads as follows:

> *Living well* consists of pursuing actions that strengthen humanity's relational goods created by relationships with nature and with each other. The added value of improved relationships can include additional material goods and services, so long as the additional material income is shared with all beings in the relationships. The aim of good living is to increase the value of all relationships without harming them.

To clarify this definition, one must describe relationships. The persons in a relationship focus on creating and sharing relational goods that allow them to act in their mutual interest. Relational goods are trust, cooperation, peace, and similar primarily subjective things that contribute to sociability. When nature is included, the relational goods create a sense of stewardship that in turn promotes high productivity of the land, ecological resilience to external shocks, and the flourishing of all species. It supports biodiversity, an environmental condition based on the relationships among different entities (Wood 2000, 39–41). In contrast, one could interpret development as the promotion of living poorly through creation of relational bads such as distrust, resistance to cooperation, war among humans, and the loss of biodiversity. Living poorly means not caring for the quality of life of all beings that form relationships with humans. In contrast, supporting biodiversity becomes a consequence of good living with nature included. Such mutual flourishing means that all beings can live their lives while also participating in relationships.

Standard economics defines wealth as the ownership of sources of commodities, which is usually physical and financial capital valued in monetary terms. An individual's wealth is his or her net worth. Some Indigenous peoples have urged a different definition of wealth. People are wealthy who have many strong relationships with each other and with all persons in the landscape, including nonhuman persons (Turner 2005, 24–36; Kelly 2017, 236–37). This economy of affection has a strong subjective component, based on the feeling of community resulting from participation in making and sharing relational goods. An empirical sociologist like Gilbert Rist would want easily observable characteristics to detect the presence of living well. Although measures of biodiversity and health broadly defined can provide such observable characteristics of living well, the subjective component cannot be removed. It depends on the creation of valued relational goods by participants in relationships. Broadly defined wealth includes the relatedness and health of all beings in a landscape, the Earth, and even the universe, an idea that some Indigenous people refer to as balance or beauty, as in the sophisticated Navajo concept of *hózhó* (Farella 1984).

The literature on well-being focuses on individual well-being rather than relational well-being, as explained by Sarah C. White (2017) in her review of the three main approaches to well-being that developed in the past forty or so years. First, "comprehensive well-being" dismisses gross domestic product (GDP) as a measure of well-being, focusing instead on a broad range of indicators that include both objective and subjective elements. The comprehensive well-being concept includes attention to the capabilities that Amartya Sen (1999, 2002) advocates when he mentions agency, freedom, and capabilities, which are supported by a well-functioning civil society. The measurement of "subjective well-being," a second approach, originated when Richard Easterlin (1974) discovered that self-reported happiness did not increase in countries as their per capita income increased, although richer people were happier than poorer people within countries. The meaning of such self-reported happiness by individuals has been questioned; it seems to be sensitive to questionnaire format. The third approach is to focus on "personal well-being" as a project for individuals to undertake, by improving their attitudes and taking actions that are fulfilling, with a focus on psychological well-being. While the focus is primarily on perfecting an individual's condition, some of the actions are developing relationships because such relationships improve personal fulfillment. The inclusion of relationships as a factor that contributes to individual well-being opens a door to consideration of relational concerns. Some measures of personal well-being are also reported to be correlated with the quality of a person's relationships, especially their marriages (White 2017, 124–28).

White prefers to emphasize "relational well-being," explaining that each of the three types of well-being assumes an individualist ontology. Well-being belongs to individuals even if relationships help. Her own fieldwork on the Indian subcontinent and Africa suggests that "the autonomous individual is a cultural myth" (White 2017, 129). Her research and that of other authors she cites suggest that well-being depends on three considerations beyond individuals:

1. Well-being is explained as something that groups, especially kin groups, share among themselves.
2. Societal structures, which are relationships at different levels, interlock and support relational well-being at different levels.
3. These structures include the natural environment; people know they depend on their land, and they care for that land on its own terms. Different parts of the environment require different types of relationships, depending on their own characteristics, not a projection of them as humans. (White 2017, 130)

These three characteristics are shared with buen vivir.

When policies are enacted, the structures of the society matter for implementation of programs to support well-being. Such programs need to be widely discussed, allowing people at all levels to express what they think will work for everyone, seeking common ground rather than competition. All beings need to be included, even marginalized people and elements of the natural environment. Policies should support relationships at all levels, with these relationships and the trust that they create replacing the ways that nation-states and their markets force people to act as individuals, unable to coordinate what needs to be done at all levels (White 2017, 131–32).

The next pages present five examples of successful relationship building. In Ecuador, Indigenous people refused to accept a payment for ecosystem services scheme because they did not want water to be a commodity, but they negotiated a solution that nonetheless did have downstream water users financially assisting upstream users of land to improve the flow of water from upstream to downstream. In Ontario, head trappers of the Pikangikum First Nation created a jointly written forest management plan with the Ontario Ministry of Natural Resources. On the coast of British Columbia, the Haida and the government of Canada agreed to set aside the issue of who ultimately owned the land in order to set up a park and a new timber harvest plan that would improve the condition of the land. In Aotearoa / New Zealand, local Māori tribes and the national government found that giving legal personhood to a river made cooperation possible while neither gave up their claims to ultimate ownership of the river. In the United States, a coalition of five tribes, supported by environmental and recreational organizations, persuaded the Barack Obama administration to create the Bears Ears National Monument. President Obama, and President Joe Biden four years later, approved a commission of five tribes to advise the federal government on management of the large area of the monument on the Colorado Plateau. In each of these cases, Indigenous people extended their relationship-building skills to including other people and the powerful states that they needed to improve relationships with their land.

Examples of Developing Relationships
The Tungurahua Project

A political movement to solve a water supply problem in the province of Tungurahua in Ecuador illustrates many of the principles discussed in this book. The movement began by recognizing the need for a solution between the upstream and downstream residents of the upper Ambato River watershed. The upstream residents are Indigenous peoples living on an agricultural frontier next to high moorlands that serve as the catchment area for the watershed. The moorlands are called the *páramo* ecosystem. The páramo was shrinking due to expansion of agriculture and the grazing of cattle and pigs, whose cloven hooves harm the vegetation. Downstream users consisted of urban customers from the capital of the province, irrigators, and hydroelectric producers. A popular mainstream economic solution for this kind of externality is to establish a program that pays for ecosystem services in which the upstream residents are individually compensated for taking action that would provide more water downstream. This approach was rejected for a solution that accomplished the same goal *without* commodifying water. Between 2002 and 2008, after much public discussion and the creation of new organizations, a solution was adopted. The water users would voluntarily contribute to a trust fund that would finance group-organized projects to improve the living standards of people in the upper zones (Kauffman and Martin 2014).

Outside partnerships with nongovernmental organizations (NGOs) and a German government organization facilitated the many discussions that led to the solution, by supporting local activists as they undertook the tasks of convincing everyone involved that a solution involving participatory governance could find the needed solution. The process that led to the outcome began in 2002 when the outside experts had recommended to the elected leader of the province that he set up a market-oriented payment for ecosystem services system run by the government. The initial proposal was that water users would pay a tax per cubic meter of water used, and the resulting funds would be paid to individual farmers in the upper reaches of the watershed. This proposal was rejected by the Indigenous people because it made water into a commodity and supported individuals rather than communities. Downstream users objected because most of the payments would come from agricultural interests, who were poorer than the urban residents or the two hydroelectric companies. Public opposition to the proposal was so strong that "the phrase 'ecosystem services' became toxic" (Kauffman and Martin 2014, 48).

Finding agreement involved considerable political activity in relationship building. Three Indigenous organizations that had not previously worked together decided to create a joint front they called Mushuk Yuyay (New Ideas). The New Ideas initiative advocated for governance that relied on dialogue and respect among people with different ideas and cultural traditions. The goal of development would be reimagined to improve the quality of life. Maintaining well-being was based on "a strategy that integrated the restoration of *páramo* ecosystem, food security, and education to create healthy communities" (Kauffman and Martin 2014, 50). These are the Indigenous ideas that describe buen vivir in the Andes.

As they confront the advocates of Western development, the Indigenous peoples of the Andes have articulated their view of how to go about managing humans' relationships with each other and their land. The principles are summarized as *sumak kawsay* in Quechua (Kichwa) or *suma qamaña* in Aymara. Both terms are difficult to translate; Indigenous peoples have said that three different translations would be "life of fullness," "good coexistence," or "harmonious life" (Villalba 2013, 1430). Speakers of the two languages object that the Spanish terms *buen vivir* or *vivir bien* do not capture the full meaning of either term, nor does "good living" in English. Nonetheless, *buen vivir* is very commonly used to describe the constellation of ideas, which are summarized as principles of relationality, complementarity, and reciprocity.

Among the main ideas of sumak kawsay and suma qamaña is the importance of relationality. Relationality applies to both humans and nonhumans. Unai Villalba reports, "The community is conceived of as a unit of life made up of all forms of existence; not just a social structure made up of humans only." He refers to relationships starting with the family unit and then progressing upward "to the community and beyond" (Villalba 2013, 1430).

The division of nature and society doesn't exist in the Andean worldview, as is common with other Indigenous peoples. In addition, attention to spirituality implies "acceptance of the importance of emotions and their relational nature, affectivity and 'all that is beyond-the-rational'" (Villalba 2013, 1431). The ideas surrounding sumak kawsay suggest that the goal of living well is achieved through support of relationships.

In the final arrangement, there is a flow of money from the water users who benefit from the restoration of the ecosystem to the upstream residents who are doing so. The difference from a payment for ecosystem services arrangement is that the seven partners who fund the Tungurahuan Fund for Páramo Management and Fight Against Poverty do so voluntarily. The fund does not compensate individual landowners; it instead supports a range of activities designed to help the ecosystem and reduce poverty. This approach was required for the Indigenous groups to support the plan. From 2008 to 2011, annual contributions averaged $480,000 per year. The fund invests 60 percent of the contributions for future support and uses the remaining 40 percent immediately (Kauffman and Martin 2014).

The support for improvement of the agriculture in the Indigenous areas focused on the well-being of both the ecosystem and the people. The community created plant nurseries to grow native plants for improving the degraded areas. Restoration also focused on food security. The cattle and pigs were replaced with local guinea pigs and alpaca, with their padded feet. Trout farms added additional protein sources. Increased output was sold in the capitol city of Ambato. Irrigation works were also improved to conserve water. A bilingual literacy campaign supported additional education. The creation of new relationships and relational goods led to increases in material living but not with a market for water.

The success of the effort of Tungurahua's new governance model contributed to the national movement that led to a new constitution for Ecuador in 2008. That constitution is famous for requiring that buen vivir be used in a new development model that would not reflect neoliberalism, which is the old development model. After approval of the constitution, the Ministry of Planning and Development used the Tungurahuan model in development of the new five-year plan (Kauffman and Martin 2014, 54). The full potential of buen vivir has not been implemented as yet in Ecuador, because the government of President Rafael Correa and his successor continued to support extractive industries. Many authors have examined the conflict between the ideals that have been enacted in the constitution and the realities of funding the national government and responding to those interested in extraction (Martin 2011; Altmann 2017; Kauffman and Martin 2018; Laastad 2019). The ideas of buen vivir have been entered into the constitution of Ecuador, revealing that the Indigenous ideas of relationships have received considerable acceptance. Much of the attention paid to the Constitution of 2008 emphasizes the rights of nature. Yet extraction harms nature.

The Tungurahuan story illustrates a group of Indigenous peoples insisting on respecting nature through not treating water as a commodity. The long process of working out a solution consisted of a great deal of relationship building. Many people are cited by Craig M. Kauffman and Pamela L. Martin as facilitating the building of new organizations. The development of local participation was very important; the emphasis on facilitation was a form of peacemaking. An international agency from Germany worked hard to assist the governor of the region in creating the relationships that the Indigenous peoples of the region desired. The governor of the region provided relational leadership by encouraging the facilitation and the resulting new efforts.

All these activities created an improvement in relationships and relational goods. The productivity of the upper part of the watershed will improve as the trust fund, supported by downstream users, provides investment funds for projects that improve productivity and protect the páramo. The projects are those of groups, not individuals, thus supporting relationships at the micro level. At the level of a watershed, living well has been implemented through relationship building.

The Whitefeather Forest Plan

In 1995 the elders of the Pikangikum band in northern Ontario had a problem. A line created by the Ontario Provincial Government defined the northernmost limit of timber harvesting; that line included the southernmost parts of the elders' hunting territories, which had been clear cut. The Pikangikum could see that the rest of their land was next. They had to find a way to stop the destruction yet allow the province to proceed without destroying the land. Their land was in the way of development, and a different kind of development had to be created. They set out to create new relationships that would allow the new kind of development.

The process began in 1996 when the Pikangikum chief sent a letter to the Ontario Ministry of Natural Resources (OMNR) proposing dialogue. The band created the Whitefeather Economic Development Corporation (WEDC) to manage their efforts; the goal was to be "in the driver's seat" in planning forest management in their territory. They created the Whitefeather Forest Initiative and began to seek partners to work with them in the effort to control forest planning in their territory. The effort would be led by their elders, consisting of the persons with responsibility for each of the traplines in their territory. These traplines are the family territories that had existed and were formally recognized in 1947. In 1998 they established another entity, the Whitefeather Forest Management Corporation (WFMC), a partnership between the Pikangikum and Timberline Forest Inventory Consultants. This was the first of many entities created to allow partnership with outside entities. The WFMC became the focus of funding for the planning process.

In June 2000 the OMNR created the Northern Boreal Initiative and developed it during the next few years; the intent was to support First Nations in northern Ontario in addressing sustainable forest management. Pikangikum was one of the communities involved and received considerable funding from the initiative to undertake planning activities. The Pikangikum set out to create a forest-planning document titled *Keeping the Land*; the plan would be co-authored with the OMNR and use information from a variety of sources. The document was written in a collaborative manner over a period of three years, from 2003 to 2006.

The Pikangikum have built connections to and been assisted in this work by faculty and students at the Natural Resources Institute at the University of Manitoba in Winnipeg. Advocates for sustainable forest management in Canada had been proposing that systems of criteria and indicators can be used to monitor forest conditions. Because of the popularity of the criteria and indicators approach, Indigenous peoples in Canada were asked to develop their own systems of criteria and indicators. A master's student at the Natural Resources Institute, Janine Shearer, took on the task of determining what criteria and indicators the Pikangikum elders would like. As she conducted her research, she made a great effort to make sure she did not dominate the process so that the elders could state their position clearly. Shearer's goal was to help the elders explain their evaluation framework. As they explained, she went through cycles of clarification (Shearer, Peters, and Davidson-Hunt 2009).

The Pikangikum elders began by examining proposed ideas that Shearer had collected from transcripts of meetings designed to lead to the planning document; in doing this, Shearer had found little to create a list of criteria and indicators. Paddy Peters and the elders found even that framework was not satisfactory, and as they worked through different rounds of considering the problem, they moved away from the criteria and indicators approach. The criteria became themes, and then the themes had to be arranged in the proper order for the elders to articulate their alternative way of viewing the forest. After considerable thought about the issues, they ended up creating a drawing to illustrate how to achieve the condition that "everything is good." They placed the elements of reaching that outcome by beginning with good relationships: "Elder Norman rearranged the layout of the themes so that the order of the themes changed to represent an orderly progression (clockwise), stating that we first need to have good relationships before we can begin planning, it won't work the other way" (Shearer, Peters, and Davidson-Hunt 2009, 76). In the final circle developed by the elders, the process started with good relationships, moving from there to good decision-making through "putting things in order." Next is a way of life based on the land, through the people's experience with a land-based livelihood. The fourth and final stage is "everything is good," which means "joy in everything," and "health," through healing mind, body, and soul (80).

Shearer completed her master's thesis in 2008, two years after *Keeping the Land* was published (Pikangikum First Nation and Ontario Ministry of Natural Resources [PFN and OMNR] 2006). Her final matrix has at its center the image used on the cover page of the land use strategy. Paddy Peters had further refined his image during their discussions; it was used in *Keeping the Land* before Shearer completed her thesis. *Keeping the Land* uses both English and the Pikangikum version of Ojibway, with the community's orthography in Ojibway and the community's rendering of its language in the English alphabet. It has a glossary that attempts to reconcile the two languages; the authors state that they had to invent some words in Ojibway to express ideas from English. In its note on language, the plan states, "Our cultural dialogue has only just begun."

Pikangikum chief Dean Owen opened the published version of *Keeping the Land* with a statement that read in part:

The cross-cultural context in which this plan was developed brought together two rich knowledge traditions in a truly cooperative effort. The results
of the collaboration between our First Nation and the Ontario Ministry of
Natural Resources can be seen throughout the Land Use Strategy. This is a
great achievement. We have achieved what our Elders asked in this regard.

Years of hard work by many people have gone into this Land Use Strategy.
In all these years, our Elders have never wavered in their dedication and
commitment to the planning process. We are grateful to them. Likewise,
during this time, the commitment of the MNR to supporting the Whitefeather Forest Initiative planning process and being a partner with us has
also remained constant. The same is true of the staff and technical support
people associated with the Whitefeather Forest Management Corporation.
I wish to thank you all. All of the effort that has gone into this Strategy is
leading to tremendous opportunity for our young people. For this we can all
be proud. (PFN and OMNR 2006, preface)

Charlie Lauer, the northwest regional director of the OMNR, followed with
his letter of endorsement:

On behalf of the Northwest Region MNR, I am pleased to endorse the Whitefeather Forest and Adjacent Areas Land Use Strategy. The Strategy is the
result of a three-year dialogue with Pikangikum First Nation, a cross-cultural
dialogue in which we have shared views and explored ideas. Together, we
followed a consultative planning process, considering a full range of environmental, social and economic factors. As a result, MNR has adopted the Strategy as provincial land use direction, contributing to the wise management of
lands and resources. (PFN and OMNR 2006, preface)

These two statements reveal the result of determined relationship building
by the elders of the Pikangikum Nation, to which the OMNR responded with
its own efforts at collaboration. The consultative planning process included
public forums as well as many meetings between the elders and employees
of the OMNR. The use of "to keep" caused some confusion, as "to keep the
land" means to be stewards of the land, to keep it productive. Some interpreted "to keep" as a statement of property interest to exclude others, causing
some concern. The plan's name has not been changed. The stewardship goal
is described as follows:

The planning tasks described in the Strategy we understand to be part of our responsibility to "keep the land" (*kah-nah-wayn-dahn kee-tah-keem*); to keep the land as it has been, in all its diversity and abundance, since time immemorial. (PFN and OMNR 2006, 2)

The publication of *Keeping the Land* ended the first part of the transformation; the actual implementation of a forest plan by the OMNR in 2013 marks the end of the planning period and the start of implementation. The joint document became the basis for a forest plan written by the OMNR and adopted in 2009 (OMNR 2009). The plan is an extensive document with detailed descriptions of how all parts of the Whitefeather Forest are to be managed.

Eventually, the Whitefeather Forest Management Corporation established another entity, the Whitefeather Forest Community Resource Management Authority (WFCRMA), which in May 2013 obtained a Sustainable Forest License for the Whitefeather Forest. Both the original WFMC and the later WFCRMA were set up separate from the band council and were operated by a council of elders. The WFCRMA is a nonprofit corporation. This complex web of legal entities enables the elders to implement their vision within an organizational framework that satisfies the needs of Ontario law.

The work on relationships included pursuing mutual understanding, which is itself a relational good. As Andrew W. Miller and Iain Davidson-Hunt (2013) report, discussions among the Pikangikum senior hunters and officials of the OMNR meant that each heard the other side's worldview and the consequential interpretation of relationships with animals such as moose and beaver. They cooperated to write an official forest plan based on the plan of the Pikangikum senior hunters. Now the Pikangikum are developing enterprises based on new ways to use the family hunting territories. They will use uplands to raise pine and reduce the reliance on lands along the rivers for fur bearers; one consequence has been a change in the role of fire, which can damage the newly repurposed pine trees to a community forest enterprise. They are now on a path to explore good living in the context of new relationships.

Relationship Building on Haida Gwaii

For a great many years, the government of British Columbia has been financing its operations with stumpage revenue from selling old-growth timber throughout the province. Because that government had signed very few treaties with the Indigenous peoples of the province, those peoples had for many years been trying to assert their ownership of the land. The Canadian government in 1927 had even outlawed efforts by Indigenous peoples to fight in court by making it illegal for lawyers to work for Indigenous peoples regarding land claims, a law that was repealed in 1951 (Tennant 1990, 111–22, 215). Once their use of courts became possible, resistance to timber cutting increased. As the Haida tried to slow down or stop the intensive logging of their islands, they created numerous new relationships between themselves and the governments of British Columbia and Canada. Two of these are comanagement of Gwaii Haanas National Park on the southern islands of the archipelago and an agreement to comanage timber lands on the large northern island.

Gwaii Haanas National Park developed over time. Among the first actions was a blockade by the Haida people to stop a proposed timber harvesting plan on one of the islands of Haida Gwaii, known at the time as the Queen Charlotte Islands. They organized the blockade with cooperation from environmental groups that also wanted to protect the islands from logging; this started a process of change on Haida Gwaii. While most of the merchantable old growth was on the northernmost large island of Haida Gwaii, one valuable watershed south of that island was also slated for harvest in 1985. A blockade may not be the best way to initiate a relationship-building process because it can create emotions that inhibit communication. Given no alternatives, however, the Haida have used blockades several times in order to prevent destruction before agreement can be reached. In addition, they have sued the province of British Columbia many times in order to have their aboriginal claims to Haida Gwaii recognized. They have won many of the court cases. Despite the animosity that such tactics can create, the Haida have nonetheless been able to reach comanagement agreements on Haida Gwaii.

Two of the main comanagement agreements begin with clear statements that each side understands the position of the other side. The first of these resulted from the South Moresby Agreement, signed in 1988. Before an agreement could be reached, the distrust and misunderstandings existing between the Haida, the non-Haida residents, and government officials had to be addressed successfully. This occurred during meetings designed to implement expenditures of $38 million allocated as part of the South Moresby Agreement. The story of how planning that expenditure led to relationship building is told by Norman Dale (1999), who was hired as a community liaison by a secretariat that had been hired by the government's Planning and Coordination Committee (P&CC). He was to liaison with the Resident's Planning Advisory Committee (RPAC), a group of residents of Haida Gwaii that included only one Haida person, who was an observer. Dale had extensive experience with negotiation and planning with Native peoples. He also immediately saw that the government's top-down approach had to be changed, even though he had been hired to carry it out. As Dale points out, the proposal he helped create was simple. The government had proposed to compensate the community as part of the creation of a park by spending $38 million for economic development. An alternative was to put the money into a trust and use the interest for an ongoing and never-ending series of projects that would support community development. The government had to be persuaded to change a grant expenditure into an interest-bearing account. The local community had to develop a plan that would convince the government of the wisdom of the decision. When the government said it could not do that, the community representatives noted that a trust account had been set up for the forest companies whose operations had been curtailed (Dale 1999, 937).

Although the proposal was simple, agreement depended on the establishment of trust among the non-Haida and Haida residents of Haida Gwaii, the Queen Charlotte Islands. The political standoffs were delaying spending the economic development money. The P&CC decided that "the RPAC needed a series of 'leadership development' workshops." As Dale also notes, "The premise was a common one: This untutored group of local people needed collaborative skills as well as greater understanding of cross-cultural relations, negotiations, planning processes, and tourism development" (1999, 929–30). Dale used the opportunities presented by these workshops to facilitate the non-Haida in learning about the Haida and the Haida's understanding of the land.

When the RPAC proposed that a feast occur where the Haida and the RPAC could get to know each other, Dale knew he had a problem, because the Haida would not attend a feast if it meant recognizing the authority of the RPAC, which actually had none because it was only advisory to the P&CC. Fortunately, the last of the training seminars would be run by a Native American from Hawai'i knowledgeable about tourism. The feast could be held to honor the guest, and everyone could become more acquainted. At the feast and at meetings organizing it, the parties began to talk and to understand each other. The Haida were able to tell stories about the islands. While attending to the formal negotiations, which were called "exploratory discussions," Dale also attended to the process of building trust among the local people who were not well acquainted with each other even though they lived in six neighboring communities. As he looks back on the process, he stresses the role of trust, a relational good of supreme importance. He reported, "Without 'small t' trust, no 'large T' trust!" The large T refers to the Gwaii Trust, funded by the provincial government, which governs a trust account with the interest on the account used to finance projects (Dale 1999, 941).

Trust had to come into existence before the local community could reach an agreement about how to spend the money that had been allocated in the compromise on South Moresby that ended logging and provided funds to the local port, Skidegate, which would be damaged by the loss of logging activity. Once the people involved came to know each other, to talk about their issues, and to start to trust each other, then the details of an agreement were easily worked out. The Canadian government added another $10 million to build the port that Skidegate wanted, and the Gwaii Trust then began to distribute funds from the interest on the $38 million that had been allocated for economic development. The trust that began to be created with this settlement later led to other settlements. The Haida and non-Haida on the island slowly came to cooperate with each other in additional conflicts, particularly about logging operations on the northern island where everyone lives.

In 1993 the government of Canada and the Council of the Haida Nation reached another agreement to establish governance of the new national park. This agreement provided a framework in which the national government of Canada and the Haida could comanage the park on land for which the province of British Columbia had ceded jurisdiction to the national government. The first section of the agreement contains statements from the government of Canada that it owns the land and from the Haida that they own the land. This disagreement was recognized and set aside, unresolved, while the rest of the agreement provides for comanagement of the park.

Although the Haida had settled with Canada about the archipelago and the Gwaii Haanas Heritage Site, setting up a successful comanagement arrangement, the Haida and the government of British Columbia had not settled their dispute over logging on the northern island, Graham Island. That dispute developed into court fights and a blockade, much as had occurred in the southern part of the archipelago. After the confrontations, a series of joint agreements signaled an increase in trust among the parties. Each agreement provided a way for each side to indicate its reliability by compliance, and as time went along the agreements became more specific and trust seemed to increase. The Kunst'aa guu–Kunst'aayah Reconciliation Protocol climaxed the process.

Three investigators set out to examine trust specifically (Hotte, Wyatt, and Kozak 2018). Their study provides ways to evaluate how a relational good, trust, can be developed in the process of resolving strong differences about how to manage forests. In the process of studying trust, they also provide evidence of increasing trust as the comanagement agreements developed. Their conclusion is that as relationships developed, they "increased the degree of influence of the Council of the Haida Nation over decisions regarding lands and resources on Haida Gwaii compared with other top-down Provincial governance approaches" (Hotte, Wyatt, and Kozak 2018, 364). This conclusion supports the assertion that developing relationships improves good living from an Indigenous perspective.

The study has another use: exploring the development of trust for different levels of relational agents. The agreements on Haida Gwaii represent development of macro-level relationships, with trust coming into existence across organizations, supported by trust developing at individual interpersonal levels. They find that unequal power in the rules at macro levels decreases trust in comparison to situations where power is equal. This is demonstrated by a comparison of two different decision-making entities. The Haida Gwaii Management Council operates with consensus and is the final decision maker on strategic issues such as setting the annual allowable cut. The Solutions Table makes operational decisions; while these decisions must conform to strategic-level mandates, they can have serious negative effects at the operational level. The province allows its ministers to make the final decisions of the Solutions Table, and, as a result, trust is low in that forum (Hotte, Wyatt, and Kozak 2018, 365).

Despite the mixed condition of trust, the Haida have been able to reduce the annual cut and direct harvest away from key stands of importance such as monumental cedar. They have been able to obtain the support of the non-Haida residents of Haida Gwaii. The study of trust in forest management refers to the earlier success with establishment of the Gwaii Haanas National Park. Many Haida are employed by the park, and the park protects lands of great importance. From the Haida viewpoint, good living has increased.

Legal Personhood for the Te Urewera National Park and Te Awa Tapua (the Whanganui River)

Another example of creating a comanagement relationship while sidestepping the state's need to have ultimate ownership over land are two agreements to provide personhood to Te Urewera National Park and Te Awa Tapua, the Whanganui River. The agreements were the outcome of treaty settlement talks resulting from New Zealand needing to deal with its violation of agreements under the Treaty of Waitangi. The Tūhoe *iwi* expressed claims to the land in Te Urewera National Park, and the Waitangi Tribunal declared that the Tūhoe claim was valid. This meant that the national government and the Tūhoe had to negotiate a settlement to the claim. Similarly, the tribunal ruled that the national government had to settle with the Whanganui iwi with regard to its claim to the Whanganui River. For some settlements, the New Zealand government transfers ownership of land to Māori entities. The government refused to transfer ownership in either case. The national park is a popular park. The national government asserts rights over freshwater and the beds of rivers. For each, the Māori with claims wanted to be able to exercise their authority under the guarantees of the Treaty of Waitangi.

Legal scholar Katherine Sanders (2018, 209) explains that the use of legal personhood addressed the dilemma created by the refusal of either the local Māori or the State of New Zealand to concede. The Māori insisted that the Treaty of Waitangi expressed "unqualified exercise of chieftainship over their lands, villages and all their treasures." The State of New Zealand refused to concede "ownership of the beds of navigable rivers" (214). In addition, the jurisdiction of the state received great public support regarding the park: "Public resistance to the transfer of ownership to *hapū* and *iwi* in this context may to some extent be due to the strength of the association of these properties with the identity of the colonial state" (221). *Hapū* and *iwi* refer to the local Māori families and tribes that assert their chieftainship. Both sides have their identity tied to the issue of who controls the land and the river. With identity involved, compromise is difficult.

The negotiators for both agreements were the same people on each side. As they sought to find a solution, the idea of legal personhood appeared to provide a solution, based on the growing literature on the rights to nature. The Māori wanted something different from ownership. Recognizing legal personhood of the river then places both sides in an equal position of responsibility for the river. As a legal entity, the river could own itself. The Māori could say that the national government no longer owned the river. Similarly, the national park could own itself. Both agreements recognize the relevance of *tikanga Māori*, the Māori belief that land "possesses an inherent, powerful personality that is logically prior to, and completely independent of human existence" (Sanders 2018, 211). In addition, Māori would be able to exercise guardianship over the land and the river. The government could also maintain that the Māori had not obtained ownership of the river or the park (208).

Once the deadlock is set aside, relationships can develop around mutual concerns for the land and water. The legal personhood idea provides a way for Māori values to be recognized as relevant to management decisions, an advance over having all decisions made by non-Māori people in the government. The government, however, defined legal personhood and can claim it exercised its jurisdiction in the decision. The Māori can work on development of relationships that accomplish their goals, even though some compromise will be necessary in the comanagement arrangements. Both acts that created comanagement set up a board. The Board of the National Park will have nine members, six of whom are Tūhoe. While the act creating the board is complicated in its delegation of powers, in general the board replaces the government in making decisions about the national park. While the government no longer owns the park, the board has the "rights of control often associated with Crown ownership" (Sanders 2018, 225).

The Whanganui River Claims Settlement Act of 2017 creates a complex comanagement arrangement that balances the various parties' concerns. Administration is carried out by a two-member board, one appointed by the Māori and one by the government, who operate with advice from two other entities, one of which has broad representation from groups with interests affected by the river. The requirements of consensus in these entities will support relationship building among the people charged with giving advice to the managers.

Relationships, therefore, extend also to nonhumans, such as the environment. The principle of stewardship of the Earth is expressed as *kaitiakitanga*, "which has layers of meaning including guarding, keeping, preserving, conserving, fostering, protecting, sheltering and keeping watch over, thus guiding relationships between people and nature." The idea includes the view that the Earth's resources "do not belong to humankind; rather humans belong to the earth" (Henare 2001, 202). The governing boards exercise power on behalf of the national park and the river. They are trustees and guardians who represent land and a river, each of which is then part of the relationships that the governing structure mandates. Sanders emphasizes that these governing structures act on behalf of the newly created legal persons, not on behalf of the Crown, even though parliament set up the arrangement and can remove it at will. The hope is that the people who care about the park and the river will work together to take care of both (Sanders 2018, 233).

Bears Ears National Monument

A final example of developing new relationships to protect valued landscapes is the innovative use of the Antiquities Act to create the Bears Ears National Monument. This action resulted from a movement led by Indigenous peoples. The history of national monuments and national parks in the United States generally involves the federal government removing Indians and Indian access to them. President Theodore Roosevelt signed the Antiquities Act of 1906 in order to protect archaeological sites in the American Southwest from the plundering that was occurring. The act, under the assumption that the Indians would disappear, was used to remove them from the lands that were declared national monuments (Krakoff 2018, 220–27). The Bears Ears effort changes this pattern. Rather than removing Indians from the land, it places them in a strong position to participate in the use of the land. Local development interests in Utah oppose the action. Instead of fighting eastern elites wanting to protect a national heritage, they are fighting a coalition of tribes, archaeologists, and recreation interests that wants to protect the lands (Necefer and Luneau 2018).

In July 2015, five tribes met and established the Bears Ears Inter-Tribal Coalition for the purpose of proposing that President Obama create a national monument that would protect the Bears Ears landscape. The Navajo, Ute Mountain Ute, Uintah and Ouray Ute, Hopi, and Zuni had known for many years that the lands needed protection. While the involved tribes did not have a history of working together, their joint interest in protecting the

Bears Ears landscape led them to organize the meeting. In expressing his support for the coalition that resulted, Willie Grayeyes stated,

> The idea of being a family, all together, one direction, is stronger than individual efforts. The unity of the group fuses all Tribes in the future. Our lifestyle, our food, our way of life seems to be the cornerstone for our position, and I'd like to express my support for that. (Bears Ears Inter-Tribal Coalition 2015, 18–19)

Willie Grayeyes is a Navajo living in San Juan County, which includes much of the area that was proposed for the new national monument. Before the meeting took place, he had led a coalition of Navajos in San Juan County, the Utah Diné Bikéya (UDB), created in 2010 as a nonprofit organization. The UDB had assembled data and maps to describe the landscape that it wanted to protect. The governing body of San Juan County opposed the idea when it was proposed. The county changed its position after an election in November 2018, when Willie Grayeyes was one of two Navajos elected to the three-member county commission (Associated Press 2019). The change in membership of the commission resulted after a court ordered the gerrymandered districts in the county to be redrawn to cease limiting Navajos to only one of the seats, as they are a majority of people in the county (Stevens 2019).

Once formed, the coalition acted quickly to consult widely and to write a proposal to submit to the Obama administration. It identified the land to include in the new monument, explained its importance, and proposed a management structure called "Federal-Tribal Collaborative Management." The proposal would create an eight-member Bears Ears Management Commission composed of a representative from each of the five tribes and one from each of three federal agencies that manage land in the proposed monument: the Bureau of Land Management, the U.S. Forest Service, and the National Park Service. The commission would plan the monument and hire a manager to oversee all management of the monument. The proposed collaborative management would use both Indigenous knowledge and Western science. The proposal recognized that considerable detail had to be worked out (Bears Ears Inter-Tribal Coalition 2015).

While the coalition worked with the Obama administration, government officials from Utah worked on a different proposal, without involving the tribes. An appendix to the October 15, 2015, proposal reported the extensive efforts of the coalition to participate in the creation of the Public Land Initiative (PLI), an effort led by members of Utah's congressional delegation in cooperation with the commissions of several Utah counties (Bears Ears Inter-Tribal Coalition 2015, Exhibit 1). The PLI proposal was for 1.35 million acres, not the 1.9 million the coalition proposed. The PLI proposal would create a conservation area and allow much less protection than would a monument. It also did not allow for tribal participation in management. The Utah congressional delegation proposed legislation, but the legislation died in Congress in 2016. After the end of the legislative session and after the election of President Donald Trump in November 2016, President Obama announced the creation of the Bears Ears National Monument on December 18, 2016 (Executive Office of the President 2017a).

The proposed monument did not have the level of collaborative management that had been requested. Rather than have the tribes and the agencies serve together on a governing body, the proclamation set up a Bears Ears Commission composed of people appointed by the five tribes in the Bears Ears Coalition. While the tribes wanted clear collaborative management, the proclamation kept final decisions in the hands of the federal agencies. The language says the secretaries of the Departments of Agriculture and Interior would "meaningfully engage the Commission" and fully consider the recommendations of the commission. If they did not follow the recommendations, they would provide "a written explanation of their reasoning" (Executive Office of the President 2017a, 1144). This structure is more like an advisory committee than a collaborative commission. It keeps final decision-making authority in the federal agencies to comply with legal requirements to avoid subdelegation of authority to entities outside the federal government (Franz 2021).

That the Bears Ears Inter-Tribal Coalition had built a broad base of support became important when Trump followed Obama as president. He quickly undertook a process that would lead to the reversal of Obama's declaration. On December 4, 2017, Trump's presidential proclamation reduced Bears Ears from 1.35 million acres to 200,000 acres (Executive Office of the President 2017b). The five tribes, outdoor recreation companies, archaeology organizations, and many environmental organizations went to court in Washington, D.C., on December 4, 2017, to oppose President Trump's action (Ruple 2019, 4). The plaintiffs argued that no president had the authority to reduce or rescind a designation of a national monument; the original Antiquities Act and its amendments only authorized the creation of monuments by the president. The different legal actions were consolidated into one, which lasted until the end of the Trump administration (Yachnin 2021).

After his election, President Biden appointed a Laguna Indian, Deb Haaland, as Secretary of the Interior, and work began on reinstating the monument to its full size (Rott 2021). On October 8, 2021, President Biden reinstated the Bears Ears National Monument to its original size, also adding 11,200 acres that Trump had included in his proclamation but had not been in the original Obama Bears Ears declaration (Executive Office of the President 2021). President Biden's declaration included the commission that would serve as an advisory council to the secretaries that would administer the Bears Ears National Monument. The Utah delegation to Congress indicated that it would sue to void President Biden's reinstatement of the monument. Thus, the political conflict over the monument has not been concluded as of the end of 2021. An anticipated objection to the monument is the reason that President Trump gave for his action reducing it: the proposal was not of the smallest size needed to protect the resources. President Biden's proclamation contains an extensive listing of the protected resources, justifying the size of the monument.

The establishment of the Bears Ears National Monument does not involve new legal theories such as the personhood of a river. The Antiquities Act already authorized a special status for valuable landscapes. The innovation in this case is to change the management structure to a type of comanagement, which is also the result of each of the previous four cases.

Focus on Relationships

The five examples in this chapter all show that relationship building in the modern era can have benefits both for Indigenous peoples and for others with whom they form relationships. The Indigenous peoples in each example taught others about relationships, even if the learning was only partial for the others involved. By focusing on relationship building, Indigenous peoples in the Andes, in the Boreal Forest, on the islands of Haida Gwaii, in Aotearoa / New Zealand, and on the Colorado Plateau have each started a process that aims at a different goal from that of conventional development. The goal is to enhance life by enhancing relationships that include the natural world. Wealth can be composed of the quantity and quality of all persons' participation in relationships. The wealth of relationships provides good living for all concerned. By pursuing relationships in these examples, Indigenous peoples have strengthened the protection of their land from excessive development; they have improved the stewardship outcomes. They have also improved their participation in the governance of the lands of concern by insisting that all beings on the land must be included in relationships.

• • •

This book explains how a focus on relationships generates a different kind of economic theory than the mainstream approach in all its variations. Persons replace the individual in standard economics; persons become active agents in the creation of the lives they live rather than passive responders to incentives given by prices. Persons combine into relational subjects of many different types that are similar in their dependence on dialogue and reflexivity among the persons who comprise them. Relational subjects can differ in scale with corresponding differences in the modes of dialogue and interaction. Relational subjects include all beings in a landscape.

The book lays out the theory of relational economics and then explores some of the implications of the relational viewpoint. Many standard issues in economics change. The middle six chapters of the book explain these changes in an exposition of the many aspects of a relational economics. Relationships create both a person's and a group's identity. The idea of property needs replacement with relationships on the land, a different kind of territoriality in which humans care for the welfare of nonhumans, and the care is reciprocated by the land providing for the humans. The dilemmas of dealing with common pool and public goods become easier to solve. Leaders are persons who enhance relationships rather than give orders or inspire followers. Entrepreneurs create firms that differ from the contractual firms of standard economics; they seek well-being as well as find ways to generate new productive activities. After chapters 2 through 7 explain Indigenous economics as relational economics, the afterword draws the contrasts between Indigenous economics and standard economics and in the process suggests some directions for further work in the field of Indigenous economic theory.

CHAPTER 2

Relationships and Persons

Persons develop in relationships and persons create relationships. This interdependence is absent in standard economics, which has no explanation for the origin of individual preferences in its analysis. In addition, economics has a special model of the individual, that of a rational person with preferences that provide motivation. Economics now recognizes preferences for altruism and inequality aversion, providing for concern for more than an individual's own well-being. The fundamental basis for theory remains individuals, who are assumed to be the main agents in determining economic outcomes. Indigenous economics cannot start with either individuals as the main focus or economic man as that type of individual because so many Indigenous peoples emphasize that relationships are fundamental to social organization. The first chapter explained the importance of relationships to five Indigenous peoples in different situations. When relationships matter, the character of individuals must consider the importance of relationships.

If each person is a creation of their unique relationships, then each person is unique. Valuing this uniqueness means that relational societies are more respectful of individual autonomy than are individualistic societies. Such societies also drop the assumption of a common human essence, or rational (even if altruistic) "economic man." An economic theory for relational societies requires a different concept of the person. This chapter provides a description of this kind of individual, a relational person. Such persons are reflexive; they talk with themselves, with internal conversations, in deciding what is best among the actions available to them. Modes of internal conversations vary among persons. The chapter describes four modes of internal conversation that have been identified among Indigenous college students in the United States. Relational persons develop ultimate concerns and use their internal deliberations to decide how best to pursue those ultimate concerns. Among their choices is to develop and maintain relationships with other people. While relationships in standard economics are formed with contracts, a relational approach to economics focuses on subjective understanding and valuing of other persons. Relational persons interact to create relationships in which the persons share relational goods, creating higher-level relational agents. This chapter focuses on persons; the next chapter examines how persons form higher-level relationships in carrying out their projects to address their ultimate concerns.

The Nature of Self and Individualism

The great value placed on individual autonomy in Indigenous societies is inconsistent with the portrayal of Indigenous societies as "collectivist." Indigenous students in university classrooms resist acting competitively, which seems to be motivated by a desire not to stand out, which is supposedly valued in individualistic societies. On the other hand, part of this motivation is that one individual isn't supposed to tell others what to do. Indigenous students describe acting assertively in a classroom as being "aggressive." When one is aggressive, one is impinging on the autonomy of other people.

Villalba (2013, 1430) provides this puzzling statement in his description of sumac kawsay: "Community does not imply a lack of individuality, since individuality is expressed through complementarity with other beings in the group." Such a community does not make everyone the same, as in collectivism. Anthony Wallace (1970, 34) describes Iroquois thought as follows: "The close connections of kinship sustained by the Iroquois clan system were reinforced by an ethical ideal of autonomous responsibility taught from early childhood in Iroquois culture." Kinship does not make everyone the same. The Pikangikum, as is typical of Anishinaabe and Cree culture, strongly urge that people should not interfere with the actions of other people or of other animals. Each one's autonomy is to be respected (Tanner 1979; Feit 1988).

On the other hand, in highly individualistic societies such as the United States, often conformity is rewarded or required. For instance, for years gay people were forced to go underground and hide their sexual orientation. In order to join the dominant society, American Indians were required to dress as settlers did and to adopt a Christian religion. When particular clothing styles are popular in a high school, everyone dresses essentially the same. Intolerance of "others" seems very high, even though the ideological position is that individuals and individualism are very important. Societies such as the United States strongly promote individualism while at the same time ranking individuals in their perceived worth, with men above women, white people above nonwhites, straight people above those with other sexual orientation. What accounts for these inconsistencies?

Philosopher Hoyt L. Edge (1998) explains this puzzle. He notes that Western individualism assumes "atomism": that the world is composed of "atoms" that combine to create everything we see. For humans, the atoms are individuals. The atomism assumption underlies the use of "reductionism" in scientific explanation; it also informs economic theories based on methodological individualism. Western individualism also assumes the idea of a universal human nature. All humans are due respect because of this shared human nature. He points out that much of Western philosophy has debated the content of human nature while assuming that the answer, whatever it is, will apply to all humans. The most common answer is that humans are all similar because they are all "rational." Ironically, because they are rational, all humans should come to the same conclusions; those who do not are suspect. This can become the basis of hierarchy, when those in fortunate and powerful circumstances doubt the full rationality of those who are not like them. When people are assumed to have a common human nature, then difference is suspect even if people are valued for what they share. Edge's explanation with its focus only on rationality seems incomplete. Another source of hierarchy is the assumption that humans are different from other beings because they have consciousness or spirit and they think. That humans are above nature has led to the idea that the beings on Earth are ranked, with humans at the top.

Edge argues that societies that do not assume a universal human nature have a more radical idea of individualism than is present in Western philosophy. In a relational culture, each person is assumed to be created by his or her relationships. Even in a family, each person will be different because of different relationships. He points out that in Aboriginal culture in Australia, each person is assumed to be different, and the difference is approved. He cites one community's view: "'That's his own business,' the Pintupi say."

He makes a further point: people develop their own uniqueness. "A person grows into autonomy" through his or her relationships (Edge 1998, 37–38).

If there is no universal human nature, if each person is formed by his or her unique relationships, each one would be expected to be different. This difference becomes the value of the individual, and that uniqueness is to be left to develop as the person wishes to have it develop. In a footnote, Edge explains that if one searches for what might be universal among humans, it is "shape." A further assumption in Indigenous societies is that humans are not separated from other animals by language, by rationality, or even by a sense of self. As unique entities, other-than-human persons can also join relationships.

The idea that relationality forms persons exists in thinking from the Andes. A young Aymara scholar, Marcelo Fernández Osco, explains the idea of a person as a continuing growing entity.

> Thus, both the piq'i [reason] and the chuyma [heart, feelings] are constitutive of the being and doing of the jaqi (social person). The jaqi, conformed by a male and a female, is not a solitary entity but a being inserted in a multi-dimensional community, which is, in turn, part of a larger collective of humans and non-humans. What from a modern Western perspective would be an individual is, therefore, invariably in an unfinished state; his or her betterment is only possible within the collectivity and through interactions with others, human and non-human. (Fernández Osco 2010, 34)

Fernández Osco is explaining the idea of autonomy from his perspective within a larger book that considers the relationship between autonomy and globalization (Blaser et al. 2010). He objects to the racial hierarchy that accompanies the Western idea of an individual, and advocates that the Andean idea of an ayllu also be given prominence. An ayllu is relationally based and includes the nonhuman persons in a territory. The racial hierarchy to which he objects is an example of the intolerance generated by assuming rational individuals would all end up the same and that humans are different and superior to nonhumans.

Another aspect of this assumption of a universal human nature is the particular form that it has taken in the West. Marshall Sahlins (1996) has summarized the origins of the ideas that describe "economic man" in a lecture honoring anthropologist Sidney Mintz. He applies cultural/anthropological analysis to support the idea that basic assumptions of the "western cosmology" originate in the origin story of Adam and Eve. Vine Deloria Jr. (1997) recommends that anthropologists apply their analysis to their own culture; Sahlins does just that. Because of the outcome of the interaction in the garden, God threw man out of the Garden of Eden, leaving man to struggle against his nature, which is to be motivated by pleasure and pain. The motivation is also egotistical, which then makes a coercive government necessary to deal with the basics of human nature. When the government is democratic, as in the United States, checks and balances are needed because humans with power will misuse it. Sahlins's presentation is long, giving many examples of how the fundamental ideas have changed over time without ever discarding the particular cosmology that originates with the story of man's fall from the Garden of Eden. He also documents how that cosmology still motivates much of social science.

There is more to this than just individualism; it takes the form of "economic man," the idea of a selfish, self-centered individual. Not only did being thrown out of the Garden of Eden make man a creature of desire, but nature also became corrupted and stopped providing for man's needs. Sahlins points out that a famous definition of economics explicitly refers to Genesis.

> We have been turned out of Paradise. We have neither eternal life nor unlimited means of gratification. Everywhere we turn, if we choose one thing we must relinquish others which, in different circumstances, we would wish not to have relinquished. Scarcity of means to satisfy ends of varying importance is an almost ubiquitous condition of human behaviour. Here, then, is the unity of the subject of Economic Science, the forms assumed by human behaviour in disposing of scarce means. (Sahlins 1996, 397, citing Robbins 1952, 15)

Sahlins summarizes his argument: "The Economic Man of modern times was still Adam. Indeed, the same scarcity-driven creature of need survived long enough to become the main protagonist of all the human sciences" (397). Sahlins is correct that Lionel Robbins's formulation is very often cited to explain what economics is about (Marglin 2008, 293); in mid-December 2019, Google Scholar reported 6,059 citations.

Edge bases his analysis of individuality in relational cultures on two examples, Bali and Australian Aborigines. They differ because Balinese culture has more hierarchy than do the Aborigines. Both are similar, however, in defining people's selves in a relational framework. When hierarchy is the background for the philosophy, possibly the valuation of each individual will not be equal as it is in Australian Aboriginal society. The main message, however, is that in a relational society, individuals are assumed to be created by their relationships, which are different for each person. Apgar found that Edge's analysis applies to the Guna of Panama (Apgar et al. 2015). Anthropologist Theresa DeLeane O'Nell (1996) reports that members of my own tribe also conceive of persons in this relational way.

Because of their emphasis on relationships, Indigenous peoples have erroneously been classified by social theorists as "collectivist" people, in contrast to "individualist" people. Each of these terms carries much baggage, such as being identified with "communism" or "capitalism." Harry C. Triandis has summarized the distinction in many works, and has distinguished the concept of an individual's loyalties from the presence or absence of hierarchy (Triandis et al. 1988; Triandis and Gelfand 1998; Triandis 2018). Untangling the differences requires a lengthy analysis, which would need to begin with Edge's observation about atomism and a shared essence. Both individualism and collectivism assume atomistic individuals; individualism assumes bottom-up social formation and collectivism assumes top-down social formation. Mark Granovetter (1995) points out that the individual/collectivism dichotomy has had great influence on the analysis of top-down corporate organizations, leading to failure to identify internal organizational structures based on development of relationships.

The expanding European settlers emphasized the benefits of individual agents operating to create new economic activities. They carried with them ideas about individuals that had strong effects on the economic development of their societies. A variety of the distinction between individualistic and collectivistic was evident in policy regarding Indians. In her book on the allotment policy, historian Emily Greenwald (2002) summarizes the thought of settler society in the nineteenth century. She explains that in the nineteenth century, people believed that "civilized society was marked by political and economic individualism, while savagery was marked by tribalism and collectivism." As a consequence, efforts to assimilate Indians meant turning them into individuals by making them owners of private property.

The combination of assumed common essence and assumed hierarchy among all beings, including humans, leads to the classification of humans into various "races," in which all members of one race have the same essence. One thus needs to find a terminology that adequately describes the many types of Indigenous peoples. Are they American Indians, Native Americans, Alaskan Natives, Aborigines, First Nations, Aboriginal people, Indigenous peoples, or something else? Each of the settler societies has adopted a variety of classification that the Native peoples of the occupied lands reject, preferring to be called by their own names as they have selected them. This issue of adopted group identity is addressed in the next chapter, using the idea of peoplehood as a way to describe the similarities without assuming sameness. This book primarily uses "Indigenous," but that term also suffers from its implied assumption of sameness. In a world where human persons are formed by their relationships, variety means single descriptive terms are never going to be adequate.

The idea that individuals acting in their self-interest would generate progress was expressed clearly by Senator Henry Dawes after he visited a successful Indigenous nation in Oklahoma. Even after observing the successes of that nation, he refused to accept the evidence that their system had virtues.

> The head chief told us that there was not a family in that whole nation that had not a home of its own. There was not a pauper in that Nation, and the Nation did not owe a dollar. It built its own capitol . . . and it built its schools and its hospitals. Yet the defect of the system was apparent. They have got as far as they can go, because they own their land in common. It is Henry George's system, and under that there is no enterprise to make your home any better than that of your neighbors. There is no selfishness, which is at the bottom of civilization. Till this people will consent to give up their lands, and divide them among their citizens so that each one can own the land he cultivates, they will not make much more progress. (Otis 1973, 10–11)

In his proposed system of taxation, Henry George maintained that all land should be recognized as collective property. Land rents should not belong to the "owner" of the land; rather, it should be taxed fully and provide the funds for a government. This contradicts the idea of private property in land, owned by individuals, which was a key basis of the expanding American economy. Rent to land in a private property system belongs to the owner of the land, who should not have the rent fully taken away.

The irony here is that the probable topic of his complaint, the Cherokee land tenure system, was neither George's system nor a private property system. It was a relational system that included the land; such systems are described in chapter 4. To explain this point fully, one needs to examine a different type of individual, one that is created by their relations and affects those same relations. One cannot just reject the "economic man" of standard economics and much of social science in the West; one needs to offer a replacement. Sociologist Margaret Archer provides a model of man that fits well with the ideas of relationality that different Indigenous people have articulated.

Although both she and her co-author, Pierpaolo Donati, are European sociologists, they have mostly separated themselves from the ideas inherited from the Enlightenment, in the process critiquing that inheritance. They argue that to free oneself from the "oscillation between methodological individualism and holism," one must find a path that is not located "midway between the individual (the Self) and the whole (the social system), nor is it a mixture or a bridge between the two." They argue for changing both by recognizing a different type of reality, the "relational order of reality" (Donati and Archer 2015, 32). Describing that framework begins with Archer's description of the person conceived as a product of his or her relations.

Relational Persons

Archer and Donati argue that persons are "personal relational subjects," who get together to form social relational subjects. "Subject" is a potentially confusing term. Simply identifying them as relational persons avoids "subject," which in other contexts means a topic of interest and doesn't necessarily refer to people. Another connection is to the idea of "subjectivity," the idea that a person's views are unique to them, as opposed to "objective" facts, which do not depend on the subjectivity of individuals. The word *subject* refers to the subjectivity of the relational goods that more than one person creates when they join to become a social relational subject, a "We," and that disappear when the "We" is dissolved, as with a divorce. A married couple shares property that can be divided between them; their shared children can also be divided between them, living with them at different times. Their sense of love as a couple, however, disappears or has disappeared when the divorce becomes necessary. When a couple separates, the personal identity of each changes and no longer includes the identity of the couple that they previously were. They continue to exchange things and share their children, but they no longer are part of a couple.

A person's subjectivity is formed through their relations to the three orders of reality: natural, practical, and social. Each person deals with his or her situation by accepting and working with the natural order by eating, walking, and swimming if necessary. People learn skills that allow them to interact with the practical order. They learn to ride bicycles if necessary. And they interact with other people, which consists of the social order of reality. In chapter 3 of *The Relational Subject* (Donati and Archer 2015), Archer explains in great detail the formation of a person and the resulting full person. She begins by summarizing one of her books, *Being Human* (Archer 2000a); part of the complexity of her exposition results from her desire to clearly explain why her approach differs from that of other sociologists. Importantly, a person develops four parts of his or her being through relationships.

A full person can be seen from four different perspectives as "I," "Me," "We," and "You." "I" is a person aware of existing continually over time. "I" has a sense of self, which is different from a concept of self. The sense of self exists even as a person changes his or her concept of self over time. To the extent that there is a shared essence in human nature, it is that everyone has a sense of self.

"Me" describes the social position in which persons find themselves, with advantages and disadvantages in the social order. Most of the characteristics determining the social position, initially, are given by or specially recognized by society. A person is born into a family. The family first places a person into society with its connections to others, such as clan members in societies that emphasize extending kinship ties. As a person grows, he or she discovers what personal characteristics mean, and whether or not he or she likes that meaning. A person develops the characteristics he or she likes. Some, like height or birth order, are really fixed. Others, such as gender, skin color, or sexual orientation, can be changed with difficulty or disguised by the person. Others, such as education level, practical skills, language, or dialect, can be changed. With a sense of self that remains, a person's concept of social self changes as he or she grows and develops.

"We" describes the person's relationships with other people, initially his or her family. Later, the "We" may be people who share the same characteristics in the "Me" aspect of a person and organize because of joint concerns.

The "We" is where a relational person, a personal relational subject, joins one or more other personal relational subjects in joint efforts to get along in the world, creating social relational subjects. Archer also uses "Agent" to describe persons joined together as a "We." One or more persons can be together as a family. "We" may organize to become a Corporate Agent, a relational subject with sufficient power to change the opportunities and constraints they face both as persons and as relational subjects. In the stratified settler societies such as those in the Americas, the creation of Corporate Agents through social movements is necessary for those in the lower strata in order to deal with the disadvantages. The resurgence of Indigenous peoples involves many relationships and especially emphasizes relationships with land. Michael Asch, John Borrows, and James Tully (2018) have assembled a group of authors to explain the recent efforts in Canada.

In connection with the previous three characteristics, a person obtains a "You," a social identity that defines a role in a social structure, such as an electrician, a teacher, or an athlete. Such social structures may previously exist or be created in a new social structure as a result of the actions of a "We" acting as a Corporate Agent. Archer uses another term to describe the "You": Actor. An Actor is a person holding a role; the role can be in a relational social structure, or it can be a position in a nonrelational Corporate Agent such as a business, university, or government.

The coming out of a gay man illustrates the distinction between sense of self and concept of self. Prior to accepting one's homosexuality, a man conceives of himself as heterosexual, possibly even with a wife and a marriage. The closet metaphor is helpful because one hides that part of oneself through denial. One's subjective concept of self is different from the objective reality of self, in that sexual orientation is a solid reality that can't be changed, only accepted or denied. One's view of his identity is fallible but real. The idea that sexual orientation is objective is contested; whether or not it is subjective or objective, it is real at any one moment.

The experience of the gay community in the United States also illustrates the notion that kinship can be a model for the "We" of a social relational subject. Gay men and gay women are kin in that they share a sexual orientation even if they do not share a genealogy as does a clan. Once a person comes out, he or she can join any number of groups. The relatively impersonal experience of entering a gay bar provides a sense of the potential change of "Me" to "We" to the isolated gay person. The negative self-image as a lowly closeted homosexual can begin to change when others of the same type become friends. Gay people formed more substantive relational subjects, Corporate Agents, when they organized as a social movement sharing the goal of removing the legal and social barriers to following a satisfying life in the United States.

Archer explains how the four components of a person change throughout one's life, in an analytic sequence of change in which at the start of a period, all four are givens. Then during that period, a person acts to address the issues created by the "Me," in cooperation with other people, the "We," and in the process may be able to obtain both a changed "Me" and a new "You," or role. Through all this, the "I" is a continuous sense of self even as the person changes.

After exploring the ways in which a person can be understood, Archer turns to exploring how a person interacts with the world in more detail. In *Being Human*, she explores how humans undertook each of the four components of their being, stressing in particular the creation of Primary and Corporate Agency. Primary Agents are too weak to change their opportunities and constraints, unlike Corporate Agents. She discusses people's "inner conversation," or "interior dialogue." She came to realize that the inner conversation would provide an answer to an important question: How does a person deal with the given conditions, the social structure and the culture of his world? She had identified that persons join together, but how does that happen? Her answer is personal reflexivity. A key preparation for the consideration of relationships is personal reflexivity. Reflexivity is "the regular exercise of the mental ability, shared by all normal people, to consider themselves in relation to their (social) contexts and vice versa" (Archer 2007, 4). She found that few sociologists had considered personal reflexivity; the American pragmatists had done so. William James tried to understand the deep meaning of introspection for an individual. Then Charles Sanders Pierce focused much attention on how a person could use an internal conversation to determine what actions to take. Pierce emphasized "interiority, subjectivity, and personal causal efficacy" (Archer 2003, 78). Archer charges George Herbert Mead, a more famous sociologist, with denying all three of these characteristics of the internal conversation (79–92). She insists that people take the facts of society and interpret them in their own personal way; there is always a context. But the internal conversation is with oneself; it is not society's conversation, which comes later. The person decides as an

"I" based on his or her characteristics that may be shared with other people, the "Me" and the social role that the person occupies, as an "Actor" (118–29).

The Internal Conversation

Included in Archer's complex analysis of a person is each person's internal conversation. Everyone can understand the idea that persons engage in internal conversations. These are conversations with oneself in considering how to relate to the world. Numerous examples can be given. We ask ourselves simple things like "What shall I have for dinner?" That is a practical question about maintaining one's life. A question that has great social content is "Shall I marry the person I think I love?" If "marry" seems too specific, one could restate the question, "Shall I form a close personal relationship with that person, by moving into a common residence and doing all the other things people do when they form relationships like marriage?" Although one would probably discuss this with the person chosen, the key point is personal reflexivity.

The internal conversation is the conduct of reflexivity: the consideration of what one is thinking and what one is doing in each set of circumstances. Reflexivity connects the person to the world around him or her. It motivates action based on thinking and considerations of alternatives. For Archer, the internal conversation solves a sociological problem: what specifically connects structure and agency, which she poses as a question: "How does structure influence agency?" Structure consists of the circumstances that confront any person or group of persons when they are planning to take action. Structure consists of material circumstances as well as the cultural ideas that are available or enacted into law and which influence or constrain people's actions regarding their concerns and goals. Action is what agents do. A person examines the constraints and enablements, the obstacles and opportunities that he or she confronts. These are objective factors that confront agents. A person then evaluates the objective factors according to his or her own concerns, the goals in life. This evaluation is an internal process and a subjective process, which then leads to actions that cause change for the person and for society.

This process of evaluation is the internal conversation. Upon coming to a decision, a person or a group of people act. What they decide to do is difficult to predict based on information about the circumstances and information about the desires of the person because deciding what to do is a subjective, personal process that cannot be fully predicted. The action can be explained, however, by asking the person why they acted as they did.

Some theorists have denied that people do have full access to their own motivations; Archer (2003, 93–150) discusses at length some of the philosophical, psychological, and sociological objections to allowing a person to be the authoritative reporter on why he or she has taken certain actions. An outside observer can look at the circumstances and draw conclusions about what might or might not be possible for a person in those circumstances. That evaluation would be the observer's subjective consideration of the facts, which may correspond to the person's own evaluation. But the internal conversation is internal, not observable unless the person reports it, and even then, the report will likely be incomplete. Once Archer had convinced herself that people act based on their internal conversations, she found that very little research had been conducted to determine how such conversations occurred, and whether all people undertook the deliberations in the same way. She discovered they did not.

Her first study involved lengthy interviews with 20 subjects in and around Warwick University, where she worked (Archer 2003). Based on the results of the pilot study, she undertook a larger study in the city of Coventry, with 128 longer interviews (Archer 2007). Both works were static, revealing different patterns of internal conversations based on onetime interviews of each subject. Realizing that the world was changing quickly, she undertook a third study, which interviewed college sociology students during their three years of education (Archer 2012). These three intensely qualitative studies allowed Archer to present some very interesting results that help greatly in understanding some key patterns among persons. Surprisingly, her results resonate well with issues in Indigenous societies. In her third book, she argues that in the rapidly changing period of late capitalism, young people as they grow up, and then as adults, must be reflexive. The rapid changes and the many choices available have created a "reflexive imperative."

The Reflexive Imperative of Colonial Encounters

Archer (2012) has argued that the time of late modernity in which we now live presents young people with a reflexive imperative: the rapidity of change and the variety of choices available mean that people's internal conversations are required to deal with the many options available. The "reflexive imperative" is that all individuals need to deliberate and decide what course to follow in their lives, as the options proliferate because of the increasing complexity of the global economy. Long ago, the reflexive imperative applied also to Indigenous peoples confronting colonists, whether the invaders are settlers or a conquering army. Once the conquerors have established their government, they proceed to take Indigenous lands and impose assimilationist pressures on individuals. As John Locke spelled out, Indigenous peoples, in order to qualify as landowners, needed to adopt Christianity and accept private property in land. Missionaries sought to convert Indigenous peoples to one or another form of Christianity. In Canada, the United States, and Australia, children were removed from their homes and placed in either foster care or residential schools. Children had to choose between loyalty to the ideas of their home communities or joining the dominant society. The choice involved coercion because they were prohibited from speaking their own language and forced to dress and maintain their hair as non-Indigenous persons. In a highly racist situation, where white colonizers rejected equal opportunity to darker peoples, sometimes the choice was easy. A dark person was not truly offered assimilation. The only ameliorative factor was that the settlers augmented their desire to take land by accepting some Indigenous peoples with white blood. By defining mixed bloods as non-Indigenous, more land was available, and mixed bloods had a wider choice about which society to join.

Indians confronted a reflexive imperative in the United States when the dominant society attempted to assimilate them into the settler society. For instance, children were removed from their homes and sent to boarding schools. They were pressured to change their identity to "assimilated Indian" or, for some, "white." The expropriation of land and confinement to reservations reduced most of the components of their "traditional" lifestyles. The application of the allotment policy and the opening of reservations to non-Indians further reduced the agricultural options. Many survived by seeking wage work in the non-Indian economy. Others lived off the meager rations that were available from the federal government. Those that could not pass as "white" had to endure discrimination based on their race or ethnicity. The policies of settler colonialism created a reflexive imperative for Indians in the nineteenth century. That globalization has presented a reflexive imperative to young people in the twenty-first century explains the useful conjunction of evidence presented by Terry Huffman and by Archer, as explained in the next section.

Modes of Reflexivity

Archer (2003, 2007, 2012) discovered that people conduct their internal conversations in at least four different ways as they develop and become occupants of social roles. Her interviews with people in England about the decisions of each type of reflexivity revealed that there were four general patterns, both in terms of what kinds of upbringing created each type of reflexivity, and what kind of deliberation each group makes. A strength of the study is Archer's attention to the "reflexive imperative," the necessity to choose among alternatives. A limitation of the study is its use of people in England; people in her first two samples, however, were purposely selected to be heterogeneous. The college students in her third sample were more homogeneous. A completely separate study by Terry Huffman (2008) of American Indian college students found four types of responses in South Dakota very similar to what Archer found in England.

Although Huffman's research on ways that young adults adjust to educational opportunity does not use Archer's framework, his results identify four types of reactions in educational settings that map rather exactly into Archer's categories (Huffman 2001, 2008, 2013). His interviews and questionnaires provide evidence to establish the relevance of her typology to interpret typical reactions that can be seen in Indian communities.

Archer's category of family follows the English and American pattern (also shared with Inuit peoples) where men and women pair up and pursue their own lives in nuclear families. Children are then raised in two-parent homes (in the main model) and depend on their parents for socialization. In other societies, couples move in with either the wife's or the husband's parents and family. Socialization occurs within the extended family. Since university students in England grow up in separate families, rather than extended families, the full possible repertoire of reflexive deliberation may be larger for communities that use extended families. One consequence might be that the mix of reflexive internal conversations may be different in extended families. Huffman's data suggest that the types of reflexive internal conversations are not affected by the different family structures: there are four different types both for British and for American Indian college students.

In order to present Archer's classification of reflexives, modified with Huffman's work, table 1 describes the different approaches, along with some factors in family upbringing and experience that may affect choice of reflexive style. The top row gives Archer's names for the reflexive type, followed by six rows containing her description of each mode. The next two rows give Huffman's names and descriptions for the similar type in his work.

Communicative Reflexives

Those persons whose internal conversations require completion and confirmation by others before resulting in courses of action are communicative reflexives. They have a circle of persons with whom they consult for advice for major decisions. They were comfortable in their upbringing and do not want to pursue possibilities much different from those of their parents. They will forego major opportunities in order to replicate their parents' or other family members' experiences. Communicative reflexives are mainly responsible for maintaining existing cultural patterns because they reproduce the thought patterns of their families of origin. Huffman identifies "estranged students" as ones who do not find their experiences in mainstream educational institutions to be acceptable; they are "estranged" from those systems, but of course they are not estranged from their natal communities. They do not want to sacrifice their connections to their friends and family in the home community, something that occurs when students are away studying in college.

Archer maintains that communicative reflexives are the type of people who served to maintain systems in the past and continue to do so in the present. The communicative reflexives, in deciding what ideas to support, do choose to replicate the thinking of their families. Part of the reason is that these people come from supportive families. Another reason is that they have stable work environments to enter when they reach adulthood, similar to those of their parents. Their actions and conversations support replicating the system.

In situations with many choices, communicative reflexives reject the need for choice; they wish to remain in the system in which they grew up. They seek a career that will replicate their current situation. They seek new friends who have commonalities with themselves. They reject the choices offered in a university and return home. In Archer's largest study, with people of many ages in Coventry, she found that the communicative reflexives had

TABLE 1 Comparison of Modes of Reflexivity

Archer's reflexivity type	Communicative	Meta	Autonomous	Fractured
Relation with natal background	Identifiers	Disengaged	Independents	Rejecters
Relation with home friends	Retention	Rejection	Selection	Absence
Reason for relationship with new friends	Commonalities	Values	Interests	Dependency
Purpose of career	Replication	Promoting change	Material benefits	Ephemeral appeal
Location of career	Family example	Third sector	Financial and public services	Uncertain
Response to today's situational logic of opportunity	Rejection	Acceptance	Competitive adaptation	Passivity
Huffman's categories for college students	Estranged (from college; not comfortable in college)	Transcultural (able to act in either culture)	Assimilated (accept the dominant culture's values)	Marginalized (on the edge either at home or in college)
Type of participation in university education	Remain connected to home; treat education as separate from their plans	Identify with both cultures, and handle both well	Adopt dominant society educational values	"Lost" between the alternatives, and unable to decide how to respond
Response in an Indigenous community	Support for continuation of current relations	Support of change and modernization within the community's values	Frustration and departure for other places	Stay or go depending on short-term availability

Source for the first seven rows: Archer 2012. *Source for the eighth and ninth rows:* Huffman 2008. The final row is the author's suggestion of possible responses.

acquired less education than the next two types (Archer 2007, 335). While this is a result from a very small sample, it indicates a certain consistency with Huffman's results.

Meta Reflexives

Meta reflexives are persons who critically evaluate their previous own internal dialogues and are critical about effective action in society. Like autonomous reflexives, described next, they decide for themselves their course of action, but in the process of deciding, they are critically reflective about the sources of their ideas and about their place in society. They ask themselves why particular ideas are appealing and compare ideas. They critically analyze the options available on the basis of values as well as opportunity.

Like communicative reflexives, "meta reflexives" come from relatively supportive families, but they do not follow their parents' and relatives' ways of thinking. At a young age, they have become aware of other possibilities, and they carefully evaluate the alternatives. If they choose to accept Indigenous identity, it is a result of careful reflection, with an emphasis on values. In the population Archer studied, the meta reflexives tended to go to work in the public sector or nonprofit organizations. They weren't particularly interested in the commercial sector. As the meta reflexives plan their lives, they seek to change current patterns and choices.

They correspond to Huffman's category of "transcultural" students. He documents how these students reach a time where they realize that their Indigenous values are a source of strength. They act in ways that work in the non-Indigenous setting without adopting the values taught in those settings. The transcultural meta reflexives are likely to accept Indigenous values, but with considerable thought and critique. They can complete their college education. One student described the advantage in college: "I feel that I have a special advantage because I have two cultures that I can draw on. I can learn from here, too. And I am learning" (Huffman 2001, 15). They would be advocates for change if need be. If the reservation does not offer opportunities in the public or nonprofit sectors, they will seek work outside the reservation but may choose to remain loyal to the tribe's values and return if an opportunity arises or for their retirement years. Huffman labels his discovery of the meta-reflexive approach the transcultural hypothesis: "the transculturation hypothesis assumes that American Indian students simply increase their cultural repertoire, adding the skills needed while keeping their native heritage intact" (18).

Autonomous Reflexives

Another group that sustains self-contained internal conversations are the autonomous reflexives. Their internal conversations lead directly to action. Autonomous reflexives emphasize individualism and their ability to decide for themselves which of the options open to them should be selected. Their tendency is to take the opportunities available, especially in business and the corporate world. Of the four types, autonomous reflexives are the closest to "economic man," in that they put material self-interest first.

They see the necessity of selecting among opportunities available, but they aren't too interested in changing existing structures. They tend to be interested in the commercial and business sector. In the population Archer studied, autonomous reflexives tend to come from families where the parents had separated or divorced. In Indigenous communities, these individuals may also have parents sent to boarding schools, where they would recognize the need to be autonomous, and where they would have been cut off from the supportive environment that encourages communicative reflexivity. Huffman's "assimilated" students fit this category; they see the opportunities available in the non-Indigenous economy and pursue educational careers that prepare them for those opportunities. The autonomous reflexives appear to be the people who take advantage of opportunities for jobs and education without selecting their direction with great guidance from the elements of their community's values. Some entrepreneurs of the tribe may come from this group, and they will leave the reservation seeking opportunity if the reservation does not provide them. They also will seek careers in the private sector outside the reservation. If opportunities exist on the reservation, they will stay. In public discussions of the tribe's alternatives, they are likely to emphasize the need to adjust to current economic realities and go along with the mainstream methods of organizing enterprises and businesses.

Fractured Reflexives

Some people have internal conversations that only intensify their distress and disorientation rather than leading to purposeful courses of action. Without supportive assistance, fractured reflexives have difficulty in making sensible decisions, or even deciding. Fractured reflexives aren't able to use their internal conversation to find direction. They are people who have suffered considerable trauma in their lives, such as having abusive parents. They reject the values from their families, but their personal makeup has been so traumatized that they are unable to take their lives in a useful direction. They tend to remain fractured if the trauma has continued, but when they have a supportive environment, they can start to have productive internal conversations that lead to decisions and purposeful action. This was the case with some of the people in Archer's studies. These appear to be Huffman's "marginalized" students, whose inability to be decisive limits their academic success.

More Evidence About Persons in Indigenous Societies

This book argues that the complicated stratified person that Archer describes is a good description of the person in Indigenous relational societies, both in the past and in the present. Four types of evidence prove that reflexive persons like Donati and Archer describe were created in Indigenous societies: child-rearing practices, the standards of leadership, recognition of personal development, and the attribution of agency to nonhumans. Although the reflexive imperative is strong today, it was not weak in the past.

First, the child-rearing practices of Indigenous communities generate autonomous persons that are much like the ones we are familiar with today. Much evidence supports the idea that American Indian societies supported their young people to find their own spiritual path and that the selection of a role in society was not preordained. Children were watched carefully to see how they acted, what they seemed to prefer. Among the peoples that believed in reincarnation, watching a child could help in determining which of the people in his or her genealogy had returned (Mills 1994, 118–19). This could perhaps cause some pressure to conform, but the judgment was usually tentative. One result was a high tolerance of a variety of sexual orientations. This wide tolerance outraged the Christian missionaries who promoted their own religion. Although there was a sexual division of labor, an individual woman could decide to take up men's pursuits and individual men could undertake women's roles. This strong commitment to individual autonomy suggests that persons of the reflexive types Archer and Donati describe were present in Indian societies (Graeber and Wengrow 2021, 37–46).

Second, American Indian societies were democratic societies of persons, all of whom were respected and able to participate. Women, for instance, were not placed in a lower category than men, although they were expected to engage in different roles in the economies of the societies. Among the Iroquois, for instance, the chiefs were selected by the women and stayed in office if the women approved of their behavior. The radical nature of political processes led anthropologist Pierre Clastres to write a book, *Society Against the State* (1987), explaining the ways in which Indigenous communities restricted the power of their leaders. Europeans mistakenly assumed there was no government among the Indigenous peoples because there were no states that looked like the ones in Europe, with royal families controlling their governments, raising their armies, and administering their systems of justice.

An illustration of the difference in governance is the concept of "sovereign immunity." In European legal systems, the monarch could only be sued with his or her consent. The king was above the law. This was not true in the Americas. Even in the very hierarchical houses on the Northwest Coast, the head titleholder was accountable to the people in his house. If he failed to carry out his duties, he was vulnerable to an arranged kidnapping or an outright execution (Walens 1981; Donald 1997). In the areas with family hunting territories where beaver became important, the head trapper or head hunter for a family's territory had authority only so long as he exercised it appropriately, taking care of the land and giving those with rights to access the land the access that they deserved (C. Scott 1986, 2018).

Third, Indigenous peoples recognize that persons are always growing and developing. Hoyt Edge writes, "A person does not have autonomy as a part of basic human nature, but grows into autonomy by developing the uniqueness and particularly found in a set of totemic relationships. Autonomy is not a capacity, but rather a project that one achieves through growth, which is basically spiritual" (1998, 38). On the Northwest Coast, young titleholders work their way up the hierarchy by assuming a series of names, each a separate identity that shows the learning that is occurring.

Fourth, even more radically, is the inclusion of nonhumans in society through relations. The inclusion of animals in human society can be illustrated by the application of ideas of "skin" in Australia. Miles C. C. Holmes and Wanta Jampijinpa (2013) explain that if one is concerned about a particular animal, say, because its existence is endangered, one step in learning about the animal is to know its skin group. This tells which humans the animal is related to and, from that, who is responsible for good relations with the animal. Once animals are assumed to have consciousness, the question arises as to how they see the world. Hunters recognize the autonomy of the animals they hunt by watching for signals to indicate an animal is presenting himself for harvest. As a person grows into an adult, he or she must attend to relationships with nonhumans as well as humans.

• • •

This chapter has explained a stratified conception of the person, with an emphasis on how persons use their internal conversations to make decisions about how to "make their way in the world." The focus has been on the interaction of "I," "Me," and "You," with passing attention to "We." The next chapter addresses how persons join a variety of social relational subjects as part of making their way in the world. By joining with other persons into relational subjects, persons are able to influence the structure of society and culture as well as to achieve their own personal goals.

CHAPTER 3

Relationships Build Indigenous Identity

The previous chapter explains how a person develops an identity through relationships with the natural, practical, and social orders. Each unique person is different because of those relationships. The person decides how to live his or her life through an internal conversation by reflecting his or her relationships to each order. The natural order affects one's physical well-being. The practical order is where one achieves competence in doing things with objects. The social order is where a person finds self-worth in connection with other persons. For most sociologists, the social order consists of humans dealing with each other. For Indigenous peoples, much or all of nature is also part of the social order because other beings have consciousness and can react to human actions and speech. The social order is the place of relationships with other persons. This chapter focuses on the "We" part of a person, the contribution of relationships to a person's identity and the contribution of persons to creating social relational subjects with their own identity.

Relational subjects, also identified as relational agents, are the associated persons who are cooperating to produce and share one or more relational goods. Because of their relationship, they can jointly become powerful or at least effective agents when acting to achieve the goals they set for themselves. Donati and Archer use "relational subject" to describe persons who are cooperating to produce and share relational goods. This emphasizes the difference between "object" and "subject," in that objects are subjected to the power of subjects. The terminology is confusing because all the citizens of England are the queen's subjects; communities that are studied by anthropologists are described as the subjects of the anthropologists' inquiry. Because agents do things, the idea of "agent" may be better. On the other hand, the idea of a relational subject emphasizes that the relational subject is held together by one or more shared relational goods. Relational goods are primarily subjective in character, as explained later. Because this subjective element is so important, the use of "subject" in "relational subject" emphasizes the subjective component. Another relevant point is that nonhumans, often treated as objects, become subjects when they are part of a relational subject. They participate in actions as they are treated well by others in the relationship.

In economics, there is a "principal–agent" literature on interactions of principals, the bosses in an organization, for instance, and the agents, who are the workers acting within a set of incentives determined by the principal. Because the agents may not act in the ways desired by the principal, interesting questions arise. It is well known that the workers on a factory floor in which each worker is being paid for his own production may start cooperating with each other to set a quota agreeable among themselves. Workers who produce at too high a rate would be ostracized from the camaraderie of the other workers. Such a situation illustrates action by a relational subject: the workers act in unison to achieve the goal of not working too hard for the boss (Granovetter 1985). To call them a relational subject emphasizes that they are no longer objects under the full control of the boss.

The chapter begins by comparing relational subjects to the idea of social capital; the two concepts are complementary but distinct. Before moving to further consideration of relational subjects, the chapter summarizes rules for creating such relationships, drawing on both Indigenous and non-Indigenous sources of advice. Then a more detailed definition of relational subject is presented before examining different levels of relational subjects: micro, meso, and macro. A society of different levels of relational subjects is compared to the public/private organization that mainstream economics uses. The chapter next examines Indigenous identity at the macro level. Indigenous peoples self-identify using the components of peoplehood. After years of work by Indigenous peoples, the United Nations adopted the Declaration on the Rights of Indigenous Peoples; its preamble clearly describes peoplehood.

Social Capital and Relational Goods

A society of relational subjects can be contrasted to a society of individuals connected by exchanges. This distinction can be explained by comparing relational goods with social capital. The concept of mana in Māori culture provides an example of a relational good generated and held by relationships. Mana is a subjective concept generated by relationships, describing the power of a person or a group to impact the lives of others, the condition of land, and the strength of generations to affect each other. Kiri Dell, Nimbus Staniland, and Amber Nicholson (2018) describe four types of mana: (1) mana from universal connectedness, (2) mana from historically developed processes, (3) mana created by connections to people and land, and (4) mana that is personal power dependent on individual attributes. Three of these are generated by relationships; the fourth, personal power, is held by persons acting in relationships. In the first three cases, persons in relationships share the power of mana. When Māori theorists describe the system of mana, some have labeled it an "economy of mana" (Henare 2001; Dell, Staniland, and Nicholson 2018). As a non-Māori reading a description of mana, the idea seems elusive; it is something powerful, it is shared among Māori in different relationships, it is created at each of them, and it can vary in amount. It can be destroyed if rules of reciprocity are violated. Māori regard it as real.

Dara Kelly (2017) describes this system as an "economy of affection," terminology that she found Māori were using to describe mana when she wrote her dissertation. Her people, the Sto:lo of the lower Fraser River Valley, reported great sadness at having lost the ability to express affection at their potlatch feasts, which had been outlawed and not revived sufficiently when she interviewed her elders. She referred also to its use to describe economic relations in Africa as explained by Goran Hyden (2006), but Hyden did not appreciate economies of affection because they seemed to get in the way of development that he was advocating for Africa.

Relationships generate relational goods through the cooperation of all the people in the relationship, who orient themselves toward the production of the shared good and the joint goals or projects of the relationship. They attend to the needs or desires of each other, through communication in the process of generating the relational good or goods. Relational goods are created and shared by persons who are able to relate to each other in a reflexive manner, through their individual internal conversations and through conversations among the individuals. The relational goods such as mana, righteousness, trust, and civil power are all subjective, held among the persons involved in creating them, and not available to persons outside the relationships.

A very common conception of social capital among economists is to characterize social capital as personal preferences for cooperation and generalized trust in other people. Data for such attitudes can be collected in surveys such as the World Values Survey; correlations between the attitudes and economic growth then demonstrate that having many individuals having social capital attitudes can promote development as conventionally defined. Luigi Guiso, Paola Sapienza, and Luigi Zingales (2011) propose the term *civic capital* to emphasize that preferences for cooperation support civil society. Samuel Bowles and Herbert Gintis (2002, F425) propose that such social capital operates best in communities because communities have enough individuals with a preference for strong reciprocity. A strong reciprocator is cooperative and willing to punish noncooperators even if it is costly to oneself. The content of social capital exists as preferences inside the individuals who act together. Although the social capital literature addresses networks of agents, preferences for cooperation remain held by individuals (Uhlaner 1989; Bowles and Gintis 2002; Tabellini 2010; Guiso, Sapienza, and Zingales 2011).

Distinguishing the effects of social preferences compared to relational goods is difficult, however, because the outcomes of both are similar. The advantage of relational goods is that they explain the source of the social preferences. For instance, Jules Pretty (2003), when surveying social capital and natural resources management, emphasizes bonding links among people as well as the role of Indigenous peoples in caring for common property resources. Rather than emphasizing preferences, he focuses on trust, long-term obligations, and connectedness, without, however, seeing that Indigenous people include more-than-humans in relationships. In an earlier article, Pretty and Hugh Ward (2001, 221n4) stress the weaknesses of the individual-oriented economic model of social capital and provide examples of groups developing trust, norms, and other types of social connectedness as they mature.

Civic capital as measured by surveys of individual attitudes can detect the presence of individually held norms, without distinguishing them from relational goods, since the persons in relationships will articulate trust and other cooperative attitudes when asked. They may or may not say that people in general can be trusted, since the sense of trust applies to those people in relationships. Although people not sharing relational goods might also answer that people in general can be trusted, probably experiencing trust assists in expressing a belief in trusting even unknown people.

Some of the social capital literature assigns to parents the task of training their children to have preferences for social capital such as trust. The assumption is that parents are the source of civic values, which they in turn inherited from their parents. Pierpaolo Donati and Riccardo Prandini (2007a, 2007b) report that persons in families in Italy with high levels of relational goods are greater supporters of civic virtues than are persons in families with low levels of relational goods. They cite studies from other countries that have found similar links between familial relational goods and expression of values that support civic participation. Their articles are ones of many considering the effects of family ties on social capital; most found positive relationships.

A system of relational subjects contains micro-level, meso-level, and macro-level relational agents. The levels may be more than three; for purposes of describing systems of relationships, identifying three levels is convenient. One could label the levels as families, villages, and nations. A family is composed of persons, a village is composed of families, and a nation is composed of villages. Other terminology is used for each of these levels. For instance, instead of "family," one could say "extended family" or "clan." Kinship designations can be very complex. An extended family includes the grandparents, parents, cousins, and children. The children of parents who are siblings would be cousins. The grandparents could be a set of older people who are related to each other because they were the children of the previous generation. A clan might be a group of extended families, or the extended families could themselves be described as a clan. While some societies distinguish aunts and uncles of children, in others all the older generation are parents.

Many observers have described the great variety of relational agents existing in Indigenous communities. The communities have their own names for them. If an outsider assumes they will find clans, villages, and nations, then the external observer needs to decide which of the names describes "clans," which describes "villages," and so forth. The external observer will not find the structures they expect because the expected structure is probably the one of the external observer's society. A better approach is to accept the classification of the community being visited. For example, the Māori report *whānau*, *hapu*, and *iwi*. Nisga'a report *wilps*. Australian Aborigines divide their groups by skin and totem.

Although there is great variety in the vertical and horizonal systems of relationships, from the point of view of a relational theory, all that is needed is an expectation that a society will have a variety of types of relationships. For Indigenous peoples, the relationships include nonhumans. The persons, human and nonhuman, in each relationship share relational goods as well as produce them.

In an article looking for "relational values" in Native Hawaiian worldviews, Rachelle K. Gould et al. (2019) found that direct questions about "values" would not work well in talking to Hawaiians because the word *value* doesn't exist in the Hawaiian language. They did find "value-like concepts," which are statements of relational goods: *aloha* seems to express sharing mana face to face, creating love and affection; *mālama* means taking care of land; *pono* seems to express righteousness in relationship to land. Each of these terms is widely used in Hawai'i; the article has pictures of signs displayed in parks to urge visitors to behave properly. The authors note that such public use of the words distorts their deeper meaning, yet they express ideas that are generated by relationships between persons and between persons and the land. Much of the difficulty in explaining the ideas seems to stem from the belief that a "value" is held by an individual. The authors are searching for such values held by individuals in expressing their attitudes toward land. They recognize that the values they are searching for are created by relationships, but the authors don't use the idea of relational goods created by relationships to explain what they have found.

These relational goods are primarily subjective. Persons in relationships share them, but persons outside relationships do not. The persons in the relationships perceive them and create them; if they leave a relationship, they cannot take their share with them because the relational good cannot be divided into pieces. It is like a "local public good," in the terminology of economics, recognized by the other persons in the relationship and shared equally, but not available to people outside the relationship. When economists define local public good, however, they have in mind something objective like fire protection services, public utilities like water and waste disposal, or a public park. The local public good is produced by the local government and the service provided to local residents. This differs from a relational good, which is a subjective entity jointly produced and used by the same persons.

If one is not careful, a circular argument can be used to demonstrate the existence of a relational good. Consider the idea of "respect" between a hunter and his prey. The prey expects to be treated properly; if it is not, then it will not offer itself for harvest and the hunter will go hungry. How does one determine which hunters have attained a high degree of respect from the hunted animal? The most successful hunters are the ones with that quality. If one asks the hunter what he does, then the objective activities required for showing such respect, such as thanking the animal, disposing of the remains properly, and sharing the meat with others, can be observed. If the prey could be interviewed, it might express the feeling of trust that has been developed. Without evidence of the subjective matters, the hunter's behavior would be the only evidence of the relational good.

Guiso, Sapienza, and Zingales (2011, 464) have charged Robert Putnam (1993), one of the advocates of social capital, with presenting a circular argument, using economic success in a region as evidence of social capital. The subjectivity of social capital adds to the problem because, unlike physical capital, social capital is difficult to measure objectively. It also does not deteriorate with use; rather, it improves. Similarly, using a relational good can make it stronger, the opposite of depreciation as in physical capital. Relational goods and social capital share these qualities. When people act in a trusting manner, thus using the relational good of trust, they also increase the strength of the trust.

Advice for Behaviors That Create Strong Relationships

There is a list of words to describe the goods (or bads, but ignore that for the moment) that are created when relationships are strong: mana, trust, solidarity, pono, aloha, and so forth. Although defining and describing these elusive things are difficult, one can describe the processes that create them. Such description serves two purposes: it aids in identifying relational goods, and it helps people form relational subjects.

Much advice is available about how to generate these goods by generating good relationships. Several sources are particularly helpful: the advice of the Haudenosaunee in creating peace, power, and righteousness; the advice of the Kluane and other Indigenous peoples in northern Canada to explain how to respect animals; and the advice of Roger Fisher and Scott Brown in preventing nuclear war between the Soviet Union and the United States. Other researchers have described the rules used by people in successful relationships to manage common property or in the establishment of groups that can survive in competition with others. The subheadings for each of the rules given here are taken from a very useful book by Roger Fisher and Scott Brown, *Getting Together: Building Relationships as We Negotiate* (1988), while the descriptions are based on many sources (Ostrom 1990; Williams 1997; Fenton 1998; Nadasdy 2003, 2007; Atkins, Wilson, and Hayes 2019).

- Learn how they see things
- Always consult before deciding—and listen
- Balance emotion with reason
- Persuasion, not coercion
- Acceptance: Deal seriously with whom we differ
- Reliability: Be wholly trustworthy, but not wholly trusting

Learn How They See Things

In order to have a good relationship, each participant needs to understand how other participants view the relationship and what they want to obtain from it. Although discussion is the primary means for development of mutual understanding among humans, observation and other methods need to be used with nonhumans.

Some of the Haudenosaunee steps in creating agreement particularly address each side, learning what the other side thinks. After a negotiating team from one village arrives at another, Haudenosaunee hosts provide a meal and give the visitors a place to have a good night's sleep. This is a time to informally learn what the other side is thinking about. The need to inquire as to the presence of a loss is part of getting to know the other side's viewpoint; if there was a death, then a ceremony of condolence is needed. As part of negotiations, the Iroquois would expect parties to "meet in the woods" outside of formal proceedings. These meetings address the need to see things from the other person's viewpoint, or at least to understand their concerns. The meetings in the woods are not formally part of the proceedings and therefore don't have to be constrained by the formalities of making proposals.

Part of understanding is to seek to know the interests of the other party or other members of a relationship. People vary in their reasons for joining a group; they all may share the attainment of the same relational goods but for their own reasons. Their abilities in different activities will lead to different roles. This differentiation is especially evident when nonhumans are members of a relational subject.

The advice for a hunter is to patiently watch what animals do. Paul Nadasdy observes, "Over time, hunters build up a vast store of experiential knowledge; they have seen the land in thousands of subtly different climatic and seasonal conditions." Based on that experience, they develop an intuitive understanding and can "feel" what animals may do (Nadasdy 2003, 98). He reports on a very experienced hunter, Moose Jackson, who could tell where a moose was by looking at recent tracks. How does he do that? Nadasdy reports, "He stressed, he can only do this because he knows what moose do and 'how they think.'" Jackson reported as well that "his father and others had taught him some things, but mostly he had learned by hunting and by being open to what the animals had to teach him. . . . One must be willing to invest the time and effort needed in order to understand the essential nature of the moose and to deal with it on its own terms" (Nadasdy 2003, 107–8).

Jorge Ishizawa (2006, 211–12), in describing the conservation of cultivated plants in Peru, reports a woman who treats her potatoes as members of the family; she speaks with all the plants in her garden, and she sleeps with the seeds.

Always Consult Before Deciding—and Listen

One of the classic contrasts in treaty making between Indians and colonists is that the colonists believed in written agreements that were assumed to then govern future relationships without modification. But the Indians were insistent that frequent meetings were needed in order to maintain the relationship. Such frequent meetings would allow consultation on issues that arose. "Always consult before deciding—and listen" is an example of the Haudenosaunee concept of "polish the chain." The chain is the relationship; meetings allow people involved in a relationship to polish it. Once people "link arms together," they are in a chain and become of "one mind."

Fisher and Brown recommend that mutual trust is enhanced when either party can assume that the other party will not take action unilaterally.

Consultation means more than simply informing about a decision that has been made before implementation; it means discussing the decision and modifying it if the other party has objections. The proposer needs to listen well enough to understand potential objections as well as making clear statements and seeking feedback to be sure that one has been understood.

Following Moose Jackson's observation, a hunter or a plant gatherer needs to listen to the land to get advice about what to do. Sometimes signs from the plant will indicate that harvesting at a particular time is not a good idea. Robin Wall Kimmerer (2013, 177–78) reports that she consulted with leeks one spring by observing them. The leeks were small and dried out; it was too early to harvest; they needed time to absorb water and become tasty. She carries this point to its conclusion: to reciprocate with nature, one needs to listen to it and follow the resulting messages. Another woman reports that she kept slipping as she tried to harvest some rushes; she took the advice and stopped, discovering later that the water was rising.

Indigenous groups insist that decisions be made by consensus. In the process of reaching consensus, every member of the group is encouraged to speak and give their opinion. Such a process can be described as fair and inclusive decision-making. The process of discussion involves listening to all opinions, airing differences, and seeking means by which a final decision satisfies everyone.

Many argue that because full consensus can rarely be attained, consensus decision-making is a recipe for inaction. Full discussion will lead to better decisions, but the veto of one person will prevent action. In the context of relationality, however, rules exist to restrain the dissenters from preventing action. Those who do not fully agree with the decision explain why they do not as well as why they no longer object, seeing that they have not been able to convince the others. They may participate in the activity they dislike, complaining all the way, conceding their error if it all works out (Umeek [Atleo] 2004, 90). I often see the views of the minority reported in the minutes of the Tribal Council of the Confederated Salish and Kootenai Tribes. After an 8–2 vote, the two people in the minority explain why they dissented. When I worked there, I often saw a 6–4 vote overturned in a later meeting. A vote of 8–2, 9–1, or 10–0 survived. Staff needed to make sure the council was in consensus before taking a decision as final.

The difference between such actions and the blockading practiced by Senator Mitch McConnell in the U.S. Senate is that the Senate operates on competitive principles, not cooperative ones. Each side seeks victory, not joint success. Moving from majority rule in a competitive polity to consensus in a cooperative one would be difficult. *The Consensus Building Handbook* (Susskind, McKearnan, and Thomas-Larmer 1999) advocates consensus processes rather than Roberts Rules of Order, based on the rules Congress uses.

Balance Emotion with Reason

A part of public discussion of issues is the need to deal with conflict within relationships. Conflicts generally cause emotional responses of anger, fear, or disgust. These emotions interfere with maintaining a relationship, but the causes of the emotion may be misunderstanding of the motives of another. It may be a simple misunderstanding, an error in communication. Dealing with conflict requires that some persons in a relationship can assist others in separating out the emotional issues from the rational ones.

Fisher and Brown begin their list of the ways to create good relationships by considering the tension between emotion and reason. Emotion cannot be eliminated, but it needs to be dealt with as it affects a relationship. The Iroquois negotiation ideal begins with steps in which the parties address their emotional issues. If one side has suffered a loss, the other side will insist on a condolence ceremony to comfort those who have lost a member of their side. When a delegation reaches a village to prepare for negotiation, the hosts are obligated to provide a speech at the wood's edge consisting of the "three rare words": clear the travelers' eyes, ears, and throat of the thoughts and issues that they may have brought with them to the negotiation. The speech reminds all parties that clear thinking is needed, which means forgetting the emotions of the trip.

Killing an animal creates several different emotions. One is joy at the success. Another is sadness over the loss of life. The need to have a level-headed approach is evident. Nadasdy reports that the Kluane do many things to temper or reduce emotions. When he was sad about the death of a rabbit, his host told him it was disrespectful; the rabbit had given itself and a gift should not be rejected. If a hunter is proud of his kill, the community will reduce his pride so that he will not become too assertive in other contexts. Often a young hunter feels both pride and sadness as a result of his or her first kill. The Kluane state that both emotions are disrespectful of the gift of an animal's life; respect has to tame emotions (Nadasdy 2003, 88).

Persuasion, Not Coercion

A consensus-based decision-making process involves persuasion rather than coercion. Trying to coerce other members of a relationship has a bad effect on emotions, as no one likes being forced to do things. It is better to persuade, and persuasion is helped by the other rules, such as communication or balancing emotion with reason. If another party is not persuaded, perhaps one's own position isn't correct; listening carefully will improve the assessment of who is correct.

Numerous coercive tactics exist: taking a position rather than addressing issues, narrowing the options to exclude ones the other side may like, threatening to cease negotiating, using majority power to coerce those in the minority, and so forth. To counter these tactics, Iroquois insisted that a respondent be able to wait at least a day before responding. The heat and emotion created by coercion could be resisted with a period of cooling off. Time is needed for a good decision or response even in a noncoercive negotiation.

The idea that a hunter should kill only those animals who have offered themselves is an example of working by means of persuasion. In this case, the animal is persuading the hunter to kill it. Indigenous people object to research methods that rely on coercing animals in some way rather than patiently watching what they do and learning from them on their own terms. Monitoring movements by use of radio collars, for instance, insults wandering ungulates or predators ranging within their ranges, an invasion of autonomy. Aerial surveys by plane or helicopter scare the animals. Because animals think and feel, humans must ask themselves if they would like to be treated in that manner (Nadasdy 2003, 110). From the Kluane viewpoint, one should not coerce animals because of their power; the consequences can be severe, such as the disappearance of a source of food. The relationship might come to an end.

Elinor Ostrom noted that in successful common pool management, members used graduated sanctions. If a rule was not being followed, a first choice for obtaining compliance would be to tease other people. There might be a small fine to give notice that a rule is not being followed. Larger sanctions would be held back and possibly never used. This is a form of using persuasion rather than coercion. If rules are enforced by coercion, over time mutual trust and the desire to rely on each other would erode (Ostrom 1990, 98).

The economists' emphasis on strong reciprocity overemphasizes punishment, when persuasion is equally or more effective.

Acceptance: Deal Seriously with Whom We Differ

"Dealing seriously with whom we differ" describes the formal part of the Haudenosaunee diplomatic system. Each step shows serious intent, led by the need to present each proposal with wampum—which indicates a serious proposal. Insisting on condolence of the other side's losses is another way to deal seriously. Meeting at the wood's edge to respect the three rare words and clear the mind for negotiation means serious intent.

The point of accepting another person in a negotiation is to accept them as equals and to agree to talk. The opposite of acceptance is rejection, a refusal even to negotiate, which in an extreme case would be the elimination of the other party. The idea that all animals and plants have a role to play, even if people do not understand it, is acceptance. The very assumption that animals are persons is acceptance, a willingness to deal seriously with all animals, especially those who are hunted and those who hunt the same food humans use. Leave some huckleberries for the bears.

Accepting the other party as worthy of interaction applies differently at different levels. At the level of humans and the land, acceptance means respecting the right of animals and plants to see the world in their own manner. At the higher level of a nation, each of separate relationships accepts others within a nation, such as, for instance, the Seneca and the Mohawk peoples in the Haudenosaunee League, and then acceptance of the other nation facilitates creation of a confederation.

A perhaps extreme example of acceptance of the view of other beings is the attitude of Tlingit and other peoples in very cold climates to accept glaciers as beings to be treated with respect. Julie Cruikshank (2005) explains their attitude in a slightly misnamed book, *Do Glaciers Listen?* She answers the question on her first page: yes, they do listen and people need to be quiet when approaching them, in respect for their power to surge suddenly over villages, to block the flow of rivers, and to do other dangerous things. John Muir's recklessness frightened his Tlingit guides, although he did listen to them (Cruikshank 2005, 163–72).

Other powerful beings such as bears and moose also need to be treated well. That they think differently is beside the point; they need to be accepted for what they are and included in relationships on their terms. Since humans are also powerful, good advice to the bears or lions would be to treat humans with respect. The result is that they reach an accommodation and don't interfere with each other, as has been reported in Africa. In discussing relationships between predators and humans, Raymond Pierotti (2010, 222) reports cooperative hunting with humans and animals such as whales, wolves, and lions. He cites Elizabeth Marshall Thomas (1994) to explain that in Africa, lions and humans respected and avoided each other. Only after colonial powers disrupted the relationships by excluding humans from parks did lions become dangerous for people. That animals have culture and can learn proper manners has been confirmed recently by mainstream scientists (Brakes et al. 2019; Whiten 2021). This confirms the views of Tsilhqot'in people, who describe the matriarchal culture of the horses on their lands (Bhattacharyya and Slocombe 2017).

Reliability: Be Wholly Trustworthy, but Not Wholly Trusting

One of the valued relational goods is mutual trust. Mutual trust depends on group members acting in a trustworthy manner. Each must evaluate their own behavior to be sure they are acting in a consistent manner. A short list of ways to be reliable is the following:

- be predictable
- be clear
- take promises seriously and follow through
- be honest, accept responsibility for errors in communication
- don't exaggerate the errors of those on the "other side"

Each member of a relationship must deal with weaknesses in trust and reliable behavior on the part of other members. Trusting too much early on in a relationship may reduce the growth of trust over time. For this reason, the hosts of a visiting Haudenosaunee delegation meet them at the wood's edge before admitting them to the village for further consultation. That meeting also has the speech with the three bare words, which means removing emotions from the encounter. The meeting is based on an agreed-upon agenda; topics outside the agenda need to be postponed for another meeting because surprises undermine trust.

Being not fully trusting means monitoring the behavior of all participants in a relationship. The monitoring includes actions by nonhumans, who monitor human behavior to assure that they are being treated respectfully. Monitors are members of a relationship, and they monitor both other members and leaders who are supposed to assure that decisions are carried out as agreed. Although persons in a relationship are advised to act in a trustworthy manner, others still need to be sure that proper behavior is occurring. Failure to monitor allows a con man to fool everyone else.

The rules for dealing with animals can be seen as ways to establish the trustworthiness of the hunter. Meat should not be wasted; remains should be disposed of properly. Animals should not be played with. These are all trustworthy behaviors; following them would convince an animal that a person could be trusted to treat it properly. But the hunter must be careful, especially with large animals such as moose or bear.

Relational Subjects and Agents

The rules for successful relationship building are not easy to follow. They require work. Learning how another person sees things requires careful listening. Accepting them as worthy of discussion is not easy if the person has many negative qualities in addition to an opposing view; it may be that relational subjects do not include persons who are wildly or widely in disagreement with other members. Taking time to widely consult before acting is not easy in every situation. Complying by being fully trustworthy is probably one of the easiest of the rules to follow.

Before describing the different levels of relational subjects, I need to present the concept of relational subject in more detail. I mentioned to the chairman of the Confederated Salish and Kootenai Tribes that I was puzzled over the issue of "how do we know when we have reversed settler colonialism?" in connection to the tribes' success in obtaining control of Kerr Dam, which the tribe renamed Séliš Ksanka Qĺispė Dam (Trosper 2019b). His answer is quite relevant here: he said the elders complain that "we don't take care of each other anymore." He gave a profound answer: if tribal members began to care for each other, we would know that settler colonialism had been defeated (Finley 2015). My tribe and others have been contending with the many efforts that promote individualism and thus challenge the maintenance of relationships and relational subjects. I now own my father's allotment as private property within a system designed to promote individualism, an effect of the topic of my own PhD dissertation. One of the characteristics of a social relational subject is that the personal relational subjects who have joined together care for each other. Following the rules for creating good relationships, they have learned how others see the world. They care about the other people in their relationship, and they always consult before deciding and listen to each other. They deal seriously with each other, and they respect the autonomy of other persons even as they care about them.

From the point of view of a person, what does it mean to form a "We" relationship with other persons? An "I" has a solid *sense* of self but perhaps a not-so-solid *concept* of self, given the need to deal with the external characteristics that define a "Me" in a social situation. If the Indigenous society holds that all young persons of a certain age who are in a certain extended family are brothers and sisters, then they can proceed to develop a sense of "We," the brothers and sisters of this age in this extended family. Given the ties of kinship and family, they see themselves as a defined group and can come to care for one another. If they are in a tribe that encourages people of the same age to create a group among themselves, they may also have joined with the youth of other families to define themselves as a particular age-grade set of people who are similar. They may form a relational subject, who have "We" relationships among themselves.

What does it mean for a group of persons to form a relational subject? Donati and Archer suggest the following standards for a micro-level relational subject composed of persons.

1. Each of the persons is an autonomous subject with their own identity, which is consistent with the respect for the autonomy of persons in a relational society. They are not anonymous people; people know who they are.
2. They all recognize that they share a commitment to the relation, each for their own reasons, and participate in creating and sharing the relational goods of the relationship.
3. They self-identify as a distinct "We," defined by their sharing of one or more relational goods.
4. They have at least one shared symbol that identifies them as distinct from other relational subjects.
5. The "We" of the group has an identity that becomes part of the identity of each of the persons in the relationship. That is, they create the identity

of the group as a relational subject, and then each of their own identities incorporates their membership in the relational subject.

This last condition must exist to be consistent with the idea that every person is unique and formed by his or her relationships. The relationships influence the person as the person contributes to the relationships, since part of a successful relationship is mutual contribution to it (Donati and Archer 2015, 185–86).

The sharing of one or more relational goods, the creation of a shared symbol, and the effects of the relational subject on the persons creating it are all characteristics of emergence. The new relational subject is a distinct entity that has emerged from the actions of the persons in it. A sign of emergence is the existence of a property for the new entity that is not a property of the entities of which the new entity is composed. The shared symbol, for instance, symbolizes the new relational subject but is not a symbol of any of the persons in the relationship. A relational good is also a property of the relationship and not of the persons in the relationship.

In order for emergence to be described for higher-level relational subjects, the list has to be changed. Consider a meso-level relational subject created by micro-level subjects. A group of families may create an organization to share babysitting with each other. A group of firms may create an organization to help them jointly purchase supplies, reducing the cost. Rewording the list gives the following:

1. Each of the relational subjects has their own identity and is not anonymous.
2. Each of the relational subjects shares a commitment to the relationship among them and shares the relational goods that they create.
3. The relational subjects self-identify as a "We" when they have joined for a common purpose.
4. They create at least one shared symbol that identifies them as distinct from other similar groups.
5. The relational goods of the group have effects on the relational subjects making up the group.

Some of these conditions create observable characteristics, such as the shared symbol. Other emergent effects may be so subjective that they only exist as shared ideas rather than as observable objects. The level of formality may be considerable, as when a group writes out an agreement that specifies each member's duties and perhaps dues.

While all relational subjects are emergent entities, not all emergent entities are themselves relational subjects. A written agreement may be a contract that commits members of the agreement to certain actions without at the same time creating a relational good shared among the group signing the agreement. Because this approach to analysis of relationality is rather new, some of the details have not been worked out.

Donati and Archer emphasize that a relational subject is not just a group of people who are connected by exchanges into a network of people sharing those exchanges, as is commonly assumed in the social capital literature. Their sharing of relational goods and identity creates an emergent entity (Donati and Archer 2015, 30). An emergent entity has at least one property that is not a property of any of the parts that create the relationship. A relational good is such a property; it is shared among the members but if one leaves, they do not have the good any more. The symbol of the relationship is not a property of the members of the relationship (Trosper 2005). Depending on terminology, the emergent entity is the relationship, the relational subject, or the relational agent. The incorporation of nonhumans in these relationships matters for Indigenous peoples. As is presented in detail in the next chapter, humans include portions of the landscape in their relationships, and identify with those parts of the landscape. While the relationships have shared relational goods, the persons in the relationships are not identical; they have different roles and contribute in different ways. Some are clear leaders. In a family, some are parents and others are children. When the different relational subjects join together to create other subjects, some of the members of the groups joining are delegates to the higher-level agents. They are spokespersons for their community.

Bruno Latour (2004, 67) proposes recognizing "spokespersons" to represent the ways in which scientists speak for the nonhumans they study in their lab. His point is that the "objects" of scientific study themselves have agency; they are also "subjects" (71). Scientists work hard with their laboratory equipment to make the objects of their investigations speak. As members of a relationship, the scientists become spokespersons for the objects of study. His point is to dispute the object–subject dichotomy that also maps onto the distinction between "objective facts" and "subjective values" (95–127). His argument does not go as far as many Indigenous peoples' do, for he clearly does not want to be claiming such an odd thing as to say that things can speak like humans do. He also doesn't say that nonhumans can respond to human speaking, but he does point out that the responses nonhumans make in laboratories are not easy to understand. That is the reason that scientific procedures and discussions among scientists about the meaning of the results of experiments take place among scientists. Once the scientists come to a consensus, they can identify "facts" (103–4). In his polemical style, Latour wants to reduce the power that scientists obtain by being able to be the only credible spokesmen for nonhumans, through their scientific procedures.

Latour wants to open the discussion of the character of "nature" by allowing other people also to be heard. Among those people in his list are Indigenous peoples. He argues that Indigenous peoples are not "in harmony with nature" because the idea of "nature" is absent (Latour 2004, 43–46). They just see other beings who deserved to be consulted and dealt with. Richard W. Stoffle, Richard Arnold, and Angelita Bulletts (2016) have pointed out that the "double hermeneutic" that exists when scientists talk about humans also exists with nonhumans. The "double hermeneutic" occurs when the objects of social scientists' research read the reports and change their behavior or argue with the scientists. A fixed reality that can be predicted doesn't exist when the "objects" are actually "subjects," able to respond and change their anticipated actions. Latour seems close to saying the same thing when he insists that nonhumans must be consulted. His main reservation is that the consultation must be through spokespeople, those who can speak for the nonhumans. He seems to constrain the spokespeople to be scientists who use their many experimental methods to determine the message that the nonhumans are conveying, yet he also states the Masai need to be included in decisions about lions or elephants (Latour 2004, 166, 170). That the nonhumans may have a message they wish to convey directly, due to their own consciousness, seems to be just outside his position.

The question naturally arises, "What is speech?" If communication can occur with methods other than the speech humans produce, then the rules of successful relationships can apply if the human side of the relationship makes strong efforts to understand the other side, even if the form of communication is not "speech." Kimmerer (2013) reports that trees coordinate the timing of periods of large seed production (masting) with chemical communication. Suzanne W. Simard (2009, 2018), in many studies, has documented how mycorrhizal fungus assists trees in communicating and sharing with each other. Tony Trewavas (2016) provides other examples of plants communicating and argues for their intelligence. Although the issues are complex, this work simply accepts that further study will make the Indigenous view of the consciousness of other-than-humans more plausible, also making their participation in relational subjects believable.

Application of Reflexivity: Different Levels of Relational Subjects

The five characteristics of relationships are stated previously at a very general level. This section applies those characteristics to distinguish micro-, meso-, and macro-level relational subjects. The Haudenosaunee provide a good example. Among them, the extended families within a village divided into two halves, or moieties, which had particular duties to each other. Highest among these duties were to offer condolence to the other side if someone died. These ceremonies became very formal when a chief died; the position needed to be filled by another person, and the condolence for the grief of one half was followed by raising up the successor. Many of the Haudenosaunee rules come from different villages seeking to solve relationship problems through use of the principles of negotiation that are initiated by one party proposing to create a "council fire." The village desiring to start the negotiation visits the other to make the proposal. The visit itself follows the rules of such visits, beginning with a meeting at the wood's edge, followed by a day of hospitality, after which an agenda for the council is agreed to. Then the parties separate and prepare for the council, at which time the larger set of rules comes into effect. At the subsequent council, proposals are accompanied by wampum; the respondent to the proposal does not need to reply immediately. While negotiations proceed, the parties meet in the woods to come to an understanding. The responding party, taking a proposal seriously, responds also with wampum. The goal of the negotiation process, which may or may not succeed, is to have all parties link arms together and assure that their minds are one. They agree to relational goods, described as a chain with the people's arms linked together. Subsequent meetings are needed to polish the chain, meaning that the agreement remains in place, changed in details if needed. These chains could exist among villages in one tribe or among tribes, as in the entire Haudenosaunee League.

The Haudenosaunee example shows that relational subjects can compose themselves at different levels. Persons can join each other in kinship groups such as families or other local groups such as a hunting party. Families can join together to make bands, and bands can join together to make higher-level groups. The different levels have different types of relational goods, which define the differences in the levels. The different negotiation rules for jointly creating the relational goods also should vary by level. Although much work needs to be done to explore the differences among levels, some initial ideas are possible.

Micro Level

Nuclear and extended families are the micro level. Persons are born into their families, and one of the main shared goods is the love among members of a family. Kinship is a fundamental component of defining micro-level relational agents. Indeed, the language of kinship extends upward to describe other levels of relational agents.

Humans in families establish relationships with nonhumans in the territories that families inhabit. The hunting territories of Algonquian peoples are a good example. These family hunting area combinations are led by a head hunter. Members of the family agree that the head hunter will lead them, and such leaders also work to coordinate the creation of relational goods on the landscape. These family leaders are expected to know the beings of the landscape so well that their advice is sought by family members before going out. The members of the family consult the leader, and the leader in turn advises them. The leaders do not coerce their family members, but their authority and knowledge mean that their advice is followed. The relational goods of trust, love, and solidarity support the development of mutual reciprocity among the humans and the nonhumans in the territory. The next chapter provides some details on such family hunting territories.

In people with seasonal rounds, the trees or berry patches become associated with particular families who tend them. This varies from the Algonquian territories, where different parts are left unharvested for some years before the people return to them. But in both, the We-relation lasts and develops over time.

The connections of families to land exist also in agricultural societies, where each family has its own gardens and cropland. Respect for the autonomy of such relationships requires that others not interfere.

In the modern era, the identity of micro-level relational subjects persists even when some members migrate to cities. With the jobs in the cities, the members of the group send monetary support home for their relatives. People back home send traditional foods to their relatives in the city. In many cases, the urban persons support each other (Sahlins 1999).

In describing the relationships of his Rarámuri peoples to their landscape, ethnobotanist Enrique Salmón (2000) coined the term *kincentric ecology* to describe the relational subjects his people use in their homeland. Using the language of kinship helps emphasize the consciousness of nonhumans who join in relationships with humans.

Meso Level

The archetype of the meso level is a village. Families have their own lands, especially for cultivation of crops or tending of plants. The village shares some land among everyone. The village may have a sacred grove that is never harvested but which serves as a reserve for key plants and animals. The forest may be a source of firewood and forage. They may have irrigation works that are maintained by cooperative effort. All are committed to maintenance of the village. They need to assure that equity exists among the people of the village, both as individual persons and as social relational subjects. Equity contributes to creating a fully reciprocal We-relation.

All families in a village may have a right to a certain amount of land. Although some have more than others, everyone has some. A village that allows some members to be paupers, landless and jobless, would seem not to be a meso-level relational subject because there is not an equitable distribution of access to the means of making a living.

Alternatively, one might say that village-level relational agents that have a fixed internal hierarchy of haves and have-nots is a meso-level relational agent that is held together by relational bads rather than relational goods. The hierarchy of rigid status maintains the systems, but not in an equitable manner. The feudal structure of Europe may be this type, with its landlords and serfs. The system of castes in villages in India could be another.

Another type of divided-up set of relational agents could be the relationship between farmers in the lowlands and transhumance among herders of animals. The herders use the mountains in the summer and live in the lowlands in the winter, grazing the stubble in the fields as their herds provide nutrients to the farms through defecation.

A characteristic of the meso level is that interactions among the families provide a different type of relational good. On the Northwest Coast, a group of houses sharing a river, such as the Nisga'a sharing the Lisims (Nass) River, needs a river-wide alliance to coordinate the relationship with each salmon run. While each house may control a stream where the salmon spawn, some of the salmon spawn in lakes and rivers that are not so easily designated as solely held by one house. A system of feasts enabled the Nisga'a to coordinate at a meso level. When asked to describe their system, the Nisga'a described it as a "common bowl" (Trosper 2009, chapter 9).

Similarly, agricultural fields in an irrigated river basin need the agricultural works to be jointly managed. The mountains of Bali present a different model, where the irrigation occurs in terraces on mountainsides with a system of irrigation communities organized through a hierarchy of water temples. The priests and the congregations of the temples determine the allocation of water and the rice-planting schedules each year. The gods, which are an example of relational goods, are also arranged in a hierarchy (Lansing 2007).

The organization of irrigation is similar to the groups that operate all the economic activity of the island. Clifford Geertz (1963, 82–106) provides an extensive description of the *seka* system, "a set of overlapping and intersecting corporate associations" (84). Each seka is egalitarian, with leaders who have "diffuse and wholly non-authoritarian directive and administrative functions" (84). The Balinese do nearly everything in groups. Geertz describes the system of relational subjects in great detail. Because he had only the individualism/collectivism division, he was hampered by a lack of language to analyze a relational system such as that on Bali. Geertz describes it as "pluralistic collectivism," stating that "Balinese society is not individualistic, but it is, nevertheless, rather libertarian in its own peculiar and traditionalist way. For all the communalism there is room for personal maneuver" (85). Edge (1998) used the Balinese to illustrate the way in which a relational society is radically supportive of the autonomy of persons. Even though Bali society as a whole is not egalitarian—it has a noble class—that type of inequality is not the same as that when there is "an emergent managerial class." The leaders, while earning more of the surplus than others, must attend to the welfare of everyone (Geertz 1963, 125).

Macro Level

The archetype relational good at a macro level is peace. We know that humans in large assemblages of meso-level relational agents can start fighting with each other over the resources they have. At this level, a lack of relationships generates relational bads, especially war. Coercion replaces persuasion; trust is nonexistent; cutthroat competition replaces cooperation.

An example of strong relational goods is the persistence of the goods identified by the Iroquois League. Deganawida, the peacemaker who is credited along with Hiawatha and Jigonsaseh with the founding of the League of the Haudenosaunee, provided three words to describe the relational goods that would result from following his principles of good relationships. These three words have been translated in various versions. The first connects health and peace—peace being generated by organized bodies of groups and persons; health being sanity of mind and health of everybody. The second connects equity among persons with righteousness in conduct and thought; its main focus is on justice. The third describes power in a civil sense of military or civil authority or spiritual power resulting from religious ceremonies and interactions. The qualities, often listed in different orders, are described as the outcome of following the recommendations of the great statesmen and stateswomen who founded the Haudenosaunee League (Buck 2016, 97, citing Hewitt 1920, 541).

Private Versus Public; Solidarity and Subsidiarity

Dividing a system of relational subjects challenges the common distinction of "public" and "private," which relies on assuming a society of individuals. The individuals' private lives are separate from the public life where governments operate. The autonomy of individuals is protected by a right to privacy. Governments may be stratified, as in a republic made up of provinces within a national state. States are responsible for the production of public goods. At the national level, such goods are things like national defense. Some public goods are local public goods, created by provinces or by entities within provinces such as cities and towns. The public sphere is run by states. Individuals make up civil societies, and their organizations are combinations of individuals associated through contracts, such as firms. When firms are treated as if they are individuals, such as with corporations, the basic analytical framework is still individual and state. In standard economics, states produce public goods and individuals produce private goods. There is no analytic unit called "relational subjects"; these entities are neither private nor public as defined for a system of individuals. This distinction will be important in the next chapter, where property comes in two primary forms, private property and state property. Land held by a relational subject is neither privately held by individuals nor publicly held by a government.

The idea of "community property" or "communal property" exists but is usually not very thoroughly described, at least within standard economics. Since the seminal work of Elinor Ostrom, however, a substantial body of work has developed describing the governance needed for common pool resources. Tellingly, the International Association for the Study of Common Property changed its name to the International Association for the Study of Commons. They faced the difficulty that the idea of "property" did not fit well as describing the governance of commons.

Donati and Archer (2015, 221–28) recommend focusing on solidarity and subsidiarity rather than debating public and private. Solidarity is one of the relational goods that bind relational subjects together. The principle of subsidiarity is that social functions should be addressed at the level where they are best performed. Central governments should not perform actions that are better addressed at lower levels. To address subsidiarity, one needs to address the multiple levels. As the third sector grows in modern economies, where nonprofit organizations emerge with goals that include production of new relational goods, the analysis of political structures needs to be addressed without assuming only individuals participate in governance. Among the organizations that do not fit into the market versus state structures of the modern era are Indigenous peoples, who can be understood through the idea of peoplehood.

Peoplehood: Macro-Level Identity in the Modern Era

When it formed, the Haudenosaunee League had only other Indigenous peoples as neighbors. They needed peace among themselves to have the power to resist their neighbors as needed. After the encounter with European settlers, Indigenous peoples formed another type of macro-level relational good, their own identity as a people. The relational agents of micro and meso levels cooperate to create Indigenous peoples with their own distinctiveness. The macro-level relational good of peoplehood characterizes their distinctiveness and has come to be used to defend their rights to self-determination, most recently ratified in the provisions of the United Nations Declaration on the Rights of Indigenous Peoples. This section explains how relationality can explain the development and persistence of peoplehood, which emerges in a relational system.

Drawing on a series of articles and books that have observed the persistence of Indigenous enclaves in the Americas, Tom Holm, J. Diane Pearson, and Ben Chavis (2003) proposed the term *peoplehood* to summarize the ways in which each people created the basis for their own self-government, their own sovereignty. "The concept of Peoplehood is important," they argue, because "Native American knowledge and philosophies [are] . . . based largely on the understanding of relationships—the interrelationship between human beings, animals, plants, societies, the cosmos, the spirit world, and the function of other natural, even catastrophic, occurrences" (17–18). Because Holm Pearson, and Chavis adopt relationships as the framework, the concepts of relational agent and relational good can be used to place their assertion solidly in the relational analysis of this book.

When persons consider themselves a "people," they describe a macro-level relational good, an emergent property of their ways of relating to each other and to their territory. As originally conceived, the peoplehood concept asserted that Indigenous peoples combine the characteristics of ceremonial cycle, place/territory, sacred history, and language into a coherent whole that has shown the ability to endure and to persist (13–14). Indigenous identity as peoplehood emerges from the association of the many relational agents making up an Indigenous society. These agents each share their own relational goods at the micro and meso levels. Identity as peoplehood occurs at the macro level but is built upon the meso-level relational subjects and their interactions.

Jeffrey Corntassel (2003) surveyed the variety of definitions of Indigenous identity that inform international debate about Indigenous peoples. He dislikes the linear and inflexible nature of many of the definitions, noting that they overlap. In searching for a better formulation, he labels the peoplehood idea "flexible and dynamic" (Corntassel 2003, 75). He elaborates the categories of peoplehood as informed by his survey of the other definitions. Each statement of the category is a direct quotation from Corntassel, using the categories from Holm, Pearson, and Chavis.

1. [Ceremonial Cycle] Peoples who may, but not necessarily, have their own informal and/or formal political, economic and social institutions, which tend to be community-based and reflect their distinct ceremonial cycles, kinship networks, and continuously evolving cultural traditions.

2. [Place/Territory] Peoples who distinguish themselves from the dominant society and/or other cultural groups while maintaining a close relationship with their ancestral homelands/sacred sites, which may be threatened by ongoing military, economic or political encroachment or may be places where indigenous peoples have been previously expelled, while seeking to enhance their cultural, political and economic autonomy.

3. [Sacred History] Peoples who believe they are ancestrally related and identify themselves, based on oral and/or written histories, as descendants of the original inhabitants of their ancestral homelands.

4. [Language] Peoples who speak (or once spoke) an indigenous language, often different from the dominant society's language—even where the indigenous language is not 'spoken,' distinct dialects and/or uniquely indigenous expressions may persist as a form of indigenous identity. (Corntassel 2003, 91–92)

This list of categories allows analysis of peoplehood as an emergent property of Indigenous peoples without assuming either an essentialist or an objective concept of peoplehood. As an emergent relational good, peoplehood has subjective elements that preclude determining a fixed list of characteristics that can apply to all Indigenous peoples. Corntassel reviews the proposed fixed lists, noting their differences and deciding that no single fixed list will work to define Indigenous peoples. He easily rejects essentialist concepts that derive identity from biology. His conclusion is that self-identification is the best way to find Indigenous peoples, with the categories of peoplehood as a way to exclude peoples who obviously do not fit. I next explain how each of the categories work.

Ceremonial Cycles: Self-Determination and Livelihood

Since ceremonies reinforce the relational goods of all relational agents, placing ceremony first and connecting it to livelihood makes sense. When carrying out a ceremony, members of a community act to reinforce the relationships in which they participate. Ceremonies both connect people to the cycles of the land and reinforce the roles of people in the social structure. Ceremonies enact the trust and affection that are needed for reciprocity. When circumstances change and a community needs to adjust, agents take the actions that are needed. They can use ceremony to create and justify the changes.

Kinship is the central model for relational agents at all levels. The agents are the entities that drive adaptation and the process of becoming Indigenous to a place/territory. Combining history with kinship is especially noteworthy among the Māori, who stress genealogy of all elements of the landscape, including humans. This means that people of the present day are always connected to their ancestry.

Agency is also needed to produce livelihoods from the material structures of the territory. The structures of agriculture, hunting, and other productive activities need humans to make them go. Livelihood depends on relationships with the territory. Leadership also depends on supporting relationships. Particular characteristics of leadership are the importance of peacemaking and having leaders defer to the judgment of the group through consensus decision-making, as presented in detail in chapter 6.

Agency is also needed to reproduce or change the social structures of a community. For instance, suppose a kinship group that is responsible for one part of the community's territory shrinks in population or even completely dies out. Someone must take care of the land, and community approval of new stewards of the land is needed. In the Northwest Coast, for instance, when a house becomes depopulated, a large feast sponsored by existing houses can be used to indicate the new responsibilities of a new group. They can learn the stories of that house, adding themselves to those stories (Mills 1994, 111–12).

Corntassel is correct to place political, economic, and social institutions in this category. One should interpret "institutions" as the stratified structure of the relational agents. They are the people who either follow or change the rules as needed for their livelihoods. The agents are maintained by conversations among the people and all the levels of relational agents.

Place/Territory: Material and Social Structures

Territory is the main location of the material and social structures in the peoplehood concept. As the people adapt to the land, they develop a land tenure system to define the connections of social roles to the land. Their territory becomes their "place." As a result, the material structures that depend on human maintenance, such as farms or irrigation systems, are integrated with the social structures of the community. The material structures of the forests and the hunting and gathering lands would have less human tending but would be tended nonetheless. The next chapter addresses the complexities of humans' connection to their land and territory. For the Pikangikum, the health of the territory, "everything is good," is the upper-level relational good for the community. The four components of peoplehood contribute to this relational good.

Sacred History: History and Kinship

How long does it take for a people to become indigenous to their place? Richard Stoffle, Rebecca Toupal, and Nieves Zedeño (2003) have provided a "diachronic model" of how a people's relationship to their place develops and intensifies over time. They argue that as a people become more adapted to their place, the connections become embedded in religion. The knowledge is sacred knowledge learned over many generations. They present analysis of people's adaptation during the first, fifth, sixteenth, fiftieth, and two-hundredth generation. Each generation is twenty-five years in length. Each generation inherits the landscape, knowledge, and social structure of the previous generation, and then acts based on that context. They learn about the land, adjust their behavior to the land's constraints, and also learn how to enhance its productivity. They establish relationships with plants and animals, learning how to benefit from relationships by understanding them. By the four-hundredth generation, much of the knowledge has been codified in sacred stories. The generations form kinship ties among themselves, and the patterns of kin relations develop. Different cultures structure their kinship and clan relations differently. Among the Haudenosaunee, villages moved in the forest about every thirty years, a long rotation type of shifting cultivation. The men cleared fields and the women raised corn, beans, and squash as the core of the domesticated plants. In contrast to such shifting, in the desert southwest, people moved in an annual cycle dominated by the seasons, moving to the most comfortable and productive areas. In the Pacific Northwest, people organized into houses with exclusive territories and control over fishing sites. Their seasonal round was dominated by the patterns of salmon migration. The people find a social organization that fits with the ecosystems they use; they modify the ecosystems to make the relationships better for all beings who are willing to cooperate and contribute to the relationships.

The tight connection of Indigenous peoples to their land results from many thousands of years of deep relationships with the elements of their people's landscape. The land embodies the history, and many stories explain what has occurred. That many peoples recount their histories in oral narratives serves to continue to bind people together. Parents tell the histories to their children, and leaders tell the narratives to everyone. The consideration of history needs to also examine the concept of time held by a people. For many Indigenous peoples, time has a circular character, and events of the past can occur again. As a result, the past is connected to the present and the future by the enduring signs on the land that have meaning because of what has gone before and continues. Individual identity is connected to kin relations, and the genealogy of those relations are another component of maintenance of identity. The Australian idea of "the dreaming" has the paradoxical character that events in the past are also seen as important today, another aspect of the circular conceptions of time.

Kinship is the basis of social structure for many Indigenous peoples. The Māori especially emphasize that a person's genealogy embodies a person's connections to other people in the Māori society. The structure of relationships is inherited by each generation. To extend history and kinship to the entire social structure of a community may seem to be a stretch. In order to have all the structural components identified, however, the roles that have developed over time need to be explicitly present.

Recent history may be especially important because of the encounters with settlers from other places. The presence of the settlers disrupts the ecosystems, the social structures, and the relations with the land in dramatic ways. Tradition changes and the ways of identifying who is and who is not an Indian also changes.

The Confederated Salish and Kootenai Tribes have used their 1855 treaty to symbolize their connection to the lands reserved by that treaty. During the fight to obtain the license for Kerr Dam, the tribes organized a treaty celebration on the mall of the University of Montana to explain the significance of the treaty to potential allies. Thomas Biolsi (1997, 145–50) reports that an anthropologist looking for real Indians among the Lakota was frustrated because the Lakota he visited had included references to the Treaty of 1868 in explaining who they were.

In her work with tribal members among the Salish people on the Flathead Indian Reservation, anthropologist Theresa O'Nell (1996) found that among tribal members, the description of who were "real Indians" changed with each generation. Joseph P. Gone (2006) found a similar pattern on his reservation. Elders whose characteristics embodied authentic identity to current young people did not describe themselves as "real Indians" because patterns of life and the content of religion had changed from what their own grandparents had done. Recollections of the traumatic events of the reservation's history, told to distinguish Indians' identity from that of the settlers, were common stories told and retold: the arrival of Jesuit missionaries to the reservation who brought Catholicism, the murder of a family while hunting, the forced relocation of Chief Charlo's band from the Bitterroot, and the opening of the reservation to white settlement. These stories all became woven into the present conception of Salish and Kootenai identity. People also argued about the relevance of Indian blood quantum (Trosper 1976), and the tribe adopted a quarter-blood rule to define formal membership in the tribe while recognizing descent as also a legitimate basis for some preference in tribal hiring when formal members of the tribe did not qualify for a job.

Language: Stories and Artistic Expression

Just as the origin story of European religions, that of Adam and Eve in Genesis, has determined many of the characteristics of European culture (Sahlins 1996), origin stories express much about the basic ideas of each group of Indigenous peoples. Stoffle, Toupal, and Zedeño (2003) propose that new arrivals in a land change the depth of their connections to the land over millennia. More than five millennia are needed for a people to claim they originated where they live. Such stories connect a people to their land, often by identifying a place of emergence from other worlds. Language names the places on the landscape, and artistic expression also ties to the land. Stories about key mythical characters, such as Coyote, provide lessons about how to maintain relationships. Language also provides the classification of levels of relational agents unique to each people. Relationships with all the beings of the landscape are emphasized. Place becomes embedded in culture, just as people have become embedded in the landscape.

Robin Kimmerer (2013, 48–59) reports that the language of her Potawatomi people treats all the entities of the landscape as living. Animacy is in the language, which classifies everything as either alive or not—most is alive. In English, everything but humans are "it," not alive. The failure of non-Indigenous languages to be able to recognize the animacy of the landscape contributes to efforts to preserve and also to restore languages when tribes have the resources to undertake language education for the children. Jenanne Ferguson and Marissa Weaselboy (2020) survey literature that connects Indigenous language to land, concluding that revitalization of language usually also involves restoring connections to land. Communities with strong language and connections to land exhibit better health.

Art serves to express the other components of peoplehood, and art is part of life rather than a separate compartment. Peoples of the Northwest Coast, for instance, post beautiful items to greet salmon as they arrive (Langdon 2007). Music becomes important as part of the ceremonies. The library of ideas is maintained through stories and histories for those people who do not have a written language.

• • •

Holm, Pearson, and Chavis recognize that the elements of peoplehood change over time and vary over space. Their focus, however, is on the identity of a group rather than upon the identity of the members of the group. A connection needs to be made between the group identity and the individuals who compose the group. This connection is made by Gone (2006) when he emphasizes that the identity of a group results from the discussions of the people in the group as they debate their own character as a group and as each individual develops his or her own Indigenous identity.

Peoplehood has persisted in the United States in spite of many efforts to eliminate Indians. One can summarize the reasons as follows: At the cultural level, the ideas summarized by "place, knowledge, history, self-determination, and language" are necessarily complementary to each other and are mutually supporting. As they consider their choices, meta reflexives realize these complementarities and support them. Indian organizations act to protect those ideas and do not give them up easily. The language describes the territory and is used in the ceremonies. Oral traditions tell the history of the people, which recounts their connections to their territory. All beings in the territory are alive, and humans welcome them into relationships. Often the ceremonies confer legitimacy on the group's leaders, who can act on the people's behalf. At the structural level, the people make their living from the land, and they treat the land in a manner that sustains their livelihood; this is the connection to economics. At the level of agency, the unity of the people's ideas and their connection to territory motivate their leaders to protect those relationships. The ceremonies annually celebrate the people's connection to their territory and to each other.

Because conversation and discourse are what hold together the relational agents, and the relational agents act to support the material, social, and cultural structures, Gone is correct to insist that identity is created by discourse. And self-identification is the way for a people to say that they are Indigenous. The meso-level relational agents interact through the rules of relationship building and continued maintenance to create peoplehood.

Holm, Pearson, and Chavis emphasize that the categories of the peoplehood matrix are complementary. With place/territory at the center, language names the place/territory, agency connects people to the place through the maintenance of the productivity of the territory, and history tells people how they have taken care of it all. The people's relationship to the place/territory is told by the stories. These ideas are necessarily complementary, as they have arisen over time as a people develop their relationship to their territory and place. One needs to examine the reflexive deliberations of the people and the micro-, meso-, and macro-level relational agents that can support and perpetuate culture and structure with the peoplehood components. Because the content of the identity is maintained through discourse, it can change over time in response to many different reasons, both internal to the community and generated from outside the community. The types of changes will be related to the shifting basis of identity for members of the community as well. Individuals decide on their life courses through internal conversations that are linked in different ways to a community's conversations.

One can ask what in particular makes a community's identity Indigenous; the peoplehood model provides some boundaries to the concept of Indigenous identity. The peoplehood components trace back to a community's original occupation of its lands, along with all the ceremonies and other matters that connected them to that land. Contact with settlers and with the technological components of the settlers' society offers new opportunities as well as presenting new constraints for a community's actions.

UNDRIP: Indigenous Peoples Assert Their Rights to Autonomy

The existence of Indigenous peoples has been established by international cooperative action by Indigenous peoples throughout the world (Tauli-Corpuz 2007). After decades of consideration, the United Nations General Assembly (2007) adopted the Declaration of the Rights of Indigenous Peoples (UNDRIP). This declaration identifies a number of features that make Indigenous peoples identifiable, but the UNDRIP itself does not include a definition. It supports the idea that a group of Indigenous peoples defines itself, on its terms, and that a definition that attempts to apply to all Indigenous peoples will encounter difficulties that Corntassel spelled out. The preamble to the list of rights provides a good overview of the issues for this chapter.

The declaration recognizes that Indigenous peoples are situated within nation-states and that they are distinctive within those states. The declaration's preamble recognizes that settler colonialism is an ongoing cause of problems.

> *Concerned* that indigenous peoples have suffered from historic injustices as a result of, inter alia, their colonization and dispossession of their lands, territories and resources, thus preventing them from exercising, in particular, their right to development in accordance with their own needs and interests.

It also explicitly identifies three of the four components of the peoplehood model of indigeneity—land, ceremony, and history—while the fourth component, language, could be seen as part of culture.

> *Recognizing* the urgent need to respect and promote the inherent rights of indigenous peoples which derive from their political, economic and social structures and from their cultures, spiritual traditions, histories and philosophies, especially their rights to their lands, territories and resources.

It interlaces the various parts because the next clause returns to the external environment, recognizing that states have made agreements with Indigenous peoples.

> *Recognizing also* the urgent need to respect and promote the rights of indigenous peoples affirmed in treaties, agreements and other constructive arrangements with States.

In addition to existing within nation-states, Indigenous peoples have organized themselves in order to address the issues created by the history of colonization and dispossession.

> *Welcoming* the fact that indigenous peoples are organizing themselves for political, economic, social and cultural enhancement and in order to bring to an end all forms of discrimination and oppression wherever they occur.

As a result of the injustices and because the peoples have organized, the statement supports Indigenous control of their own affairs.

> *Convinced that* control by indigenous peoples over developments affecting them and their lands, territories and resources will enable them to maintain and strengthen their institutions, cultures and traditions, and to promote their development in accordance with their aspirations and needs,
> *Recognizing* that respect for indigenous knowledge, cultures and traditional practices contributes to sustainable and equitable development and proper management of the environment.

The situation is based on power relations, in particular the use of military force.

> *Emphasizing* the contribution of the demilitarization of the lands and territories of indigenous peoples to peace, economic and social progress and development, understanding and friendly relations among nations and peoples of the world.

The declaration also addresses families, children, and the training of next generations.

> *Recognizing in particular* the right of indigenous families and communities to retain shared responsibility for the upbringing, training, education and well-being of their children, consistent with the rights of the child.

The following section returns to emphasis on the relationships to states, giving those relationships the rationale of international action.

> *Considering* that the rights affirmed in treaties, agreements and other constructive arrangements between States and indigenous peoples are, in some

situations, matters of international concern, interest, responsibility and character,

Considering also that treaties, agreements and other constructive arrangements, and the relationship they represent, are the basis for a strengthened partnership between indigenous peoples and States.

After this excellent preamble, the declaration proceeds to spell out rights in lengthy and somewhat repetitive clauses intended to provide reasons for actions by states in the United Nations.

• • •

Indigenous identity stresses the connections of peoples to their territories. The next chapter focuses on these connections, explaining in the process why the word *property* does not properly describe those connections.

CHAPTER 4

Territory

The organizers of the National Museum of the American Indian, which opened on the National Mall in Washington, D.C., in 2004, used plants from around the Americas to create an elaborate landscape around the building. The landscape also includes four stones from the edges of the Americas: Hawai'i, South America, northern Canada, and the eastern United States. The stone from Hawai'i can only remain at the museum for twenty years, to be replaced by another. Like the plants, stones are living entities, and they need respect and time at home. Pele, the god of volcanoes, would be unhappy otherwise. That plants and stones must be present at the National Museum of the American Indian emphasizes that the land and all its occupants are part of Indigenous communities. A museum about Indians has to include the entire community.

This chapter explores the ways in which land tenure systems in Indigenous communities embody the importance of relationships with land as part of the community, thus elaborating on the central role of land in Indigenous identity. It also incorporates a key feature of Indigenous worldviews: the idea that all the landscape, in addition to being alive, is conscious and able to react to human activities. Consequently, humans must take account of the responses of other beings in the landscape to human actions. Although humans live by using the products of the land, the land is not purely their instrument for use.

A consequence of this view is that people are not separated from their land; they live in relationship to it. Trying to explain to a court the relationship of his people to their land, Chief Delgam Uukw used the idea of marriage to express the existence of the relationships.

> For us, the ownership of territory is a marriage of the Chief and the land. Each Chief has an ancestor who encountered and acknowledged the life of the land. From such encounters comes power. The land, the plants, the animals and the people all have spirit—they all must be shown respect. That is the basis of our law.
>
> The Chief is responsible for ensuring that all the people in his House respect the spirit in the land and in all living things. When a Chief directs his House properly and the laws are followed, then that original power can be recreated. That is the source of the Chief's authority. That authority is what gives the 54 plaintiff Chiefs the right to bring this action on behalf of their House members—all Gitksan and Wet'suwet'en people. That authority is what makes the Chiefs the real experts in this case. (Gisday Wa and Delgam Uukw 1992, 7)

In this statement, Delgam Uukw describes the relationships that he as chief and the members of his house have with their land. He needs to use English terms such as *ownership, marriage,* and *power* to convey his meaning. Each chief has descended from an ancestor who established the house; the connection to land is old. Each of the chiefs in the case of *Delgamuukw v. the Queen*, [1997] 3 S.C.R. 1010 (Can.), represented their houses. Each house consisted of humans and all the inhabitants of the house's territory. Each house is a meso-level relational subject; Delgam Uukw describes the resulting relational good as power. A similar system is described later in this chapter, in the section on the family hunting territories of the boreal forest in Canada.

This cooperative view of the landscape has large implications for the rules that humans use for interaction with the land. This chapter and the following one explore the rules and their consequences for economic activity. The cooperative view of land assumes that all entities on the land deserve to be treated with respect and will respond positively to reciprocity. When one harvests, one is also obligated to return something to the land. This return could be immaterial and subjective, such as a simple giving of thanks or an offering of tobacco before harvest. The return can be more substantial, as humans enhance the flourishing of the plants that they rely on year after year. Based on her study of California before settlement, M. Kat Anderson (2005) argues that the productivity of the land was enhanced by human intervention, increasing the amount of useful material above what an untended landscape would provide. Intervention involved correct use of fire as well as proper harvesting techniques. Perennial plants were tended in place. This is consistent with the discovery by early settlers that the landscape was very productive, both with wildlife and with edible products such as nuts and berries. This chapter explores the kinds of rules that allow humans to enhance the productivity of the land as they use it.

This chapter begins by summarizing the characteristics of private property as used in capitalist economies and lists the reasons for avoiding using the idea of "property" in Indigenous territorial systems. Next, using a systematic way to describe territorial systems, the chapter describes a well-known example of Indigenous systems in North America, the family hunting territories in the boreal forest. The chapter then explains why the family hunting territories are not private property, even though some economists have claimed they were. Although Indians treated some things, even songs, as property, the idea of property should not be applied to land. After dealing with private property, the chapter describes the variations in other Indigenous territorial systems. The chapter closes by exploring some consequences of Indigenous territorial systems for economic outcomes.

Property Is a Troublesome Term

The idea of property should be avoided in describing Indigenous territorial systems because *property* does not correctly describe the relationships of Indigenous peoples to land. Avoiding *property* is very difficult because no other concepts seem available to describe the relationships of people to things and to other people regarding things. To define their claims to land, Indigenous peoples need to use the language of property since powerful states insist that ownership be based on "property." As a matter of accurate analysis, however, *property* should not be used even if it is narrowly defined as only the ability to exclude others, a characteristic often observed among Indigenous peoples.

The standard idea of property in the modern time is "liberal individual private property." It has five key characteristics: (1) property is owned by an individual; and the individual has the power to (2) exclude others, (3) use and manage the property as he wishes, (4) keep all the surplus earned by using the property, and (5) sell it. Ownership of the land is governed by a nation-state, which keeps track of ownership records and protects owners against trespass or other violation of individual private property rights. This is a short list; in his extensive survey, Bruce Rigsby (2014, 51–52) also notes that ownership has an indefinite term, the owner is not supposed to harm others in using the land, and the land can be taken to pay debts. All private property can be sold under this concept. To "own" something means for that something to be property; for this reason, *ownership* is also a troublesome term because it applies to private property. The distinction between common property and private property is that common property has many owners, each with the same rights. State property is owned by the nation-state. If there is no property, the system is "open access." Indigenous peoples have neither open access nor property in their economic systems.

There are a number of problems with using *private property* to describe Indigenous territorial systems, among them the following: Land is held not by individuals but by relational subjects that include nonhumans. Other persons respect the autonomy of the relationships with the land, thus excluding themselves unless they, too, are part of the relationships that hold the land. Holders of land are responsible for maintaining the health of the relationships with land; they cannot do anything they want. The surplus generated by relationships with land must be shared among other persons in a variety of ways, including sharing with nonhuman persons (some berries need to be left for the bears). While land may be transferred among relational agents, making land a commodity for sale is not allowed. Above all, relationship to land is not impersonal. The role the state plays in protecting property is held instead by the Indigenous community, which sets and enforces the rules by which relational subjects develop relationships that include land.

At the same time that English settlers were moving to America, the feudal land tenure system in England was being turned into a private property system as the lords found ways to remove their tenants from rights to land (Marglin 2008; Sato 2018). As settlers took land from Indigenous peoples, they created a system of private property among themselves, purifying the idea of its feudal roots. John Locke, one of the early theorists of the nature of property, presented his interpretation as occurring on the frontier in North America. He was employed by the aristocrats who controlled the colony of Carolina and provided a theory of property that could be applied in a frontier situation where settlers were occupying the land held by other people

(Arneil 1996, 60). Locke imagined land without people who had ownership, what was later called *terra nulius* in Australia and British Colombia. The origin of property, he argued, occurred when a person transformed land through his own labor. The original inhabitants had not done this, merely harvesting from the land rather than transforming it. The settlers could treat the land as unowned, obtaining their right to the land by farming it. The colonial governments recognized the ownership rights of the individual settlers, rarely recognizing occupation of the land as creating property rights for Indigenous individuals. Locke allowed for an Indigenous person to become a landowner if he became Christian and lived as a European. While some in England defended the rights of the original inhabitants, eventually the argument that hunters and gatherers did not own land dominated the ideology of the settlers (Jennings 1976). Even as they transported corn, beans, squash, potatoes, tomatoes, peppers, tobacco, cotton, and other domesticated American plants to Europe, they purposefully denied the existence of significant agriculture among the Indians.

Because of the dominance of the market system that developed as England and other European states expanded their influence, *property* has become identified with the land tenure system that settlers created as they took land from other people. As their ideas eventually dominated talk about land tenure, any land tenure system came to be referred to as a property system. Terminology that could be used to described the land tenure system used by the Indigenous peoples was discarded or never developed. The settlers created terms like *aboriginal title* to describe what they considered a less-than-property relationship to land.

Many scholars have instead used the term *land tenure* to describe the general category of a people's relationship to their land. The field of American Indian studies in the United States, or Indigenous studies generally in the settler societies, has tended not to use the more general term *land tenure*. Rather, the practice has been to describe different systems of "property," as if the baggage attached to the idea of "individual private property" could be jettisoned. Part of the motivation for this practice may originate in the prestige that became attached to the word *property*; any land tenure system that was not private property was not seen as a legitimate connection to land. The strong people, settlers, had property. Other people, to assert their rights to the land, had to call their relationship property in order to justify it at all.

From the point of view of Indigenous economic theory, the "private prop-erty" system of land tenure describes a weak system of relationships regard-ing land compared to the Indigenous idea in which humans create strong re-lationships with land. A private property system allows humans to dominate their own parts of the landscape, without requiring attention to connections among components of the landscape. All land is judged by only one metric, its market value, rather than by other metrics that are available. Land has value only in the market, and realizing that value requires selling the land, cutting the connection between owners and their land. Allowing such sep-aration weakens the connection to the land. A further source of weakness is that underneath the idea of private property is the notion that the sovereign, originally a king or queen, is the ultimate owner of the land, and each of the titles to land held by individuals is actually a grant provided by the king. The most extensive grant, "fee simple," private property, still asserts that the law that justifies the ownership comes from the king, the sovereign, which in modern times has come to mean the state, which replaced the authority of kings, queens, and emperors as democracy replaced autocracy. When the settlers obtained independence from the king in the American Revolution, they kept the idea of a sovereign being the source of land titles for individu-als. That a community could govern the allocation of land, as in Indigenous systems, was an omitted idea.

Delgam Uukw describes a stronger relationship, where title comes from the relationships among humans, animals, plants, and land, not from the sovereign. Power comes from the relationship to land and disappears if the relationship disappears. To emphasize the power of these relationships, In-digenous peoples often say the land owns them, turning the language of property on its head. Delgam Uukw goes further, stating that law comes from the land, not from people.

How to Describe Indigenous Territoriality

Before presenting a longer analysis of the absence of liberal private property among Indians in North America, fully describing one of those systems pro-vides a concrete example to use in contrast to a private property system. A major group of Cree living in Quebec, who call themselves Eeyou, have pub-lished the "Eeyou Hunting Law." It describes a system whose fundamentals have not changed since the time of the fur trade (Cree Trappers' Association

2009). Other Indigenous peoples living in the boreal forest have retained similar systems (Berkes et al. 2009; Tanner 2009). Economist Harold Demsetz (1967) was wrong when he claimed the fur trade led to the creation of a private property system, because the Cree system never was and is not such a system. Anthropologist Frank Speck, wishing to prevent the expropriation of the hunting territories and other Indian lands, was also wrong when he claimed the land was private property, although it did belong to the Indians (Feit 1991). In order to prove these assertions, one needs a systematic approach that captures all the elements of a territorial system. Elinor Ostrom and Susan Crawford provide such a system. It can be used to fully describe any territorial system. The next section describes Ostrom's approach, and the subsequent section applies it to the Cree territorial system.

The ADICO Grammar

To analyze the embeddedness of territory and humans, one needs a flexible analytical framework to use in making descriptions and comparisons. Nobel Prize winner Elinor Ostrom and her student Susan Crawford have provided a method of analyzing tenure systems that can provide the required flexibility (Ostrom 2005, part II). Her method contains two parts: (1) a grammar for consistent and tractable statement of the rules that govern the tenure system, and (2) a system of classifying the rules into seven categories that can capture the complexity of tenure systems. This section introduces the system Ostrom has proposed. The next section gives an example of application of the system to family hunting territories in Algonquian societies. The grammar and classification system is also used in one of my previous works (Trosper 2009, 66–86) to demonstrate that the territorial systems used in the Pacific Northwest are also not private property.

In explaining the system, Ostrom and Crawford label the rules "institutions." This choice follows from a practice common in the literature on common property. Unfortunately, "institution" risks confusing people who think of an institution as an organization, such as the Smithsonian Institution. Organizations are part of social structure, while rules are part of the cultural ideas. An "institution/rule" can have three forms: a law, a norm, or a shared strategy. Ostrom uses "rule" to describe what is labeled a "law" below. This approach keeps the categories clear: all three types are a rule; the strongest rule is a law. Because rules are components of a cultural system, when people are expected to comply with them, the rules either constrain or enable agents.

Ostrom has created a memorable short form (ADICO) for a statement of rules:

[A] ATTRIBUTES of participants who are [D] OBLIGED, FORBIDDEN, OR PERMITTED to [I] ACT (or AFFECT an outcome, an aIm) under specified [C] CONDITIONS, [O] OR ELSE. (Ostrom 2005, 187)

Each of the components has a letter:

A: "**A**ttribute" signifies the entity or entities, the agents, to whom the rule applies.
D: "**D**eontic" describes the requirement of the rule.
I: "a**I**m" describes the action that is the goal of the rule.
C: "**C**onditions" refers to when, where, how, to what extent the rule applies.
O: "**O**r else" specifies the sanctions for violation of the rule.

A "law" has all five of the components; with the sanction stated, it has more force than the other two types of rule. Its components are **ADICO**.

A "norm" is a statement that provides guidance but without an "or else"; it doesn't have the force of a law. Its components are **ADIC**.

A "shared strategy" omits the deontic; it merely describes an action that one or more people undertake, even though the action is not required. Its components are **AIC**.

Some examples from Indigenous communities include the following: A law commonly used for hunting, in full ADICO format, is "A hunter of deer must thank each deer for giving up its life or else the hunter's luck in hunting will deteriorate." An example of norm is "Berry pickers should leave enough berries for bears to eat." An example of a shared strategy is "Farmers plant corn, beans, and squash together."

After developing the grammar for stating rules, Ostrom provides a useful way to classify rules using the "aIm" part of the rule. Her classification system is quite complete and uses seven categories: Position, Assignment (Ostrom uses "Boundary"), Agreement (Ostrom uses "Aggregation"), Information, Payoff, Choice, and Scope. This presentation changes the names of two categories whose meaning isn't obvious: boundary and aggregation.

The order of consideration of the categories is also changed, putting the two "catch-all" categories last.

Position rules, usually stated in the form of shared strategies, define the roles that are available in the system. For instance, in a clan-based system, the roles in the clan are shared strategies: "Each clan has a clan mother, usually one of the oldest women in the clan." In a property system, "Land is divided into distinct parcels" and "Each parcel has an owner" are shared strategies; if the rule is "Each parcel must have an owner," then the rule is a norm. "Parcel" and "owner" are attributes. "Has" or "exists" is the aIm. An example of condition is "usually one of the oldest women in the clan." A description of a territorial system needs to specify the various positions, both for the land and for the people who have a relationship to the land.

Assignment rules specify the persons who can hold positions. Because "boundary" refers to the edges of something, and is especially confusing in regard to land tenure, "assignment" better describes the idea. Continuing with the previous example, one could say that "Mary" is the "clan mother of clan X." This is again stated as a shared strategy. A corresponding norm, which makes sense, is "The clan mother must be a member of the clan." This places a condition on the appointment to the role.

Agreement rules are ones that describe which combinations of positions must agree for an action of any kind to occur. The category has been renamed here, as the meaning of the original term, "aggregation," is not immediately obvious. Because "aggregation" means "adding up," it does describe whose views are added up to decide something. Potential other terms, however, carry their own baggage to make the distinctions unclear. For instance, to call these rules "decision" rules would introduce other possible conditions on a rule rather than a list of the positions that can make the decision. Continuing our examples, an agreement rule that describes selection of a clan mother would be "The women in a clan must agree to the appointment of a clan mother."

Information rules describe what kinds of information certain positions are allowed to have or must have. An example of an information norm is "A clan mother must know the traditions of the clan." A similar law from the Pacific Northwest is "A prospective head titleholder must demonstrate his deep knowledge of the history of the house, or else he or she will not obtain the position."

Payoff rules describe the distribution of costs and revenues among the positions in a system. They are among the most important of the rules when assessing the motivations of people within a system. In a liberal private property system, the owners of a parcel pay the costs and receive the revenues, leaving the difference, the rent, for their use. In many Indigenous reciprocity systems, those who control land are required to share the rent with other people. The others may have to share their income in their turn.

While classifying rules is less important than making them clear, Ostrom does suggest a priority: if a rule is one of the five just listed, use that as the classification of the rule. If it cannot be so classified, then classify it is as a "choice" or a "scope" rule.

Choice rules describe actions that involve choice by the actor. In the Pacific Northwest, for instance, a norm is "A titleholder must allow the first arriving salmon to swim upstream without being caught." One relating to hunting is "A hunter may harvest a deer that has indicated consent to the harvest."

Scope rules apply to outcomes. Because outcomes are often the result of many actions, scope rules can be vague about how an outcome is to be accomplished. A major norm for titleholders in the Pacific Northwest is "The titleholder must assure that a run of salmon returns when it should." Titleholders were responsible for the health of fishing runs in their territories.

Algonquian Hunting Territories

The application of the ADICO approach to territorial systems can be illustrated by applying it to the family hunting territory systems used by many of the Algonquian peoples of North America. These are the Cree, Anishinaabe, and others that live primarily in the provinces of Quebec and Ontario in Canada, in the boreal forest region of the continent. This example is important for several reasons:

1. The family hunting territories were used by the Algonquian peoples to manage themselves and beaver during the fur trade, one of the earliest and most studied trading relationships between Europeans and Indigenous peoples of North America.
2. The territorial system has survived to the present in many locations, such as among the Pikangikum in Ontario, in addition to the Cree. Similar systems exist in British Columbia both along the coast and inland.
3. The anthropological literature has debated the extent to which the family territories are private property, thus providing detailed descriptions of

the family territory systems. Two important collections of articles were published by *Anthropologica* in 1986 and 2018 (Morantz 1986, 2018).

4. Based on the information from the early anthropological debate about the significance of the hunting territories for anthropological theory, some economists incorrectly used the family territories as evidence to explain the emergence of private property, arguing it increased efficiency.

5. Indigenous peoples in the interior parts of the Northwest Coast purposely adopted similar territorial systems because they decreased conflict and improved livelihoods. (Fiske and Patrick 2000, 105)

6. The Eeyou of Eeyou Istchee published the Traditional Eeyou Hunting Law in 2009, in which they state of their own law in great detail (Cree Trappers' Association 2009). Analysts need not rely on anthropologists or economists when the people themselves have codified their system.

People have argued about the origin of the systems, examining whether they were caused by encounters with European traders such as the Hudson's Bay Company. Two reviews of the debate are provided by Toby Morantz (1986, 2018). Whether or not they predate the colonial encounters, clearly the hunting territory systems have persisted among the Indigenous peoples of the boreal forest, and they are not private property systems.

Before providing details about classifying the rules of the Eeyou Hunting Law into the ADICO framework, a brief summary is helpful. The Eeyou Istchee territory is divided into family hunting areas called *indoh-hoh istchee*. Each of these has a hunting leader, often called an *indoh-hoh oujemaaou*, who provides good hunting every year by directing the times and methods for taking certain animals. An Eeyou leader, Philip Awashish (2018), writes, "The Indoh-hoh Oujemaaou has the authority and responsibility for proper stewardship, guardianship and custodianship of the Indoh-hoh Istchee." People in the households of the extended family have use rights in a given territory and cannot be refused access if they follow his instructions. His position as hunting leader depends on the continued productivity of the hunting territory and his fair allocation of access to it. If he fails in taking care of the territory or restricting access without reason, his control slips and eventually a different hunting leader will be installed. The process of changing the person who is hunting leader requires consensus of the hunting group and the broader community (C. Scott 1986, 165). In his introduction to the family hunting territory system, Awashish (2018) avoids using the word *property*; he stresses governance of territory. In 2018 there were about eighteen thousand Eeyou living in ten communities with about three hundred hunting territories. The following section summarizes the Cree system using the seven types of rules.

Position

Because individuals and groups have varying degrees of access to land, one begins by examining the positions attributed to various types of land, and the people who then have a relationship with each of the types of land. In Canada, the Cree and Ojibway peoples, among others, have used a system of "family hunting territories." Each territory is called an indoh-hoh istchee and access and use of the territory is managed by a *kaanoowapmaakin*, also indoh-hoh oujemaaoo, which is variously translated into English as "steward," "head trapper," "hunting leader," "tallyman," or "hunting boss." One important position is "family member," describing people who need to have access to the hunting territories. Animals such as beaver, moose, and so on can occupy positions appropriate to them too. The "terminology" section of the Eeyou Hunting Law lists positions for people, territory, and animals. The position rule for the hunting leader is as follows:

> 4.15 *Kaanoowapmaakin* or *Kaanoowapmaakin Esquow* (female): the Indoh-hoh Eeyou responsible for an Indoh hoh Istchee and recognized as such by the Eeyou community, also known as the Indoh-hoh Istchee Ouje-Maaoo or in English as the Hunting Leader or tallyman. Kaanoowapmaakinch is the plural form. (Cree Trappers' Association 2009, 6)

The family hunting territories themselves are positions, and part VI of the law describes processes for identifying each Indoh-hoh Istchee, the family hunting territory.

Assignment

As with the house system on the Northwest Coast, where heads of the houses had to demonstrate knowledge of the house's territory, a hunting leader in the Cree system is a person with several important characteristics: knowledge of the land in question, as shown by successful harvests; recognition of the duties to other members of the family regarding access to the land; and respect for other family members by consulting before deciding. Most often, a hunting boss's son has the first opportunity to obtain the position held by his father if the father has trained the son adequately. The formal rules are in part V of the Traditional Eeyou Hunting Law; when the transfer occurs normally, the general rule states:

> 13.1 When he decides to transfer his responsibility the Kaanoowapmaakin shall select, in accordance with community custom, the Eeyou to take care of the Indoh-hoh Istchee in the manner his predecessor(s) have done. He must transfer responsibility for the Indoh-hoh Istchee to another Eeyou male or female, with sufficient competence, understanding and knowledge of the lands and animals of the Indoh-hoh Istchee and understanding and knowledge of Eeyou laws and traditions to carry out the responsibilities of a Kaanoowapmaakin. (Cree Trappers' Association 2009, 27)

Section 13.16 is very clear that the role of hunting boss cannot be bought or sold: "No Kaanoowapmaakin may demand or accept payment for passing responsibility for his Indoh-hoh Istchee to another person" (28).

A person could also be removed from the role of hunting leader. If he was not fulfilling the duties, people would stop listening to him or taking his orders. His role as steward of the hunting territory depended on continual consent. Mélanie Chaplier (2018, 69–70) tells of a situation in 2010, when one brother replaced another when the family became dissatisfied with the one brother's conduct as hunting leader.

In the form of a shared strategy, section 9.8 describes how a hunter becomes the position of owner of individual kills. Once hunters have been authorized to use an area, the first person to kill the animal, or the first one to find its den, becomes the owner. This is the only part of the law that uses "ownership." The use of "owner" in this set of rules does not mean the hunter has full control of the resulting kill; he claims it, and then other rules require sharing as described under payoff rules.

Agreement

The selection of a new hunting leader already addresses one of the decision-making rules: a hunting leader is selected by agreement among the family after nomination by the current hunting leader. In the current era, heads of the territories meet together. Among the Pikangikum, decisions are made by consensus among all the senior hunters on matters of joint interest.

Dispute resolution is important. Part VII of the Eeyou Hunting Law describes a two- or three-step process for resolving disputes about any decision. Section 5.7 describes giving elders significant roles in resolving disputes. The law itself was adopted through a process described in sections 33 and 34; agreement was based on consensus among all the people.

Information

The hunting leader is expected to be the most knowledgeable person about a family territory. Section 6.2 states clearly that the hunting leader must be capable and knowledgeable:

> 6.2 The Kaanoowapmaakin must have sufficient competence and sufficient understanding and knowledge of the lands and animals of the Indoh-hoh Istchee to carry out his responsibilities. (Cree Trappers' Association 2009, 9)

A hunter must consult with the hunting leader to acquire information about where to hunt, how much to harvest, and such matters. If the hunter does not consult, the hunting leader can restrict his access to the territory. Elders have a special role in being a source of knowledge about the "traditional ways of the Eeyou" (section 5.7a, p. 8). Parents and other adults must educate children about Eeyou customs and the "traditional practices for showing respect to animals" (section 9.3, p. 18).

Payoff

Payoff rules describe how the surplus generated by economic activity is distributed among people. A person in need of food may harvest animals or plants for that purpose. A person who harvests food when in need, without permission, must eventually reciprocate with the hunting leader. A hunting leader must give access to any family member who complies with his instructions about how to harvest, without demanding payment.

> 9.5 The Kaanoowapmaakin may not demand or require payment in exchange for granting access to or use of the wildlife or other living resources of the

Indoh-hoh Istchee for personal purposes or for trapping. (Cree Trappers'
Association 2009, 18)

In spite of rule 9.5, rule 9.6 states that hunters are expected to show respect to hunting leaders by sharing what has been harvested with them. In
addition, hunters are expected to follow traditional practices of sharing "the
fruits of their Indoh-hoh activities with their families and communities" (19).
This payoff rule makes the community have an interest in the productivity
of each indoh-hoh istchee.

Choice

Because many of the above five types of rules could also describe the choices
made by the hunting leader or hunters, one must remember that if a rule is
mostly about the preceding types of rule, they should be classified there.
"Choice" then is a category for all other rules involving choices. Section 9.6
provides a long list of choices. Some involve following traditional rules to
"respect the land, the animals and the environment" (18). Others give details
about following the instructions of the hunting leader regarding when and
how to hunt and trap, following safe practices, and respecting the personal
property of other hunters. The section ends by stating:

> These rules may vary according to the traditional practice of each Eeyou
> community and may vary according to the season in which Indoh-hoh ac-
> tivities take place. These rules may also be temporarily varied in emergency
> situations as directed by the Kaanoowapmaakin. (Cree Trappers' Associa-
> tion 2009, 19–20)

Scope

That the entire landscape is alive affects the scope rules for the hunting leaders
and all the hunters who ask for access to a hunting territory. One can summarize the rules in ADICO format: "A hunting leader must maintain good
relationships with all the conscious beings of his territory or else he will lose
his position." The Eeyou Law does not explicitly refer to other beings on the
land as conscious. Although the Cree do believe that, one can guess that to
say so explicitly might cause non-Indigenous authorities to cast doubt on the
legitimacy of the law. References to "knowledge of Eeyou customary laws" is

a way to refer to such ideas but not state them. Section 6 of the law spells out general scope rules and the specific rules as well, beginning as follows:

> 6. Role of the Kaanoowapmaakin as a Steward, Guardian and Custodian
>
> 6.1 The Kaanoowapmaakin must have knowledge of Eeyou customary laws, rules and practices and is responsible for ensuring their respect within the Indoh-hoh Istchee in accordance with the Eeyou values and guiding principles.
>
> . . .
>
> 6.3 The proper stewardship, guardianship and custodianship of the Indoh-hoh Istchee is carried out both for the benefit of the Kaanoowapmaakin's family and hunting group and for the benefit of the whole community in order to ensure the productivity and sustainability of the Indoh-hoh Istchee both for present and for future generations.
>
> 6.4 As a steward, guardian and custodian the Kaanoowapmaakin sees to the Anaacatawaayiitaacanouch/conservation of wildlife and other living resources of the Indoh-hoh Istchee and of their habitat.
>
> 6.5 The Kaanoowapmaakin has the responsibility to oversee and ensure the just sharing of the wealth of the land and the distribution of its resources among the members of his hunting group, their families and the Eeyou community. (Cree Trappers' Association 2009, 19–20)

The section proceeds in parts 6.6 through 6.12 to provide specifics about planning and coordinating with neighboring hunting leaders. Because geese fly over many different family territories, one section of the law provides specific rules for dealing with geese; among these is appointing one hunting leader as specifically in charge of all activities regarding harvesting geese.

Contrast to a Private Property System

Some have used the family territory system as an example of private property, beginning with Speck, the anthropologist who wanted to assist the Cree in holding on to their land by asserting that they had property interests in it (Feit 1991). In a widely cited article, the economist Harold Demsetz (1967) relies on Speck and another anthropologist, Eleanor Leacock, to argue that the fur trade increased the value of beaver, which led the Algonquians to develop a private property system to replace an open-access system. While

Locke advocated that colonists would replace an open-access system with private property, Demsetz argues that Algonquians had already done so.

Many anthropologists in recent years have argued that the family hunting territory system was not a private property system, a correct analysis that needs to be explained here (Chaplier and Scott 2018). The issue matters because many people have urged Indigenous peoples to adopt a private property system in order to become prosperous through development. Terry L. Anderson has been leading this movement (T. L. Anderson 1992, 1995, 2016; T. L. Anderson, Benson, and Flanagan 2004). The argument relies on the fact that capitalist economies are based on individual property ownership, even if the individual is only a legal individual, and an assumption that other approaches to economic activity are inferior to capitalist economies.

An economic system based on relationships that include nonhumans cannot use a private property system or even a property system because to do so fails to recognize the consciousness and agency of nonhumans who enter relationships. The owner of a thing as property has control over it in a way that is inconsistent with treating it in a respectful manner. The Cree Hunting Law specifically cites respect as one of the values and guiding principles for the law; according to section 3.1, *"Eeyou show respect to everyone and everything"* (Cree Trappers' Association 2009, 5). The terminology section of the law states:

> 4.16 *Naacatawaayatacano* or *conservation*: refers to the concept that the land and its living resources are precious to the Eeyou and that their good and respectful management will ensure the continuous well-being and renewal of the land and its living resources and will allow future generations of Eeyou to maintain their way of life. (Cree Trappers' Association 2009, 7)

Note that "management," which implies control, is modified by the adjective "respectful."

This rule of conservation applies to the hunting leader; among his or her duties is to "ensure that respect for animals is maintained, in accordance with Eeyou tradition" (section 6.9.d, p. 11). All Eeyou are responsible for education of the youth, which includes Eeyou traditional practices for showing respect for animals (9.3.d, p. 18), which in section 9.6 is expanded to read, "respect the land, the animals and the environment" (18). The Cree word for respect is *Chishtaiimiiduuwin*. It is one of the seven values listed on the first page of the law; in discussing the use of English to express the law, the appendix states the principle of Chishtaiimiiduuwin is one of their most important values.

To show that the Cree system is not private property, one needs to use a correct definition. The legal and economic literature on the idea of property is extensive. Two representative definitions are provided by legal philosophers John Christman and J. E. Penner. They differ in the way they describe property as it is used in law; both point out that economists do not use the legal definition of property. Many economists state that property is a "bundle of rights" that provide persons with a flow of income (Barzel 1997, 3–15). Any source of income then can be treated as property, which is incorrect for legal analysis. Property must be a separable thing; hence the flow of income resulting from the capabilities of an individual is not an example of property as a legal matter. Christman (1994, 23–27) classifies property rights in things into two main categories: the right to control and the right to income. Penner (1997, 152–54) narrows the definition to one key part of the right to control, the right of exclusion; he also maintains that the right to sell the land is part of contract law, not property law. A market depends on contracted exchanges; other types of exchange, for Penner, can occur with property defined as the right to exclude. A system of sharing outside a market system can still include this narrow definition of property. While Penner's narrow definition is fine for legal philosophy and provides a way to find that narrow idea of property in Indigenous systems, the broader idea that property can also be sold is the more common usage. In either of these definitions, the income from property belongs to the owner. The title of a recent article on the Cree system, "Property as Sharing" (Chaplier 2018), is thus a very confusing use of the word *property* because the income from private property need not be shared.

Clearly the hunting leader has the right to exclude persons who do not follow his or her orders regarding respecting the land. Exclusion is one lever that provides the hunting leader's control over the people who hunt; other sanctions are referred to but not elaborated in the Hunting Law (section 11.1). The hunting leader, however, does not have control of the animals; hunting leaders are expected to have respectful relationships with animals.

The hunting leader does not have full control of the income from the land, as members of the family must be given access to the land as long as they obey the rules. This rule would make the family the owner of the land, except that even the family, through the hunting leader, is expected to give access to other Eeyou who wish to hunt when sufficient resources are available to be shared within the broader requirement of conservation (section 6.5).

Neither the hunting leader nor the family can sell the land. One of the new rules added to the Eeyou Hunting Law is part VIII, "Guidelines for the Approval of Economic Development Projects or Activities Affecting an Indoh-hoh Istchee." Section 29, "Collective Interest," indicates that no individual Eeyou can give consent for a project and that any project requires consent from all hunting leaders for territories affected as well as consent from all Eeyou First Nations in which the territories are located or who may be affected by the project. The modern law states clearly that each of the ten First Nations within the greater Cree land base controls access to its territory.

To what extent does the Hunting Law recognize property in anything? Section 9.6.1 says that each hunter is expected to "respect the property of other hunters, including cabins and equipment," which applies to human-made things (Cree Trappers' Association 2009, 19). Section 9.8 provides rules for establishment of ownership of individual kills. Generally, an animal belongs to the person who kills it; the word *property* is not used, correctly, because the hunter may be required to share some of the kill with other persons. This is codified in section 9.6.o, requiring a hunter to "share the fruits of their Indoh-hoh activities with their families and communities in accordance with Eeyou Weeshou-Wehwun" (19). Recall that Weeshou-Wehwun refers to all the traditional teachings and laws of the Cree.

Although the hunting leader has control over the family hunting territory, he or she cannot exclude those who have rights to enter unless they fail to follow orders. He or she also must share the fruits of the hunting territory with those who may enter. And the hunters must also share what they catch. Because the leaders and the family do not own the income, the hunting territories are not private property of the hunting leader or the family that is identified with the territory. They are also not private property because they cannot be sold by the family without community approval. If a family territory is used for modern projects, they must pay compensation to the family of any other territory that is harmed by the activity.

A further point establishes that the territories are not property. They are not "things" in the sense of the English common law and by other legal systems inherited from Europe. Consider the very narrowest definition of property, that of Penner. After consideration of many arguments, Penner settled on a definition based mostly on exclusion, defining property in law as "the right of exclusive use" as follows:

the right to determine the use or disposition of a separable thing (i.e., a thing whose contingent association with any particular person is essentially impersonal and so imports nothing of normative consequence), in so far as that can be achieved or aided by others excluding themselves from it, and includes the rights to abandon it, to share it, to license it to others (either exclusively or not), and to give it to others in its entirety. (Penner 1997, 152)

Penner stresses the lack of a moral connection to the "thing" that is owned. Such an impersonal connection would rule out a subjective connection through a relational good. Neither the family nor the hunting leader of the family has this sort of distant relationship to the territory. Rather, they have a relationship or a set of relationships with all the animals and plants of the territory. These relationships lead to the principle of conservation.

While Demsetz (1967) is clearly wrong with the assertion that the Algonquian peoples adopted a private property system, a related but more correct story comes from the west coast of Canada. The people of the Lake Babine Nation adopted the potlatch governing system of their coastal neighbors in order to create peace among themselves. The potlatch governing system is very similar to that of the family hunting territories, except that it focuses on fish more than on terrestrial animals such as the beaver. Jo-Anne Fiske and Betty Patrick (2000, 105–8) report that other interior tribes acted similarly, as reported by Antonia Mills (1994, 38) for the Wet'suwet'en. A chief reported that, because "the Indians were all killing one another over the land," before they adopted the coastal system, they "decided to divide the lands and make laws" (Fiske and Patrick 2000, 105). It appears the Lake Babine people adopted an Indigenous territorial system to deal with open-access problems rather than a property system. Demsetz has the causation right but the answer wrong! Indeed, chapter 5 presents arguments that support Indigenous systems as better able to deal with common pool resources than private property systems do.

Other Examples: Agricultural, Horticultural, and Links to Hunting Systems

Information about other territorial systems in Indigenous North America is not as detailed as is available for the Cree and other Algonquian peoples; traditional systems that have survived are on the edges of settlement. Indians with agricultural land had their governance of land ended as settlers moved in. Farmers in the U.S. Southwest had their water taken, and then later they had their remaining agricultural land allotted in a system that imposed a flawed imitation of private property. Tribes held on to lands on the margins, and management was taken over by the federal government. Forestland and rangeland became subjects of short- and long-term leases. A consequence is that good evidence on Indigenous tenure systems must be obtained from other countries. While those systems have been disrupted, the Indigenous systems have survived in some form, often coexisting with a system imposed in an effort to create private property in land.

Land Tenure Among Indigenous Mexican Communities

Systems in Indigenous Mexican communities vary their tenure types by types of land. In their descriptions of Indigenous communities in the lowlands of Mexico, Victor M. Toledo and his co-authors identify many different types: home gardens, milpa (cornfields), *potrera* (cattle-raising land), secondary forest, and mature forest. Their article is too short to include the kind of detail that is required to apply Ostrom's system; it focuses on the ecological fit of the system, calling it a "multiple-use strategy" (Toledo et al. 2003). One can infer from the types of land that different rule systems apply to each type of land. One can also see relative equal distribution of assets among the households. The article presents the distribution of types of land among the households of the Totonac Indigenous community of Plan de Hidalgo, in the state of Veracruz. Six types of land use are divided among the households in different ways; the authors identify six different types of allocations of the types of land. The data show that each type of household has about the same amount of land. Each has a home garden. Those with milpa also have some secondary forest, which is fallow from producing corn but still producing other useful products. Interaction with the outside market occurs for the cash crops, cattle, and vanilla forest. The distribution of uses shows a strategy of diversification as a good way to handle risk. The authors note that the Totonac are using the pattern of succession in tropical forests as part of their strategy; they note also that the amount of land used in shifting cultivation has shrunk over time as some land has been devoted to cash crops and cattle, both of which are single rather than multiple use of the particular parcels. They have a dual economy, part of which provides basic commodities for their own use, and the other part of which produces products for sale outside the community.

The pattern of use in the lowland Indigenous communities in Mexico has resulted from the protection of the Mexican national state, which Janis B. Alcorn and Toledo (1998) argue results from the existence of a tenurial shell provided after the Mexican Revolution by allowing communities to hold their land either as ejidos or *comunidades*. Similar shells exist in a few other countries, such as the *comarcos* in Panama, which protect the Guna (Apgar et al. 2015). To be a tenurial shell, the policies must protect the right of the community to defend its territory against outsiders, to be able to decide how to allocate land and resources among the members, and to be able to settle disputes internally. The publication of the Traditional Eeyou Hunting Law is part of an effort to maintain a tenurial shell in Quebec. Indian reservations in the United States do not have such tenurial shells, even in a situation such as the very strong self-determination exercised by the Confederated Salish and Kootenai Tribes. Although the tribal government has considerable powers, it still is subject to strong outside controls prescribing rules for transferring and managing land. Federal law has frozen the property rights systems on reservations, limiting tribal ability to control their own systems (Leeds 2006; Shoemaker 2019).

At the macro level in Mexico, the tenurial shell of comunidad provides the community control of its land, but to assert ownership would be a mistake. Alcorn and Toledo observe in Indigenous communities they studied that the people said, "The real owners of the land and forest are divine beings." As a result, the community must treat the land as divine beings require. They are responsible to maintain the land in good condition, just as they do for their society. Part of maintaining their society is that all members are assured of access to land or forest needed for subsistence purposes (Alcorn and Toledo 1998, 230).

That the land is in good condition and that even the poorest members of a community can make a living creates the relational goods of stewardship and solidarity. These goods indicate the presence of a meso-level relational subject. Although the Huastec and their neighbors the Totonac have similar relational goods, the two communities have different mixes of products in their agriculture, with the Huastec selling sugar from sugarcane and the Totonac using pasture for cattle. Both share another aspect of Mesoamerican Indigenous life: the identification of milpa systems with the core cultural characteristics of the societies. The families maintain the cornfields in order to carry out important rituals, even if the corn is no longer their main agricultural crop. The milpa system connects the corn to the forest, as milpa systems are examples of swidden systems that involve using the forest to replenish the quality of the soil for corn. For this reason, Indigenous lands in the lowland tropics maintain forests as part of their land.

Alcorn and Toledo provide detail on the internal divisions of land in other Purépechan people in the subhumid temperate forest in the state of Michoacán. One group of Purépechan communities lives on the shores of Lake Pátzcuaro and therefore has tenure rules for the lake as well as for the forest and uplands. Collectively established rules recognize different parts of the lake and its shore as fishing grounds for each fisherman (Alcorn and Toledo 1998, 238).

The other example from the temperate forest is the San Juan Nuevo community, which has established a community forestry enterprise that relies on individually held parts of their forest for supply. A consequence of establishing the enterprise was that individual forest owners, who had been dependent on outside middlemen to sell forest products, accepted a reduction in individual rights in order to support the community enterprise and to improve the condition of the forest, which had been overexploited. This new enterprise resulted from the community's ultimate responsibility for the forest even if the forest had been divided among families.

After describing their case studies, Alcorn and Toledo summarize as follows:

> As among the Huastec and Totonac, Purépechan culture supports values placed on reproduction of the community, conservative use of resource, protection of natural processes, economic equity among community members, consensus building, and collective resistance to intrusion by outsiders. (Alcorn and Toledo 1998, 239)

The pattern of land tenure in Mexico's Indigenous communities fits into the pattern Daniel Fitzpatrick (2006) identified generally for local communities, with a variety of types of relationships among members of the community and the land the community holds.

Precontact Tenures in the USA

Great numbers of Indigenous residents of North America were farmers; many remain farmers. The farming communities seem to have been of several types: ones that engaged in shifting cultivation using woody species to restore soil productivity; ones that farmed along river bottoms, using water from the river for irrigation and periodic floods to restore soil nutrients; and the "horticultural" peoples, who tended plants in the wild, based on perennial plants living in a supportive community of other plants.

R. Douglas Hurt (1987, 113), in his survey of land tenure systems, notes that knowledge about agricultural methods in precontact societies is greater than knowledge of land tenure. Despite the low levels of knowledge, however, Hurt was willing to venture some generalities about the agricultural groups. He has sources from early anthropologists for his short chapter 5. Hurt titled the chapter "Land Tenure"; in the text he uses ownership and property terms quite extensively, following the usual practice of the time.

Consistent with not focusing on individuals, Hurt insists that the proper unit of analysis for Indigenous systems is the village, a meso-level relational subject in this analysis. People associated in villages, and the larger tribal confederations did not exist everywhere. Where they did exist, the basis of the confederation remained villages. Most villages asserted jurisdiction or sovereignty over an area of land they considered theirs and that they held, although they had internal rules about allocation of the lands. Individual farmers, be they men or women, had rights to hold on to the land that they farmed, although they did not have rights to sell the land. In many cases, these individual holdings could be inherited or passed to other people through gifts or other means, subject to approval of the village. Individuals and families could only hold as much land as they could cultivate (although Hurt does not stress this); connected to this, any member of the village who wanted to farm land could start to do so on unclaimed land and thus claim it. Ironically, it appears that the principles of holding individual tenure followed the initial part of Locke's theory of property: people could hold land under usufruct tenure as long as they used it with their own labor. But the exception to the Lockean principle—that more land could be held if the owner could store the products and not have waste, or that he could participate in a market and sell the surplus—was not part of the system. There was relative egalitarian holding of land. This is reported even for the large irrigated areas in the Southwest.

Hurt documents inheritance rules at length. There seems to be wide use of the rule that a family could not own more land than it could cultivate. That rule is reported for many different regions. Some peoples were matrilineal and some patrilineal. The Zuni are reported to sell land within their community (Hurt 1987, 72). Hurt does not investigate ideas of relationship with the land. The village would support their joint relational good by making sure that each family has land to farm. The problems of inheritance would be handled depending on the family's circumstances.

As with the systems that relied on family or house territories, the usufruct systems in the agricultural areas provided for the certainty needed for a person or family to invest in a parcel of land along with flexibility that allowed the village or community to change the allocation of land as conditions changed. In the areas of shifting cultivation, such as among the Iroquois in the northeastern woodlands, the allocation of farming land changed each time a village moved, which occurred approximately every thirty years (Trigger 1969, 1990).

Some hunting and gathering peoples also used individual tenure in productive areas of their land. The Paiute recognized usufruct holding of individual trees. Particular plant-gathering areas were recognized as used exclusively by particular families. With such recognition, a family gathering from an area could invest in tending the plants of that area without fear that others would enter the area and use it for their own purposes. Their relationship with the plants would be respected by others. This would be an application of the principle of noninterference with other persons and families.

Implications of Indigenous Territoriality for Economic Activity

The descriptions of Indigenous territoriality systems just surveyed share a number of features that create distinctive characteristics for economic activity in Indigenous communities:

1. the creation of relational goods for families, clans, and villages;
2. the inclusion of nonhumans in those relationships;
3. the requirement that those controlling land are accountable for using it well;
4. the flexibility of land assignment when usufruct is the principle of individual or family control of land;
5. the prohibition on selling land; and
6. the requirement that the net return from using land is shared among a defined group of people, animals, and plants.

This last characteristic, reciprocity in relationships, requires additional treatment in the next chapter to work out all the implications.

The first three features combine to provide an explanation for the widely observed correlation between hotspots of biodiversity and the presence of Indigenous peoples (Pretty et al. 2009). As is explained in the next chapter, proper harvest rates for common pool resources, which are most of the products of land, depend on relationships providing the basis for human cooperation in their actions on the land. When humans include nonhumans in their relationships, they increase their ability to understand the land and to support its health. A further reason for good support of biodiversity is that stewards such as the hunting leaders are held accountable for the condition of the land that is their responsibility.

The flexibility of the system allows it to adjust to changes that would be described as "disequilibrium" by both economists and ecologists. If the relationships between people and the land get out of balance, the flexibility of usufruct allows adjustment. Relative equality among families can be upheld through adjustments in the assignment of usufruct tenures.

The prohibition on sale of land interacts with the principles of usufruct tenure. Most mainstream economists and most people who advocate standard forms of economic development will object to the prohibition on the sale of land. The basic objection is that efficient use of land is hampered by restricting its ownership from moving to those who will maximize the market value of the land through selecting the most profitable form of use; they also say the lack of a market will not let the owner know the real value of her land, as if all value is monetized (T. L. Anderson and Leonard 2016, 7). They will also object that the incentive to use the land well is attenuated if the people controlling the land don't have full tenure security. The focus is on efficiency without taking nonhumans into account, without attention to external effects, and with little concern about development of inequality. Because private property systems do not take these factors into account, they also cannot claim that market value is the true value of the land with all externalities considered. These criticisms ignore the ways in which Indigenous territorial systems do have incentives to use the land well; those with leadership responsibility are expected to have solid relationships with the beings living on the land. The valuation of the land includes the relational values created through relational goods.

In his survey of privatization efforts in developing countries, Thomas Vendryes (2014) notes that peasants typically oppose efforts to create private property systems, for many significant reasons, among them the following:

1. Creation of land markets allows rich outsiders without knowledge of agriculture to purchase land.
2. Capital markets are poorly developed and discriminate against the relatively poor. Rich people can finance purchases with mortgages not available to everyone.
3. The pervasive externalities in rural systems make privatization hamper dealing with externalities and common pool goods.

In short, efforts to impose private property systems in the current era have often failed.

• • •

The complexity of the territorial systems among Indigenous peoples is partly a result of the need for different rules for different types of land and different types of interaction among land parcels, such as through irrigation or through the migration of animals. The rules for different "resources" on the land are influenced by the character of those resources when regarded as "goods." This analysis leads into the next chapter, which provides an emphasis on externalities and interdependencies with nonhumans and humans.

CHAPTER 5

Common Pool and Public Goods

The second and third chapters demonstrate how Indigenous peoples create relationships and through them, relational goods. The fourth chapter argues that Indigenous tenure systems are best understood as relationships among humans and nonhumans in the landscape. This chapter explains why Indigenous peoples, with their emphasis on the priority of good relationships, are well able to deal with common pool and public goods. The chapter begins by distinguishing private and toll goods from common pool and public goods. It then shows why individualism creates dilemmas that limit production of common pool and public goods. That the potlatch system in the Pacific Northwest supported a productive fishery is explained next, followed by an examination of social preferences, which economists call on to possibly provide good management of common pool goods. Merely having the right preferences is insufficient to solve the dilemmas. The chapter concludes by showing that strong relationships can solve dilemmas. Elinor Ostrom and her collaborators have discovered and verified twelve principles that provide good commons management. Five of those principles create good relationships, five of the principles describe relational goods, and two of the principles provide the tenurial shells that a community needs to govern itself.

Good commons governance results from the emphasis on maintaining good relationships through mutual respect as well as attention to equity and empowerment as key relational goods. The principles of reciprocity used in sustaining such relationships also support relational ethics, concern for the effects of actions of a relational subject on all those entities that are affected by them.

Types of Economic Goods

Economists have classified economic goods into four categories using two characteristics: excludability and divisibility. Excludability refers to the ease of preventing people from having access to a good. When there is low excludability, people can easily access the good or service. With high excludability, it is possible to charge money for access to the good. Divisibility refers to the ability to divide a good into parts. As shown in table 2, the resulting four categories are private goods, which have easy excludability and divisibility; common pool goods, which have difficult excludability and easy divisibility; public goods, which have neither excludability nor divisibility; and toll goods, which have excludability but lack divisibility (Ostrom 2010, 645).

The goal of this section is to describe the dilemmas that each of these four types of goods create for individuals acting noncooperatively. Private goods create externalities, which affect the production of other private goods. Common pool goods end up overexploited, and public goods end up underproduced, in comparison to the benefits the goods could provide. Because of high excludability, toll goods can be managed by charging for their use, as with a toll road or tickets to a performance hall.

Private Goods

Most economic analysis has focused on commodities, which are items that are bought and sold. Commodities can be goods, physical entities, or services. Services involve humans or organizations providing advice, work on a project, or other work involving humans; as such, services are easier to understand as involving relationships. Goods, on the other hand, have become disconnected from their human origin. In order to be traded on a market, a

TABLE 2 Types of Goods

	High Divisibility	Low Divisibility
High excludability	Private	Toll
Low excludability	Common pool	Public

good needs to be stabilized as a well-defined thing capable of having a single owner and that can be counted and priced. Latour (2004) and Michel Callon (1998), among others, call this "taming" a wild entity. Others have simply labeled the practice as "commodification." Commodification makes an item a "thing," subject to becoming property, being owned.

Commodification also involves making a thing suitable for buying and selling in a market and setting up the market. A market is where buyers and sellers trade, usually money for commodities. Commodities are also called private goods, to contrast them with public goods, discussed later. In comparison to public goods, private goods can be "consumed" or owned by one individual. A private good has the quality of being "divisible," meaning that when one person has each of the identical goods, others do not. Some analysts use "subtractable" or "rivalrous" as alternatives to "divisible." A second characteristic of a commodity is that its individual owner can exclude other people from access to the good. A public good has neither of these qualities.

Objections to commodification focus on the separation of goods from their conditions of production. The impersonality of the item, its detachment, allows for effects on other things that become disconnected from the item. Production of goods generates waste, which becomes garbage. Some garbage is a good with a negative price; the owner must pay to have the waste disposed of. Other things produced are released from factories with no charge to the factory owners. For ease of distribution and prevention of shoplifting, many commodities are packaged in plastic, which has externalities in production and adds volumes to the quantity of garbage (Cirino 2021). The result is pollution of rivers, lakes, the air, and land. Superfund sites epitomize this effect of private good production.

For instance, lumber can be produced in a way that destroys rather than renews forests. Without a connection to the place of origin, consumers cannot take account of the external effects of the lumber production. The Forest Stewardship Council (FSC) tried to create a brand that would differentiate wood by its relationship to sustainable forest practices. Creating the brand involved verifying the forest management of each producer with third-party verification, licensed by the FSC. The effort met with some success, and forest industries in North America responded with their own brand for sustainable management. The result was a change in types of lumber available, differentiated by the distinct sustainability brands (Tikina et al. 2010).

Another objection occurs when producers exploit labor in the production of commodities. Whether or not some workers are exploited is a contentious issue, but the point is also made that their labor itself has become commodified and subject to competition in the labor markets.

Common Pool Goods

Common pool goods are ones like fisheries in which independent actions by harvesters can create overharvesting and reduce the productivity of the fishery. The good, fish, is divisible because when one fisherman catches a fish, that fish is no longer available to others. But many fishing grounds are open to all; exclusion is expensive if it is at all possible. Other examples of divisible but nonexcludable goods are groundwater reached by unregulated wells, herds of free-roaming animals hunted by individuals, copy machines in offices that are open to all without any monitoring of the amount of use, and fields of oil that, like water, are accessible by unregulated wells.

Each of the four examples just given can be overharvested. Take too many fish, the fishery collapses. Take more water from the ground than is flowing into the underground reservoir, and the level falls; wells must be deeper and deeper in order to obtain water. The land can also subside. If the groundwater is near the ocean, extraction of too much fresh water will lead to infiltration by the ocean, and all the water will become salty. Free-roaming animals will be overharvested, and the budget supporting the copy machine will eventually fail to cover its costs. Similarly, production of commodities produces varieties of pollution, which can be described as a common pool bad: rather than too few fish, there are too many poisons in the water.

The problem with a common pool good is overharvest; to limit harvest, people must reduce their investment in harvesting technology, such as fishing boats or wells. A better solution would be not to invest in too many boats in the first place. The problem with overfishing has been known by economists since H. Scott Gordon (1954) modeled the problem in the early 1950s.

Public Goods

Public goods occur when people jointly use a good that is not divisible or excludable. The problem with a public good is underproduction. Economists' explanation for the underproduction is the phenomenon of "free riding": if other people create a public good, many can enjoy it without contributing. Local public radio stations, for instance, are unable to raise sufficient operating funds via advertisement. They need to plead with listeners to have them contribute the needed funds. Success in such fundraising occurs when stations adopt ways to simulate a relationship. Many people, however, can free ride: listen without contributing. The difficulty with indivisibility and difficult exclusion is that people can enjoy the public good whether they contribute or not.

While writing this chapter, I visited the fireworks show over the Reflecting Pool in Washington, D.C., on July 4, 2018. We all enjoyed the government-supplied fireworks together, crowded on the steps of the Lincoln Memorial or the grass west of the Washington Monument. Although each one of our enjoyments of the fireworks did not reduce that of others, it was possible for the National Park Service to restrict access to the immediate area. But anyone nearby could see the high fireworks and hear the explosions. The fireworks were not divisible, in that one person's viewing did not reduce the amount available to others. They also were not excludable, except at very high fencing costs around downtown D.C.

Because local public goods are available in a relatively small area, it is possible to devise ways to convert them into toll goods. But if a community decides to privatize firefighting, there remains an externality in that it would be in the interest of neighbors of a house to see its fire extinguished, even if the homeowner has not paid for fire insurance.

Toll Goods

When a good is not divisible but exclusion is relatively easy, the good is a toll good. A fine example of a toll good is a public event with admission for those who purchase tickets, as for a concert or an athletic competition. The dance floor at a powwow is another example. As discussed in the previous chapter, a special case of club goods is a relational good, which is available only to the members of a relationship. A relational good is not the same as a concert or a baseball game because the spectators for such events are not at the same time producers of the event. A successful team may have its own relational goods generated by the awareness and reflexivity of the team members. But the spectacle produced when two teams play a competitive game is not such a relational good for the spectators. As a marketing strategy, professional sports teams try to create a sense of relationship between their fans and their teams. These efforts are successful because they are an attempt to create relational goods.

Why Individualism Creates Dilemmas

The qualities of nonexcludability and indivisibility in common pool and public goods create dilemmas for individuals if they are unable to coordinate their actions. The dilemmas result from individuals maximizing their own benefit when such maximization reduces the total amount of benefit available to the group.

The settlers who confronted American Indians emphasized individuality and individual freedom. The practice of individualism among the settlers has inhibited their ability to deal with important dilemmas in economic activity. As a result, the settlers have an especially poor record in the management of common pool goods. Their record in providing public goods is better, and the creation of the national government of the United States is an example of an organization that has helped the settlers create some public goods. Two examples are a judicial system that enforces contracts and protects private property and a national army that protects the government and the country. Both of these may have expanded more than they should have because individuals are too disorganized to counter governmental power.

The settlers have not dealt well with common pool goods, however. Their actions have resulted in the decline and elimination of many fisheries, the extinction of easily hunted birds such as the passenger pigeon, the decimation and near elimination of bison, the inefficient exploitation of oil fields (Libecap 1989), and poor management of electricity grids. Such failures of common pool management also extend to insufficient provision of public goods such as clean air and water. Such public goods are supplied at less than satisfactory levels. In the United States in 2021, people widely acknowledge that the country's infrastructure, its roads and bridges, are in poor shape and need repair. John Kenneth Galbraith (1964) long ago noted the general failure to provide public goods.

The general idea of a commons became famous when Garrett Hardin published his article "The Tragedy of the Commons" (1968). He used a prisoners' dilemma model, which is presented in several versions, all of which depend on individuals acting independently to decide how much to harvest. He also drew upon the literature surrounding the enclosure of common fields in England; in that debate, the proponents of enclosure argued that privatization would improve efficiency because owners of a commons would naturally try to graze too many animals. The commons was portrayed, falsely, as an open-access resource. The issue for the lords of the manors was that the people with rights of access to the common fields were obtaining too large a share of the surplus produced by managing the commons. The anti-efficiency argument was a cover for the desire for a larger share of the value of agricultural production (Marglin 2008, 299–307).

The prisoners' dilemma model is well named if we recognize that the situation is a nice metaphor to describe individualism as modeled by economics. In the story, two accused people are isolated from one another and offered a choice by the police and prosecutors. Each is told that if he confesses, he will receive a small sentence, but if he does not confess and the other prisoner does, he will receive a very large sentence. He needs to know that if neither confess, the police will have no evidence and both will go free. If both confess, they will receive a sentence that is less than would be imposed on the one that does not confess. The cooperative solution for each prisoner is not to confess. The noncooperative solution is for both to confess; the police create isolation in order to prevent cooperation. The incentive is set up to make "confess" the best response whether the other party confesses or does not confess. This solution is called the "Nash solution" because it was first proposed by the game theorist John Nash (1950; see also Milnor 1995). Notice the prisoners are not able to communicate with each other, even to say that they will not confess. Without a mutual agreement, the cooperative solution is unlikely to be chosen by both prisoners.

This story is used to present by analogy the choice offered to fishermen in competition with each other. Consider just two fishermen who are using a fishery. The fishery has the characteristic that the annual production of fish depends on the existing population of fish; if the population is reduced, the harvest falls. To "confess" in the model is to catch too many fish: the fishermen don't go to jail if they mutually confess; they simply catch too few fish or destroy the fishery. If one fisherman buys an expensive big boat, he will harvest many fish if the other person purchases a small boat. If both buy large boats, then they split the harvest but have to pay for the boats. The best solution is to split the harvest by using small boats. If they both buy large boats, it will also be easier to harvest too many fish and deplete or destroy the resource.

Key to the prisoners' dilemma story is the context, which amounts to coercion (Ostrom 1990, 39). The police keep the prisoners separate. The judge does not notice that the prisoners were put in the dilemma situation. A personal statement is given heavier weight by a jury than is other evidence. In the summer of 2019, the movie *When They See Us* on Netflix portrayed the interrogation of five young Black men accused of assaulting a jogger in Central Park, New York City. The police obtained confessions from the young men. While the movie did not clearly indicate that the young men, the boys, were given a choice exactly like the prisoners' dilemma model, the movie did show clearly that each one was on his own. The police lied, saying that others had confessed and named the person being interrogated. Parents were kept away from the boys, who also had no lawyers. They were told what to say in private before recording a confession. One of the boys had a black eye caused by a policeman in an event witnessed by another of the boys. When four of the five were placed together in one room, they immediately checked with each other and discovered that they had confessed falsely. The one told the other he had seen the police beat him. They all immediately agreed to deny the confessions. The damage, however, had been done. Prosecutors used the false confessions to convince a jury of the boys' guilt, even when there was no other evidence to connect them to the crime. Subsequent research has shown that coercion of confessions is relatively easy when a prisoner is isolated from other people (Starr 2019). The police can supplement isolation with other techniques, particularly by lying to the suspect about other evidence. The power of interpersonal dialogue by police persuades a prisoner who is deprived of interpersonal dialogue with those who could support him.

Economists have given the prisoners' dilemma model more attention than other models of common pool dilemmas, such as the difficulty of assuring that other parties make the same choice. Actual situations involve problems of appropriation of harvests; of provision of capital to assist the commons, as in an irrigation project; and of monitoring mutual actions. When the police impose separation among the prisoners, they create a situation like the basic model of economics with uncoordinated customers purchasing in a market. The story does apply when prisoners are being coerced, but does it really apply to actual common pool problems? Are people who could cooperate being prevented from cooperating because they have been deliberately separated from one another? Behind the prisoners' dilemma story is an assertion of deliberate creation of individual isolation. Such a story also suggests that reducing that isolation can help solve the dilemma.

Senator Dawes, the advocate for allotment, promoted the privatization of land by arguing that "selfishness is the basis of civilization" (Otis 1973, 10 – 11). Senator Dawes was not the first in this advocacy. Another major source was the reasoning of colonists who viewed North America as open land that was not held as property by the original inhabitants. One can cite Locke, who held that property ownership originated when an individual captured a portion of territory by mixing his labor with it, by building fences, plowing the land, and putting it into agricultural production. The idea that capture provided ownership also extended to wild game and fish. The system of establishing ownership by capture presumes conditions of open access. The idea that resources are not owned by others and are free for the taking is of course a popular one with settlers wishing to find land for themselves after leaving another country. At an extreme, such settlers considered the land to be terra nullius, empty and unowned, as was the theory in Australia and British Columbia. In the early French and English colonies, however, the colonizing governments recognized that Indigenous peoples held the land and that they needed to be approached diplomatically if war over the land was to be avoided. A theory was needed to justify taking land from the people who remained, and the idea that Indians only roamed the land rather than cultivated it developed into a strong ideology (Jennings 1976).

The tension between the assertion of dominion and control by the colonizing government and the desire for open access by the settlers is a major theme of American history. The dominance of individualism as the basic theory for economic development is also a major theme. That individual uncoordinated action, which appears to work for the creation of private goods, creates dilemmas for the management of common pool and public goods is well recognized by economists.

Potlatching Solves the Prisoners' Dilemma

Canada outlawed potlatch ceremonies in amendments to its Indian Act in 1885. While a complex institution, it was a foundation of the governing practices of people who relied on salmon as a main source of wealth. Most interpretations, such as that of historians Douglas Cole and Ira Chaikin (1990), do not connect the sharing of wealth at potlatch feasts with the prosperity of societies that depended on a fishery. Outlawing the potlatch occurred as the settlers in British Columbia were taking fishing away from the Indigenous people; that expropriation was probably more important than the outlawing of ceremonies in creating the open-access problems that led to severe reductions in the number of salmon returning to the rivers each year. The settlers outlawed Indian fishing technology, such as weirs and fishing wheels located at the mouths of rivers, and licensed their own citizens to harvest fish in the open ocean (Harris 2001). As Robert Higgs (1996) pointed out, moving the fishery to the ocean reduced the efficiency of the harvest. Making the potlatch illegal and removing the authority of titleholders to control access establishes the idea that enforcing individualism is a way to create a prisoners' dilemma situation for people relying on a common pool resource for generation of wealth.

A numerical example helps in demonstrating why sharing wealth solves the prisoners' dilemma and why outlawing such sharing imposes the dilemma. A numerical representation of the choice available to a single fisherman can be illustrated by these alternatives. The model assumes two players who have the same relationship to a fishery. The choice for each player is to invest in a big boat or a small boat. The small boat is an efficient way to fish if everyone shares the catch, but if the fishermen are allowed to keep their own catch for themselves, then a big boat is a way to capture a larger share of the fish. If one fisherman buys a big boat, then the other one, with a small boat, cannot catch as many fish. If the other player also purchases a big boat, then he can compete, and obtains the same number of fish he would have before, but he has to pay the cost of the large boat. From the point of view of one player, the payoffs, after deducting the cost of the boat, can be expressed as in table 3.

What is the best decision for the first fisherman? No matter what the second fisherman does, the best decision is to use a big boat. The second fisherman reasons in the same way. Look at both decisions in one table by

TABLE 3 Payoff to One Fisherman in Two Situations

	Second fisherman uses a small boat	Second fisherman uses a big boat
First fisherman uses a small boat	20	5
First fisherman uses a big boat	25	10

entering the results as a pair (first fisherman's net return, second fisherman's net return), as in table 4.

The first line in each box shows the individual payoffs; the second line the total between the two. Clearly, total social product is greater if both purchase the small boats, but to do this they need some kind of agreement or incentive.

The potlatch institution in this simple model would make each fisherman share his catch with the other fisherman. An easy way to model this would be for them to pool their catches and divide them between each other. When they use different-sized boats, then the joint return is thirty, which would be fifteen for each. From the point of view of the first fisherman, table 5 gives the value of each choice, given the other fisherman's choice.

Under sharing the catch, what is the best decision for the first fisherman? No matter what the other fisherman does, the first one earns more by using a small boat. There is no private incentive to buy a big boat. Sharing the catch encourages purchasing small boats. If the sharing is done in public, both fishermen can see the joint result. Although they may know that sharing is a better strategy, they may not agree. A society can enforce sharing, however, which is what the potlatch institution did on the Northwest Coast.

TABLE 4 Payoff to Both Fishermen in Two Situations, Separately and Together

	Second fisherman uses a small boat	Second fisherman uses a big boat
First fisherman uses a small boat	20, 20	5, 20
	20 + 20 = 40	5 + 25 = 30
First fisherman uses a big boat	25, 5	10, 10
	25 + 5 = 30	10 + 10 = 20

TABLE 5 Payoff to One Fisherman in Two Situations When They Share the Catch

	Second fisherman uses a small boat	Second fisherman uses a big boat
First fisherman uses a small boat	20	15
First fisherman uses a big boat	15	10

Objection: Did Humans Evolve to Be Selfish?

The potlatch example was presented at the Fourth Biennial Meeting of the International Society for Ecological Economics in 1996, demonstrating that reciprocity could solve the fishermen's dilemma. Audience members objected: humans are too selfish and agreements to cooperate would be "just talk"; without enforcement mechanisms, selfish people would violate informal agreements. Furthermore, evolution selects for selfishness, not cooperativeness. A presentation at the Sixth Annual Conference of the International Association for the Study of Common Property in 1996 met with slightly more success. While people did not dismiss the evidence from the Northwest Coast, those who worked with fishermen insisted that most were individualists who would not accept sharing their catches. Several people who didn't accept the idea that reciprocity was actually part of human nature provided some references. These tapped into an ongoing debate in both evolutionary biology and economics.

Some argued that cooperative groups could outcompete selfish groups. They noted many examples of cooperation among animals. The idea of "group selection" was ridiculed by some evolutionary biologists; the debate became acrimonious. Those convinced by the evidence of cooperation developed a theory, called "multilevel selection theory," which modeled both selection within groups and selection between groups. The debate was settled and in 2007, David Sloan Wilson and Edward O. Wilson (2007) co-authored a summary article. Their summary is that both evolutionary forces are at work: "Selfishness beats altruism within groups. Altruistic groups beat selfish groups. Everything else is commentary" (345). The people commenting on the presentation of the potlatch were not completely wrong; selfishness can dominate within a group of evolving entities. Evolution, however, occurs at many levels; altruistic groups have an advantage because they can increase payoffs for the whole group, the members of which can have many descendants. Commentary addresses the issue of which selective forces are stronger in each case; the commentary can be complex, as Wilson and Wilson show.

One experiment demonstrating that group selection works used the breeding of docile chickens, preventing them from fighting in pens. The fighting problem arises when breeders select the most productive individual chickens. These chickens are more productive because they fight well. Selecting productive chickens also selects the best fighters, who are able to obtain more food than the other chickens. The individual does well, but many other chickens do not. A breeding researcher studying alternatives decided to select chickens from the most productive groups. He went through several cycles of breeding, selecting only chickens from groups with little fighting to be parents of the next generations, eventually achieving a breed that would not fight (Muir 1996; Atkins, Wilson, and Hayes 2019). Total egg production is greater in nonfighting groups.

Multilevel selection theory also applies to humans. Many humans are inherently willing to cooperate. When such persons are numerous in a group, they can enforce cooperation by punishing defectors. The cooperating groups will be more productive than the ones with high internal conflict, thus surviving in competition. This point will be developed further in focusing on the economists' concept of the individual.

Persons do not have to rely only on inherent human characteristics. The Canadians who objected to and then outlawed potlatch ceremonies were particularly upset with the *hamatsa* dance among the Kwakiutl people (now known as Kwakwaka'wakw), the centerpiece of winter ceremonials. Translated, *hamatsa* means cannibal. As Stanley Walens (1981) has explained, the dance portrays the taming of a cannibal, making him into a responsible member of society. The dance begins with a wild human attempting to eat everything he sees, including other humans. Since humans eat salmon, their flesh is also salmon flesh; thus, the cannibal is also greedily eating salmon. People struggle for days during the dance to tame the wild cannibal, finally succeeding in making him a moral human being (Walens 1981, 157). Often the cannibal dancer is the person who will replace the current head titleholder; thus, a person who will have the most power over a house is being tamed by the people of the house. The simulated cannibalism during the dance greatly enraged missionaries, adding to the resistance to what seemed like profligate distribution of wealth (Cole and Chaikin 1990, 72–75). Each year, the hamatsa dance reinforced the importance of restraining consumption and restricting selfishness, a main theme that Walens explains in his book *Feasting with Cannibals*. The dance also emphasized the socialization of children to be generous. By banning the feasts that contained the dance, Canadian authorities were forcing Kwakwaka'wakw people to become selfish individuals. They could no longer annually remind themselves of the importance of controlling hunger and sharing with each other. The Canadians, as would be predicted by the dance, were indeed cannibals, harvesting all the salmon and nearly destroying the fishery by removing the controls and sharing of harvests that the Indigenous peoples used to avoid depleting the salmon upon which they depended. Outlawing the potlatch ceremonies forced individualism and the prisoners' dilemma upon the people of the Northwest Coast.

Economists Find Individuals Have Social Preferences

That humans are a species in which group selection did have the effect of creating individuals who are not fully selfish is supported by research among economists who conducted experiments to test whether humans were truly fully selfish. The assumption is so important for economics that it deserved testing. Game theory, in particular the prisoners' dilemma, provided a way to organize the experiments. The data gathered by experimental economics showed that substantial proportions of people in laboratory settings, faced with a prisoners' dilemma or other dilemma situations, did not act as if they were fully self-regarding; they had "social preferences." This work has improved their concept of human motivation. In 2002 Vernon Smith and Daniel Kahneman received a Nobel Prize in Economic Sciences for leading researchers in developing a more realistic model of human motivation. To keep the two views separate, in what follows "individual" refers to the economists' agent (economic man) and "person" refers to the personal relational subject that Archer describes and that was discussed in chapter 2.

Economists' individuals are motivated by their preferences, which are characteristics internal to the individuals. "Preferences" can be modeled in many ways. One way is to assume that individuals make decisions to maximize their utility, which is gained from a set of material items that a person has or uses. The idea of utility suggests that it can provide a common measure among people. If an analyst does not want to assume that such utility is comparable, then preferences are modeled on how an individual ranks a set of alternatives. The utility concept can be called a "cardinal" approach, giving a score to each alternative, while the ranking approach is "ordinal." A third way is to say that preferences are reasons for behavior; these reasons can stem from many sources, including addictions and emotions (Bowles 2004, 99). If the preferences are defined over what an individual has and wants, then they are individual preferences. Social preferences are utility values, preferences, or rankings that include what other individuals have.

In the games used by experimental economists, an individual will evaluate the outcome of a game differently if she values the outcome for the other player as well as the outcome for herself. Because the individual values the outcome for the other player, the individual will act in a way that appears cooperative, where to cooperate means to benefit the other player at a cost to oneself. Narrow focus on the payoffs leads to description of social preferences as inequality aversion, altruism, or reciprocity. Inequality aversion looks at the distribution of material goods among people and tries to avoid inequality. Altruism means valuing what another individual has independent of what the valuing individual does. A preference for reciprocity means an individual is willing to have a net reduction in material payoff by either rewarding a friendly actor or punishing a hostile or uncooperative one. The focus of preferences, thus, is on the value given to an action by an individual. It does not depend on what other individuals feel about the item. Different laboratory experimental setups allow testing for different kinds of social preferences. Colin Camerer and Ernst Fehr (2004, 55) call conducting laboratory experiments "measuring social norms and preferences."

Underlying the idea of social preferences is that they are in some manner hardwired into human nature. This hard wiring resulted from evolution of human nature in the past. Experimental games can help reveal what these preferences are. Because the preferences turn out to vary in different societies, some economists propose that what evolved is the capacity to learn social norms, which then become hardwired after being learned. Different norms would be learned in different cultures. Thus degrees of inequality aversion, altruism, or reciprocity would vary but would be hardwired in adults (Camerer and Fehr 2004, 78–79). A further elaboration is to allow adults to select preferences that they find to have good results through interactions with other individuals. Bowles (2008, 1607) calls these "endogenous preferences."

The economists' model can be understood to use just three of the four parts of a person as presented by Archer and embraced by Donati. The self, the "I," is conceived as an individual with preferences that govern decisions. As originally conceived, the preferences were defined only over objects that affected the individual, with no preferences referring to other people. These are "self-regarding" preferences. Work within experimental economics revealed that individuals also have "social preferences" as well as the ability to internalize norms. This work then gave a more complicated view of individual preferences. People like to act in altruistic or cooperative ways if they can

(Bowles 2004, 96–97). In this way, economists have expanded their original interpretation of the "I" component of a person.

The "Me" part of Archer's model is assumed by economists to be the given "endowments" of each individual: their wealth, their skills, their education, all the personal characteristics that allow participation in markets as workers or owners. Over time, a person can change their endowments of skills and material goods through various types of investments. The "You" part, where people have roles in society, results from owners creating firms, and individuals obtaining jobs in those firms, thus becoming actors of various types. Owners of material wealth can become the bosses; owners of personal skills become the employees. In credit markets, some people are borrowers and others are lenders. The personal characteristics of "Me" and the income from the job in "You" provide the endowment of each individual. For economists, the three parts of "I," "Me," and "You" are sufficient for creating economic models and explanations. Individuals satisfy their preferences as best they can with their endowments and the way they are treated because of characteristics such as gender or race.

Economists do not recognize the "We" component, the sets of relationships that each person has in the approach of Archer and Donati. Economic theory needs to explain the source of norms that individuals internalize and then use to guide their behavior. The concept of "We" provides an answer in Archer and Donati's concept of "person" instead of "individual." A person can work with other persons to develop relational subjects, relationships in which the participants share relational goods. Once they have established such goods as trust, solidarity, and identity, they can work together to solve the economic dilemmas posed by common pool goods, public goods, and externalities. Persons can agree to norms while creating relational subjects. When people care for each other within relationships, they can act in ways that to economists look like "social preferences": altruism, inequality aversion, reciprocity, and a willingness to punish defectors at one's personal cost.

Stephen Cornell and Joseph P. Kalt (1992a, 244) explicitly state that economics can't provide analysis of the sources of preferences or norms; they refer the reader to sociology or anthropology for the explanation. Bowles doesn't agree; he claims that norms are the outcome of games in which the norm is a solution to the game. He gives the example of driving on one or the other side of a highway. The resulting norm is the outcome of an "assurance" game, in which the dilemma is to select the same strategy by both players. When individuals are satisfied with this equilibrium, then one or the other particular outcome is solidified by a law. As long as everyone follows the proper law, then there are no head-on crashes on the highways (Bowles 2004, 100). In southern Africa, when one crosses a border between countries, often one needs to switch the side of the road to use. If there were a tunnel under the English Channel that accommodates cars, drivers would similarly have to switch from the right side to the left side when driving from France to England. When individuals come to adulthood in France, they acquire the norm to drive on the right side of the road. When they grow up in England, they learn to drive on the left side. That tourists traveling from one type of country to the other can adjust their driving, with some difficulty, shows that such norms are changeable; one just needs to know which norm, or solution to the game of driving on a highway, is shared among the residents of the country one is visiting. The location of the driving wheel in a rental car helps in detecting the right norm. In the terminology of the previous chapter, this norm is actually a shared strategy, a solution to a simple game that is self-enforcing once adopted. Most common pool and public good dilemmas are more complicated. If the analyst is committed to having individuals as the unit of analysis, explaining coordination to solve common pool and public good dilemmas is difficult. Making relational subjects the unit of analysis provides a way to explain how humans can solve dilemmas created by individualism.

How Relationships Solve Social Dilemmas

As explained in chapter 3, relational subjects come in four types: persons and three levels of social relational subjects. A person's characteristics result from his or her relationships, and the person's decisions depend on an internal conversation and conversations with other persons. They care about the desires and ultimate goals of other persons as well as their own desires and ultimate goals. Persons are motivated by their natural and practical needs as well as their desires for social interaction and their appreciation of relational goods created by relationships. As they grow and change, persons choose to operate by certain rules and continually evaluate the results with their internal conversations. Persons join other persons to create relational subjects that depend upon the mutually created relational goods among the persons in a relationship.

The following text demonstrates that good relationships provide commons governance by generating the principles of commons governance that Elinor Ostrom and her co-authors developed. In 2009 Ostrom received the Nobel Prize in Economics for her work that established the capacity of people to govern themselves when dealing with a common pool resource or a group of such resources. Based on a study of communities with grazing land in the Swiss Alps and mountains of Japan, irrigation in Spain, and irrigation in the Philippines, she had proposed eight design principles for addressing the dilemma of commons governance. Each of the nine case studies was a community with many centuries of successful commons management; because she used so few case studies, she was tentative about their generality. She called them "speculative" but was also confident she had made good progress (Ostrom 1990, 90–91). By 2009 many other scholars had studied those principles. Her prediction was correct; further research led to a list only slightly changed from her original one. She provided a slightly modified list in her Nobel lecture in December 2009 (Ostrom 2010). The revisions were reported by the authors of a paper considering the amount of evidence supporting the eight principles. They determined that two-thirds of one hundred studies found the principles were satisfied in successful situations and were not satisfied in unsuccessful ones (Cox, Arnold, and Tomás 2010).

Ostrom's work with long-lasting commons showed that humans could solve the two types of dilemmas. They found the rules that allowed them to avoid overuse of their commons, and they found a way to agree to the public good dilemma, finding a governance structure in which to decide on the ways to solve the dilemmas created by a common pool resource. Her many counterexamples refute the inevitability of the tragedy of the commons. She also worked with experimental economists to determine how individuals placed in a variety of laboratory situations could solve the dilemmas they faced. She and her collaborators offered the individuals ways to form short-term relationships by talking among themselves before going into the laboratory to act again as anonymous people trying to cooperate. They found that "cheap talk" worked; the laboratory participants agreed to solutions and implemented them without punishment. They also offered participants the ability to punish players who did not cooperate and also options about how such punishments would be arranged. These experiments showed the laboratory subjects able to reach agreements that allowed them to come close to the strategies that would maximize their returns from using a common pool resource.

Ostrom's list is at a higher level of generality than the actual rules that any particularly successful governing group adopts. Local rules vary greatly, due to geography and history. Ostrom emphasizes principles that guide the development of local rules. Relationships can deliver good management of common pool resources because developing and supporting relationships also use these eight principles.

The revision of Ostrom's original eight principles created a list of eleven principles by splitting three of the eight into two principles each. Another should be added: trust. Ostrom emphasized trust in both her American Political Science Association and Nobel lectures (Ostrom 1998, 2010). She did not appear to realize that some of the principles would themselves contribute to generating trust through the ways in which people can build relationships. The resulting twelve principles fit into three groups:

1. five principles that contribute to forming good relationships;
2. five principles that describe the relational goods that result from good relationships; and
3. two principles that describe the external circumstances that good relationships need in order to function.

This grouping of Ostrom's principles creates a new order. She and those who followed put two of the results of good relationships ahead of principles that support good relationships. The first group of principles is connected closely to the six rules for generating relationships that are described in chapter 3. The second group of principles describes the characteristics of relational goods and the consequences of good relationships, namely the creation of trust, identity, fairness, equity, and reciprocity. The third group of principles describes how minimal rights to organize are required for relational subjects to come into existence and how relational subjects treat each other, by respecting each other's autonomy. The third group of principles also addresses the problem of scaling up the management of local commons to the management of global commons, a difficult but necessary topic, which Ostrom called the problem of polycentric governance.

Forming Good Relationships in a Commons

Four of the eight principles, with one of them divided into two, all address forming good relationships: collective choice arrangements, monitoring (of users and of the resource), graduated sanctions, and conflict resolution. What follows is a description of the five principles that address the formation of good relationships.

Collective Choice Arrangements. The principle regarding collective choice is that all persons affected by the operational rules of a common pool arrangement can participate in making and changing the rules. The relationship-building rules that address collective choice are these: always consult before deciding, learn how others see things, and balance emotion with reason. The consultation rule leads to support for consensus among all such persons; consensus assures that no one is left out of the decision-making process. Discussion among the members of a relationship means that all persons express their views from their own viewpoints. In a relational society, each person is respected for his or her viewpoint. When nonhumans are included in a relationship, humans study how the nonhumans think and take account of that. Nonhumans are consulted in decision-making through understanding of them and communicating with them. Learning how others see things also means attending to emotional matters and recognizing such emotions as legitimate while also giving reason its due.

Monitoring. The principle addressing monitoring has been split into two parts. The first is that users monitor each other or appoint monitors to do that job. The second part is that the condition of the common resource is also monitored by the users or their appointees. Monitoring corresponds to the rule "Be wholly trustworthy, but not wholly trusting." Each member of a relationship should be personally trusting, but since humans aren't always trustworthy, then they must be watched to assure other members of the relationship that they are participating fairly. If the relationship is made up of both humans and nonhumans, then the nonhumans are also monitors. The user/resource distinction does not apply if nonhumans are participants in a relationship; according to Indigenous thought, nonhumans such as deer, salmon, and beaver also monitor the behavior of people who harvest them. Such nonhumans demand that they be treated respectfully and that their needs are recognized by humans. In both parts of the monitoring principle, monitors are accountable to users, the community, not to outsiders such as a government agency. Ostrom's original presentation of the fourth principle emphasized a link between monitoring and sanctioning. She used the idea of contingent cooperation, or quasi-voluntary compliance, to argue for the importance of monitoring by users. Compliance is contingent and depends on users recognizing that other users are cooperating; if the others are not, a particular user would feel like a sucker. Monitoring each other through communication contributes to and is a key part of building and maintaining relationships. Monitoring also provides transparency.

During a visit to Kakadu National Park in northern Australia, I learned that the Aboriginal people there monitored their neighbors. As with other Indigenous peoples, each part of the park had a traditional "owner," a person responsible for decisions about his or her territory. That person's decisions, however, would be reviewed by another person, a "policeman." They were using English to describe their system, and *policing decisions* was the word that came closest. In the context of that review, there would be extensive community discussion about what should be done. This is similar to the Northwest Coast, where if a titleholder disapproved of the decisions of another titleholder, he would refuse the potlatch distributions or not attend a feast because of the disagreement.

Graduated Sanctions. The idea that people should persuade each other rather than use coercion supports the use of small sanctions in most cases of rule violation. That small sanctions seemed sufficient to ensure compliance surprised Ostrom in her original work, and it continues to surprise those who focus only on selfish motivation for compliance. The concept of strong reciprocity assumes significant sanctions and needs to be modified to consider graduated sanctions.

When a relationship is well functioning, each participant finds that benefits outweigh costs. Small sanctions remind a person that the larger interest is to remain in a relationship rather than be excluded. Exclusion from a relationship would be a large sanction, and it waits in the wings for those who do not respond to small sanctions. Ostrom (1990, 98) correctly points out that large sanctions can disrupt relationships and create resentment, especially because the violation of a rule may have occurred because of exceptional personal circumstances rather than a desire to violate the conditions of the relationship. The larger relationship rule is that persons should use persuasion rather than coercion in deciding what rules are correct as well as encouraging each other to abide by the rules that have been selected.

Conflict Resolution. Another important part of explaining successful common pool management systems is that participants have inexpensive and rapid methods to resolve disputes among themselves. Ostrom expressed this as "there must be some mechanism for discussing and resolving what constitutes an infraction" (1990, 100). This is an example of the relationship rule

"Deal seriously with whom we differ." Ostrom notes, "Those that are selected as leaders are also the basic resolvers of conflict" (101). The role of leaders in maintaining relationships is an important topic that is discussed more fully in the next chapter.

Results of Relationship Building

The five rules just discussed are good advice for creating good relationships and the resulting relational goods. Three relational goods are especially emphasized in the commons literature, in the same manner that relationality theory suggests: trust, identity, and equity. These three relational goods include five of Ostrom's principles, two with identity and two with equity.

Trust: The Additional Principle. Trust is a key result of relationship building. Both Ostrom and Cox, Arnold, and Tomás (2010) did not state that trust results from the rules just listed. Trust is a shared good and individuals are more trusting as a result of the relationship. In her address accepting her Nobel Prize, Ostrom (2010, 661) noted that she and others analyzing collective action had put more attention to "payoff functions" than to how people using a commons develop trust among themselves. She credited another Nobel Prize winner, Kenneth Arrow (1974), for claiming that trust is "the most effective mechanism" for enhancing exchanges, and also noted that empirical studies confirmed the importance of trust. She pointed out that trust creates a positive feedback loop: the more success people have in trusting each other, the more trusting they become. She explained this point at greater length in her presidential lecture to the American Political Science Association (Ostrom 1998). In their review of the studies that provide support for the list of principles Ostrom provides, Cox, Arnold, and Tomás note that some of the contributions have pointed out that more fundamental issues need attention. They quote one of the studies, asserting that "it has become clear that that the real 'glue' that keeps an institution alive over time are the social mechanisms, i.e., trust, legitimacy, and transparency" (Cox, Arnold, and Tomás 2010). Trust appears because four of the original eight principles support building strong relationships, which then produce trust.

Identity: Create Clear Boundaries. Good relationships also produce identity. Ostrom's first principle addresses the territorial and social identification of a common pool resource by stating that boundaries should be clear.

Cox, Arnold, and Tomás (2010) determined that clear boundaries should be stated as two principles: (1A) legitimate users should be clearly distinguished from other people and (1B) the specific resource the users are sharing should be clearly separated from other parts of the larger social-ecological system. The clarity of such boundaries is another way to state that the system should have its own identity.

User boundaries are well defined when the users mold themselves into a relational subject. A relational subject creates one or more relational goods that only members of the subject can access. This provides a way to define the persons contributing to the relational good. When nonhumans are treated as sentient beings and brought into relationship with humans, that relationship creates a "resource boundary," although the nonhumans should not be regarded as "resources."

Equity: Reciprocity, Congruence, Sharing with All Beings. The original congruence principle has been subject to considerable discussion and modification since originally proposed and revised into two principles. Congruence between appropriation and provision rules should be replaced by "equity" or "reciprocity." Congruence with local conditions can be described as congruence, but equity with nonhumans is better terminology. Ostrom was very concerned about the solution to two separate problems for commons management: appropriation and provision. She meant by appropriation the rules for harvesting or using the resource, the extraction of units from a common pool. Provision means investing in the resource, contribution to actions that improve the productivity of the common pool. The rules are different for different kinds of resources. For a fishery, appropriation looks more important than provision, although for a fishery the spawning grounds need to be protected, as does the source of food. In an irrigation system, provision is very important for the creation and maintenance of the diversions and canals that deliver water to the fields. One way to have congruence of appropriation and provision is to make the distribution of costs proportional to the distribution of benefits, which would seem like a fair rule. Another rule would be to make the share of harvest equal for everyone when provision costs are not large. Other authors in considering the congruence rule have advocated stating it as follows: "equitable distribution of contributions and benefits" (Atkins, Wilson, and Hayes 2019, 36).

Good relationships both among persons and between people and the resource units would depend on all participants paying attention to the needs of other participants, whatever they are. This attention improves on the two-part principle by providing a way for equity to emerge as a relational good.

Appropriation and provisioning benefits and costs should be roughly proportional; such proportionality would appear fair to all participants. The proportionality can include status as well as material matters; one group of fishermen in Japan supplies status to the best fishermen; when they pool their catch, all receive the same number of fish but the best fishers also obtain status (Gaspart and Seki 2003). The reciprocity that enables development of a solid relationship should address this issue, as all participants would be aware when some do not feel that they are being treated fairly. Relational subjects, however, may expand the range of reciprocal relationships to allow for sharing in a broader sense than one-to-one correspondence with particular amounts of provision and appropriation.

Another part of the congruence principle states that appropriation and provision should be appropriate to the resource in question. This could be viewed as taking account of the characteristics of the nonhumans involved in a relationship. In addition to stressing good relationships among people, most Indigenous peoples also emphasize building good relationships with nonhuman entities. Constructing such relationships is possible because all of creation is conscious and capable of responding to actions to create relationships. Universal consciousness extends to entities such as rivers, mountains, and glaciers. Two approaches explain such consciousness. The first assumes the entities themselves are conscious. The second assumes that each entity has a guardian spirit who will act intentionally on behalf of the mountain or river. Many non-Indigenous peoples find the idea of universal consciousness hard to accept. But anyone working with Indigenous peoples and wishing to pursue economic activities involving land, water, ecosystems, and other living beings needs to recognize that Indigenous worldviews involve accepting such consciousness or the existence of guardian spirits.

Two External Requirements

Ostrom and her co-authors also recognize that strong central governments can destroy local governance institutions through the imposition of many rules, including individual rights. They recognize that in the world as it currently is, subsidiarity is weak in the presence of strong central governments. While James C. Scott (2009) has pointed out that diffuse leadership is a way to avoid "being governed" (actually, avoiding domination), he has also recognized that the tactics that used to be successful in the highlands of Southeast Asia weren't successful after the modern nation-state arrived in those countries. The hill people, however, remain somewhat successful just as Indian tribes have in the USA and Canada and local communities have in the Andes.

Central governments have used their authority and power to change power relations in local communities, as through imposition of private property and other ways to promote individualism. These interventions may create relational bads that result from unequal power relations. They also make people act as individuals.

Minimal Recognition of Rights to Organize. Ostrom's seventh principle is that "the rights of local users to make their own rules are recognized by the government." This principle applies to the context in which relationships are created rather than to characteristics of the relationships themselves. The ability of a group to self-organize without interference is a necessary condition for creation of relationships. A major part of relationship building is respect for the autonomy of relational subjects, from the individual to all three levels of social relational subjects. The principle says that higher-level relational subjects respect the autonomy and dignity of lower-level ones. In the United States, for instance, the Intertribal Timber Council refuses to tell each member tribe what to do with its forest. Activities of the council are focused on enhancing the autonomy and capacity of each tribe as well as their tribal members. The council does not take political positions on policies of the U.S. government without the consent of all members that would be affected.

The authority of a state to create laws that interfere with the organization of relationships can be very disruptive. Such interference in Indigenous communities has been pervasive in the settler societies of the USA, Canada, Australia, and New Zealand. In the United States, tribal governments have been abolished during the allotment period. During the reservation period and the self-determination period that began in the 1970s, federal law was often imposed on tribes. The rules for land tenure have to conform to federal law. Use of resources requires leases approved by the federal government. All these actions represent a lack of respect for the autonomy of tribal governments. By allowing tribes to contract for operation of programs on reservations, some room for autonomy has occurred after 1975. Some Latin American states, such as Mexico and Panama, have policies to allow

Indigenous peoples local autonomy; implementation, however, is an issue. Kristina Maud Bergeron (2010) describes how both the Grand Council of the Crees and the Saami Council have defended their autonomy in recent years.

One of the most destructive policies a government can impose is to prohibit local people from policing the boundaries of membership in their organizations and in keeping nonmembers from extracting from a common pool resource. Governments by law can make a common pool resource managed by a community into an open-access resource by allowing anyone to harvest. In an article about world fisheries, Fikret Berkes and his co-authors call external fishermen, often with large ships, "roaming bandits" when they are allowed to harvest from inshore fisheries (Berkes et al. 2006, 1557).

States have enabled the creation of relational subjects with tax laws that recognize nonprofit corporations (called societies in Canada and other terms in other places). A nonprofit corporation is allowed to earn a profit (survival requires doing so), but it is not allowed to distribute the profit back to owners, the members of the corporation. Many such nonprofit corporations are also not taxed. Usually a corporate structure is required, with a board of directors taking responsibility to supervise the corporation. If the hierarchical structure is not desired, a relational group could use other procedures for internally made decisions.

Nested Enterprises. Ostrom's eighth and final general principle sought to make another point regarding the external relations of a system of governance for a local common pool good: "When a common-pool resource is closely connected to a larger social-ecological system, governance activities are organized in multiple nested layers" (2010, 653). In her work, she calls this the problem of polycentric governance. The idea that the organizations that govern a commons should be nested relates to the idea that relational subjects can exist at micro, meso, and macro levels. The issues that need attention with operation rules may vary by level for complex systems. The Haudenosaunee League consisted of nested entities. Villages composed tribes, and tribes composed the entire league. The league also respected the autonomy of the lower levels, and each tribe respected the others. They enacted plurinationalism among their subnations. In their international relations and negotiation with settler societies, they insisted on following their relationship protocols.

To summarize the argument, the twelve design principles that have been developed by Ostrom and her followers is a great contribution to the literature on commons management. The reorganization laid out in this chapter shows that the principles also describe the creation of relational subjects. While many of the cases that have been studied do not involve Indigenous peoples, many do. Ostrom's main examples in her 1990 book are all from communities that had lived in one place for a long time. They are not communities, however, for whom a belief in the consciousness of their landscapes has been reported.

Complexities in Application

Each of the examples presented in the first chapter demonstrates how Indigenous peoples use relationship-building principles to address complex common pool situations. Two of the examples are about water and two about forests. Maintaining the health of a watershed is complex. Indigenous peoples in the Ambato River valley united with others in the valley in opposing treating water as a commodity. They recognized that such an approach involved individualizing the ownership of the water through creation of a market. That would complicate the relationship issues that people face in trying to share the water from a river. In the case of the Whanganui River, conflict between the descendants of the settlers and the Māori about who owned the river threatened to derail agreement about how the State of New Zealand would recognize the treaty rights held by the Tūhoe and Whanganui iwi. Setting aside the question of ownership, letting the river own itself allowed the two tribes to join in a comanagement arrangement that would allow for better consideration of the health of the river.

Management of the many different resources of a forest is also complex. Development of trust was a key issue between the Haida Nation and the province of British Colombia about joint management of the commercial forest lands on the islands of Haida Gwaii. Both sides worked hard to develop trust, and as it develops, their ability to work together increases. The Pikangikum elders could see that if timber harvest licenses were awarded to standard lumber firms in Ontario, their forested lands would be clear-cut and severely mismanaged. The elders had commons management already through their use of a family hunting territory system much like the one described in chapter 4 for the Eeyou. Their agreement with the province of Ontario achieved the creation of a shell that allowed them to keep the basic structure of the family territory system. Their successful negotiation with the province allows the Pikangikum to acquire forest licenses in their territories. Their jointly written plan with the ministry responsible for the land lets them maintain the control they need over their forest.

●　●　●

When relationships include the entire landscape, sustainability of the relationships among humans and the landscape should be a good recipe for resilience and sustainability. Ostrom (1990, 101) notes that leaders in the societies that successfully manage their commons are also the people who resolve conflicts. The next chapter argues that Indigenous leaders have the maintenance of relationships as a top priority, and that such maintenance contributes to sustainability.

CHAPTER 6

Sustainability and Relational Leadership

The previous chapters show that relationships have been used and can be used by Indigenous peoples in addressing key issues: maintenance of identity, management of territory, and solving the social dilemmas created by externalities in the form of common pool goods and public goods. Success in solving social dilemmas should lead to sustainability. Because they solve social dilemmas, successful relationships create sustainability. This chapter begins with a brief survey of Indigenous concepts of sustainability before examining the ways that leadership can promote sustainability by encouraging and supporting relational subjects.

A major concern in current discussions of sustainability is the failure to achieve it. A lack of sustainability results from the reality that "development" means the destruction of nature and the transformation of social relations at the service of the production of goods and services, which occurs in the context of selfish individualism (Rist 2002). Certainly, much of the damage occurring is due to the world's inability to deal with the externalities of common pool and public goods, with the rise in the average temperature of air, land, and water the leading example of failure. The decline of fisheries and mass extinctions are others. The promotion of sustainable development distracts from the failure to implement sustainability.

The principles that support good relationships among humans are the same as those that create good relationships between humans and other living beings. Good relationships create relational goods. Relational goods provide benefits to every being in the relationship. The value of the relational goods contributes to the value of the relationships. When these values are high, the participants in a relationship want to continue it. The relatively long list of actions that persons take to support relationships suggests that the relationships are fragile and the relational goods hard to maintain. Yet some societies did maintain their systems of relationships over long periods of time. Good leadership contributes to this success.

This chapter addresses sustainability. Because Indigenous leaders place maintenance of relationships as their top priority, Indigenous peoples sustain the relationships that create the benefits identified in earlier chapters. If problems arise, Indigenous leaders intervene to improve and support relationships. Such leaders may be internal to a relationship; or, in a system of nested relational subjects, the leaders may be in a system above or outside the relationships being assisted.

Indigenous Sustainability

Several journals that emphasize sustainability have recently shown interest in Indigenous concepts of sustainability: *Sustainability Science, Current Opinion in Environmental Sustainability, Ecological Economics,* and *Ecology and Society*. Among these many contributions, the collection of articles in a 2020 special issue of *Current Opinion in Environmental Sustainability* stands out for its focus on Indigenous perspectives.

Indigenous conceptions of sustainability start with relationships among all the beings in a landscape. Based on relationships, Indigenous sustainability emphasizes the characteristics of good relationships. Several authors have proposed other names for sustainability. Andrea M. Vásquez-Fernández and Cash Ahenakew pii tai poo taa (2020, 65) propose "respectful inter-being-relationalities" focused on desired futures. Robert H. Winthrop (2014, 208) suggests "culturally reflexive stewardship." Deborah McGregor, Steven Whitaker, and Mahisha Sritharan (2020, 37) appreciate the Latin American concept of buen vivir, which they translate as "living well." Eduardo Gudynas (2011, 441) points out that the many versions of buen vivir all share two characteristics: they emerged from Indigenous traditions and they are critical reactions to Western development theory.

In their introduction to a journal issue on Indigenous definitions of sustainability, Pirjo Kristiina Virtanen, Laura Siragusa, and Hanna Guttorm (2020, 77) seek the core dimensions of sustainability in Indigenous thought, as do the authors cited in the previous paragraph. They list the core characteristics as (1) context-based relationality, (2) recognition of nonhumans as life givers, (3) local community-based governance and accountability, and (4) use of powerful symbols marked by community rituals. The first two characteristics when combined provide a concept of the sacred: interactions between the vitality of all objects in their relationships with humans (Kealiikanakaoleohaililani and Giardina 2016, 63). The importance of relationality among all beings enters language through the importance of links to land and landscape (Ferguson and Weaselboy 2020). Ideas of justice have to be expanded to consider all species, recognizing that humans are just part of all life on the planet (Celermajer et al. 2021).

Although the Indigenous definitions are not uniform among themselves, they agree that sustainability cannot be defined with an assumption that humans and nonhumans are separate, with humans consuming the services provided by the nonhumans, as in the idea that an ecosystem provides services to humans considered as a set of individuals with their own preferences. The various conceptions all reject the idea that ecosystems should be sustained for the benefit of humans, an idea motivating international efforts such as the United Nations' Sustainable Development Goals or the Millennium Ecosystem Assessment or its successor, the Intergovernmental Science-Policy Platform on Biodiversity and Ecosystem Services. Even the concept of strong sustainability in ecological economics has this problem. Strong sustainability means not decreasing the quantity of natural capital by substituting for it with man-made capital. The idea of "capital" describes nonsentient things that are owned by humans, thus preserving the separation of humans and nonhumans. The proponents of strong sustainability, however, do recognize that they are advocating for the idea of making sustainability "consistent with biological and physical reality" (Gowdy 2000).

Indigenous conceptions of sustainability all embody the two fundamental principles that organize this book: relationality and the consciousness of all beings. As they develop relationships, humans and nonhumans generate relational goods that are valuable to them, and for this reason local subjectivity has to be recognized. There is no universal definition of sustainability because the beings that are sustained along with the symbols of their mutual relationships vary from place to place. The search for a single phrase to capture the concept of sustainability for the many Indigenous peoples is probably as difficult as making a fixed list of characteristics to define Indigenous identity conceived as peoplehood. All Indigenous conceptions of sustainability emphasize that relationships are fundamental.

Leaders Support Relationships

The previous chapters explain how relationships serve in addressing many problems in society. Good relationships generate trust. Trust aids the coordination of actions that preserve the productivity of common pool resources. Good relationships that include animals help make commons productive as well. The many relational goods produced by strong relationships directly satisfy human sociality as well as enable people to deal with the many dilemmas of life. People in a relational society need to know how to create and maintain their relationships. Leaders are the ones that make and keep relationships strong. Because maintenance of relationships is not automatic, Indigenous leaders have a special role in sustaining relationships. Several authors, such as Pierre Clastres (1987), Miles T. Bryant (1998), Carolyn Kenny and Tina Ngaroimata Fraser (2012), and Gary Sandefur and Philip J. Deloria (2018), have described characteristics of Indigenous leaders. These characteristics together make sense when interpreted as supporting and sustaining relationships.

The following are ways leaders help relationships persist:

1. leaders nurture the collective and facilitate dialogue and discussion of major challenges throughout the community;
2. leaders support relationships with nonhuman elements of their territories;
3. leaders support the autonomy of persons and relational subjects;
4. leaders assist dispute resolution through peacemaking processes;
5. leaders promote socialization of the next generation into relationality; and
6. leaders promote social memory.

All these actions create, support, and maintain relationships and relational subjects among Indigenous communities. By doing so, relational leadership supports sustainability.

Leaders Nurture the Collective and Assist in Community Decision-Making

Leaders are responsible for facilitating community decision-making using principles of consensus, one of the keys to successful relationships. This kind of leadership is spread among many different people. Sandefur and Deloria

(2018, 130) point out that Indigenous leaders do not attempt to dominate; "questions are more readily talked to consensus (or exhaustion) rather than enunciated as a winning argument aimed at establishing the dominance of one position over another." This pattern of supporting community decision-making is reported for many different Indigenous peoples; the following is a small part of the total evidence available on this point.

In his book explaining the Nuu-chah-nulth worldview, Chief Umeek, E. Richard Atleo, reports attending meetings in the 1940s of his grandfather, a traditional chief of the Ahousaht, one of the bands of Nuu-chah-nulth of western Vancouver Island. He observed that every one of his grandfather's councilors were able to speak on each of the issues to be addressed in the meeting. This resulted in a need for patience.

> Ahinchat [his grandfather] and his councilors would sit in a circle and place each item, or issue, of an agenda into the middle of the circle. . . . A major feature of this traditional process was the acknowledgment of every member of a council concerning each issue at hand.
>
> While this decision-making process ensured every council member's input on every issue under discussion, it also required an unusual amount of patience, self-control, tolerance, trust, faith, and respect. Patience was required because of the likelihood that there would be a constant repetition of ideas. Every member had the right to speak even if that right meant constant repetition. Hence, whereas a modern meeting might address an issue in ten minutes, Ahinchat's meetings might have expended thirty or more minutes on the same issue. (Umeek [Atleo] 2004, 88–89)

A payoff from such long meetings was better decisions. Members of the meeting had to understand the diverse opinions.

> If a council member of sound reputation suggested a solution that at first appeared ridiculous, too radical, or impossible in some way, he wasn't dismissed out of hand. Who knew, so the philosophy goes, whether the radical suggestion was not the result of some spiritual insight given to one council member and not to the others? (Umeek [Atleo] 2004, 89)

Umeek reports his grandfather let everyone speak because he did not know to whom the spirits had spoken. Each person's connection to the spiritual world is seen to be unique. Nurturing the collective involves respecting and therefore nurturing persons in the collective as well. Part of being a reflexive person is being able to participate in conversations (dialogue) about what to do in the face of challenges. The diversity of knowledge contributes to solving problems created by challenges of all types, thus contributing to resilience and sustainability.

Obviously, if everyone has a right to speak, the meetings will last a long time. Another rule that might help the situation was reported to me by Seth Pilsk when giving advice to outside academics presenting to the Council of Elders that he worked with on the San Carlos Apache Reservation. Elders judged the wisdom of speakers by their ability to get to the point and not to talk too long. People who talked too long would lose the attention of everyone else. Just as people training academics to communicate with television and other media are advised to get to the point and make it quickly, the Apache elders also expected short speeches. The two rules complement each other: everyone can speak, but each is expected to get to their point quickly. One should think of this when at meetings where interruption is prohibited because the rule of respect dominates, but the other rule, give short speeches, has been forgotten in too many intertribal meetings in the United States. Patience has become particularly needed, but to dispense with hearing everybody is a high price. One never knows to whom the spirits have spoken. This second rule may explain why Ahinchat's meetings took thirty minutes to deal with an issue handled in ten minutes when only majority vote is needed.

The collaborative study by Apgar and her co-authors with the Guna reported on how leaders would conduct themselves when problems needed to be addressed. The study organized groups of Guna to reflect on the results of interviews.

The reflection group found that Guna leaders traditionally foster community adaption primarily through facilitation and guidance during the communal gatherings that are central to collective governance in communities and at the Comarca [Indigenous territory] level. Today, governance is manifest through a mixture of traditional structures and their associated roles, i.e., ritual specialists and spiritual leaders, and contemporary administrative and political processes and their associated roles, i.e., administrative and political leaders. The communal gatherings take a dialogical format, using principles such as respect, from the *Bab Igar*. Another *Bab Igar* principle is the ability to use the heart in decision making, which refers to the ability to allow emotion, identity, and intuition to help guide decisions. The way the Guna come together in dialogue is still largely defined by their spiritual and cultural framing, with leaders as the facilitators. (Apgar et al. 2015)

The ability to facilitate meetings needs to be learned. Apgar et al. report that the Guna leaders travel and study with different leaders with special knowledge across the territory; their skills are built through apprenticeship. The *Bab Igar*, the Way of the Great Father, is the origin story of the Guna.

On the Northwest Coast, the parents of persons who are expected to become leaders must train their children to be generous, to speak well, to facilitate discussions, to comply with community standards, to encourage youth, to train their successor, and to mediate. The principles of training titleholders were explained to me when I visited with the Nisga'a to learn how they had achieved their modern treaty with Canada. For the Nisga'a, the treaty negotiators kept their public well informed, following the principle that leaders are accountable to their public through making all governing processes transparent (Trosper 2009, 148, 151). Part of the negotiations with Canada involved revising their governance system to include elections rather than having leaders selected through holding titles conferred at feasts. The new government has a legislature, but it does not have a single elected president or chief. The executive functions of government are supervised by an eleven-member executive council; there is no single leader. The government also has an elected Council of Elders to advise them. Leadership is dispersed among many leaders (Nisga'a Lisims Government 1998).

As they worked with the officials of the Ontario Ministry of Natural Resources, the Pikangikum elders would meet among themselves and achieve consensus before discussing forest management issues with the provincial officials. In this way, the elders would speak with one voice, an approach desired by the more hierarchical ministry.

During the ceremony among the Iroquois for replacing one chief with another, there is a point at which the new chief receives instructions from elders. He is encouraged to become able to accept criticism from the people, to have a skin that is "seven fingers thick" in order to cope. Such leaders nurture the collective by allowing emotion to surface and be handled.

Historian Mary Druke reported that an English deputy agent, John Butler, expressed frustration with the lengthy negotiation process in dealing with the Haudenosaunee League, which would be long because everyone in the delegation on the Indian side would have a chance to speak (Druke 1985, 93; 1987).

Sandefur and Deloria report that the variety of leaders is a general characteristic of Indigenous leadership.

> Across a range of social roles and needs, different people move through different positions as leaders in, for example, ceremony, war, governance, teaching, or subsistence. They might, in other contexts, be followers, according to their expertise and the circumstance. Few individuals are leaders in every context. This diffusion requires a more flexible posture on authority, which shifts situationally across a range of individuals. Such decentralized structures produce leadership that is less directive and even noninterventionist. (Sandefur and Deloria 2018, 130)

A consequence of leaders being noninterventionist is that outsiders have difficulty identifying leaders. This difficulty easily occurs for those accustomed to hierarchical governance, where a "chief" is a "chief executive," who organizes people by telling them what to do. Helping people decide what to do is not seen as leadership by those accustomed to a structure that depends on leaders giving commands or making decisions after consulting staff.

Leaders Support Relationships with Nonhumans

Another feature of the emphasis on relationships is the role of leaders in ensuring that humanity's relationships with nonhumans are maintained. This role is a key responsibility for leaders throughout Indigenous communities. In the Pacific Northwest, titleholders were responsible for the health of the salmon runs and of the territory of their house. Among the peoples with family hunting territories, the senior hunter is responsible for the health of their territory. Failure to conduct himself properly would lead to people losing confidence in his leadership.

As Umeek (Atleo) continues to describe the process of reaching agreement, he explains how the need to respect all beings is connected to the need to listen to every member of the council. His great-grandfather Keesta required that all interactions between life-forms be guided by respectful protocols (Umeek [Atleo] 2004, 89). These protocols meant including non-humans in relationships.

For the Guna, leaders help the community with the responsibility for good relationships with all elements for their world. In this case, the role of the leaders is to assist the community in fulfilling its obligations. The Guna use their *Bab Igar* to emphasize the role of leaders in reminding people that "all things and beings are part of one system, and all material things have *burba*, i.e., life or spirit. Plants, animals, rocks, minerals, and people all have *burba*" (Apgar et al. 2015).

Many examples—from the peoples of the Northwest Coast, from the Pikangikum of northern Ontario, from the family hunting territories of the Cree, from the Guna of Panama, from the Māori of Aotearoa, from Aborigines in Australia—illustrate that the recognition of the consciousness of all elements of the landscape is complemented by holding leaders accountable for assuring that relationships with those elements are conducted properly. The analysis of family hunting territories in chapter 4 explained this responsibility; although many kin have a right to hunt in a territory, they are required to obtain instructions from the senior hunter before hunting. A similar rule applies in the house territories in the Pacific Northwest: if the salmon do not return as they should, the people of a house may collude with neighbors to have them abduct a titleholder who is not governing well; the people then refuse to pay to have the titleholder returned and he becomes a slave (Donald 1997). The responsibilities of the leaders are clear in those two cases.

Leaders Support Autonomy of Persons and Relational Subjects

The high degree of respect given to persons in the Nuu-chah-nulth worldview is connected to respecting the autonomy of each person. Leaders are reluctant to tell people what to do because that interferes with each person's autonomy. Sandefur and Deloria (2018, 130) report that leaders don't diagnose problems and then organize others to fix them, because to do so would imply a leader doesn't trust others and somehow knows better than others what to do. Rather than giving orders, relational leaders make suggestions, or wait until someone solicits their opinion about what should be done. Giving advice when requested respects another person; giving orders does not. Hunting leaders among the Eeyou are careful not to directly give orders, even though hunters are obligated to seek advice and take that advice when hunting. The common custom that not looking someone in the face is good manners also avoids being too directive.

That Indigenous peoples encourage children to think for themselves supports the development of people with good internal conversations and reflexivity. Among the Guna of Panama, the coming-of-age ritual for young women encourages "the capacity for critical self-reflection and creativity." They develop a "heightened sense of identity" as a result of periods of isolation and also a series of rituals in which they develop their personhood with the guidance of elders (Apgar et al. 2015). Many tribes also have youth engage in vision quests in which a person seeks guidance from special places or develop their own connections to particular animals. Elders help guide the vision quests and the analysis of the experience afterward.

Supporting the autonomy of individuals and of relational subjects means that leaders are self-effacing while also being significant in nurturing these entities. Because leadership needs to be dispersed throughout the community, everyone needs to have their opportunity to lead and to nourish the relationships in which they participate.

In the past, these methods of upbringing would have created conversational reflexives to a greater degree than meta reflexives. But the roles of meta reflexives are probably increasing, since a person selects among a number of role models to determine what kind of person he or she or it is going to be. Sustainability needs persons who are able to sustain relationships, and these are primarily the communicative and meta reflexives. The autonomous reflexives are more likely to act in the manner of individuals as encouraged by the dominant society.

Supporting individual autonomy presents difficulties if a person is misbehaving, especially if a person is affecting other people or destroying relationships with nonhumans. Dealing with misbehaving in the context of supporting autonomy presents an important tension in a relational economy. One should expect disputes because of these tensions.

Leaders Support Peacemaking

One of the most important actions is for leaders to facilitate the resolution of disputes within their communities. Failure to resolve disputes increases community tensions and threatens relationships among community members. Supporting autonomy of all persons and relational subjects requires resolution of disputes and support for the rules for maintaining good relationships and relational goods.

Political and spiritual leaders have authority from the community to engage in dispute resolution. Leaders remind people of the norms of the community that support relationships and use the norms to guide solution of the dispute. Rather than being an adversarial process, disputes are mediated with the goal of maintaining good relationships or ending them in a reasonable manner that doesn't upset other relationships. All affected persons participate in resolving disputes and take responsibility for keeping the difficulty from perpetuating anger and disagreement. Respect for personal autonomy supports persons who feel wronged; compensation or understanding is offered by those involved with guidance and mediation from leaders. Once everyone agrees to the solution, the community enforces the resolution (Porter 1997).

On the Northwest Coast, settlement of serious disputes requires a feast at which the solution to the dispute is announced and acknowledged by all present. Then everyone is required to forget the incident. If it is mentioned again, the person who does so is told that the matter has been settled and is not to be talked about again. This prevents disputes from festering and continuing to interfere with good relationships (Mills 1994; Fiske and Patrick 2000).

While peacemaking was a widely practiced way of resolving disputes in Native America, much attention recently has focused on Navajo peacemaking, which has been supported by the Navajo government as an alternative to the use of litigation in courts that was copied from the dominant society (Nielsen and Zion 2005). Carole Goldberg (1997) has summarized the Navajo peacemaking practices while also pointing out that they would be hard to transport from a relationship-based system to an individualistic one. Navajos seek hózhó, described as balance, harmony, and a well-ordered society. The order depends on the obligations of kinship solidarity, or k'e: "A Navajo practicing k'e expresses love, compassion, kindness, friendliness, generosity, and peacefulness" (1013). Navajo peacemaking supports the idea that the true clients of a peacemaker are the relationships that are involved. Rituals emphasize all the connections of the people involved, and a resolution also involves all of those people as well as balance with nature. Even the idea of health is not purely an individually focused concept. With its focus on "the world of nature," peacemaking also includes keeping nature in balance. Within this framework, the goal of peacemaking is to restore harmony in the broad sense of hózhó and k'e. That Navajo support relational persons follows from the observation that the Navajo belief "is noteworthy for its emphasis on the equal worth of individuals despite their differences." Although peacemaking is focused on restoring balance in relationships, persons are also to be treated equally (1012–13).

That peacemaking supports sustainability of relationships seems obvious. Relationships are vulnerable to the specific interests and concerns of the people involved. One cannot expect the participants always to act correctly. Some actions require compensation or other action to redress wrongs committed. Peacemakers can assist in redressing wrongs and finding acts of compensation that settle the issue.

The contrasting approaches to dispute resolution are perhaps one of the most telling examples of the differences between a relationship-oriented society and an individualistic one. Robert B. Porter (1997) compares the peacemaking practices to the norms of dispute resolution through adversarial processes in Anglo-American courts. Consistent with the individualistic orientation, litigation focuses on the individual's behavior, and the procedures are set up to assure that individuals are treated fairly. Fairness is required because the goal is to assign fault and determine consequences. The judge is impartial, not related to any of the parties to a dispute. In a criminal matter, the judge makes sure the rights of the accused are respected. Both parties in a dispute have a lawyer speak for them. The power of the state to enforce the decision of a court underlies all negotiation about resolving the dispute. In criminal matters, if a person is incarcerated for the crime, the fact remains on his record, meaning that after release from jail he remains under a cloud, often cannot vote, and has trouble obtaining work. While he is imprisoned, his family must make do as best as it can, and little attention is paid to the effects of the crime on the family of the perpetrator. Some attention is paid to restitution for the victim, but that is not a goal of the process. Punishing the guilty party is the goal; crime is not seen as a community issue in dispute resolution. Community effects of crime are addressed in other ways if they are addressed at all.

Leaders Support Socialization of Persons and the Next Generation

In working with First Nations people in British Columbia on a variety of projects, I learned that in seeking approval from the University of British Columbia (UBC) institutional research board (Behavioural Research Ethics

Board [BREB] in Canada), I had better create a permission form for parents to allow their children to participate. Whenever we consulted with elders and set up a project, they would insist that youth participate. Even if the participation of youth had not been identified by elders in the early design of the project, eventually they would ask youth to join in. Hence, we should have our permission form approved by the BREB to avoid a delay in progressing on the project. Many other Indigenous communities share this desire to provide training to the next generation.

The titleholding system was very explicit in its structuring of the training of successors to the chiefs. In the matrilineal systems, a male titleholder's successor would be the oldest son of his oldest sister. That sister would be responsible for training her son, and that son would be given a title indicating he would succeed his uncle. He would sit behind his uncle at feasts. A chief's successor also held a title, the one always held by the next in line. Similarly, for other lower-level titleholders, the successors were in line and being trained.

Future Guna leaders are well trained and knowledgeable about a variety of relational subjects within their community; they serve apprenticeships and also travel to study under other specialists who are leaders throughout the comarco (Apgar et al. 2015). Another important factor for the sustainability of relationships is to socialize each generation into the idea of supporting a relational view of organizing society and nature as well as to train them on how to do it. That every society trains its youth as part of maintaining its society is of course a trivial point; requiring that leaders be educators is less common. Training leaders requires teaching the youth to become experts at creating and supporting the kinds of relationships that promote sustainability.

Leaders Support Social Memory

For both the peoples of the Northwest Coast and for the Guna of Panama, leaders are expected to know and to repeat the stories that contain the basic ideas of their cultures, their history, and their agreements. Titleholders in the Pacific Northwest need to know the history of their houses and to repeat those histories to public satisfaction in order to become a successor to the previous titleholder. Among the Guna, leaders know and repeat the many stories that comprise the *Bab Igar*. The chapters of the book *Living Indigenous Leadership* provide many stories of contemporary leadership (Kenny and Fraser 2012). Many of the chapters are by teachers and address training the next generation.

While ideas have a separate ontological reality, they seem to require use to survive. Their representations can survive in the form of books, codices, summer counts on skins, or images on magnetic or optical disk drives. People can remember them in the form of stories. People can remember language by speaking it and teaching it to their children. Such speaking requires conversations. The content of the conversations is also a way to perpetuate and continue the knowledge of ideas in a community. Oral cultures, those without a tradition of recording their thoughts in written form, develop ways to remember what they have been told by repeating it and discussing it.

The Art of Not Being Dominated

Leaders who support relationships and the relational governments that the relational subjects create do not look like the form of government that is now called a "nation-state." The divergence between monarchies in Europe and the democracies in the New World was especially stark. Even though the colonists found the Iroquois, Cherokee, and other peoples to be formidable, the idea that the Indigenous peoples did not have governments when they did not have monarchs was widespread. Pierre Clastres (1987 [first published in 1974 in French]) titled his analysis of Indigenous leadership *Society Against the State*. He documented the ways in which Indigenous societies in the Americas kept their leaders under control, with an emphasis on South America. He argued that these societies appeared not to have governments because they did not have the hierarchical systems prevalent in Europe.

James C. Scott (2009), in *The Art of Not Being Governed*, points out that the societies living in the mountains of Southeast Asia kept the despotic states in the lowlands from dominating them by making their leaders hard to find as well as practicing kinds of agriculture that are difficult to tax. Scott agrees with Clastres that societies do not progress from simple, locally governed bands, through tribes, kingdoms, and, finally, states. Rather, the states exist alongside peoples who appear not to have governments because those peoples have succeeded in avoiding dominance by using many of the principles of dispersed leadership that are characteristic of relational societies. They had governance but not despots. For both Clastres and Scott, "governance" means domination either by a European monarch or a Southeast Asian ruler.

Scott subtitled his book "An Anarchist History of Upland Southeast Asia"; in the anarchist spirit, he opens the book with a quotation from Clastres. Both books erroneously argue that a society without a hierarchical or despotic government is an anarchy, a society without governance. Support for anarchy has a strong individualistic basis. Although the societies on the margins were not dominated by despots, they did govern themselves. Governance by relational leadership should be classified as a type of government, not an absence of government or governance. The societies on the periphery in Southeast Asia avoided domination by adopting a relational style of governance. By cooperating with the nonhumans in their territory, they could provide for themselves without allowing a state to find ways to tax the food. If the peripheral people are using the principles of governance that work for common pool goods, the central government also discovers that if they try to dominate, the goods disappear. Trading for the goods rather than trying to manage the people is a better strategy. To anarchists, the governance of common pool goods may look like domination over individuals, resulting in anarchy also having problems with common pool goods. Relational societies such as those on the Northwest Coast of North America, the Haudenosaunee and others, had and have hierarchies without domination. Their leaders are accountable and removable.

Scott maintains that states are now (after World War II) much stronger than they were. The globe is now covered by states, each able to dominate its peripheries. Modern technologies in the form of railroads, highways, airplanes, electronic networks, and remote sensing make states stronger than they used to be when armies on foot or horseback were used to dominate populations. The failed military operations of the United States in Vietnam, Iraq, and Afghanistan may suggest that many people remain able to resist domination even in the face of such military technology.

Albert Hirschman argued to me in 1967 that modern states are too busy governing their centers to worry about their peripheries, and for that reason Indigenous peoples could survive simply because they were being ignored. Scott argues that the people on the peripheries were ignored because they had found ways to avoid domination. Both views may be correct. The best contemporary examples of Indigenous relationality live on the peripheries of modern states: the Algonquians of the boreal forest, the Nisga'a and Inuit of northern Canada, the Guna of Panama. Other examples are historical: the Iroquois Haudenosaunee League, in particular. While relational societies may be good at preventing centralization and emergence of dominating states, once those states get going, they are able to dismantle local governments and impose their own methods, particularly private property and individual freedoms. A disorganized populace unable to overcome the dilemmas caused by individual freedoms and private ownership is also unable to create resistance to the state governments. Such states suppress the ability to cooperate. Now, with global warming requiring planet-wide cooperation, the fierce independence of nation-states is preventing them from cooperating with worldwide challenges.

Because all people of Aotearoa / New Zealand learn the Māori concept of cooperation, *manaakitanga*, that island nation met the challenge of COVID-19, capable of a pandemic. New Zealand's ability to organize against COVID-19 could be a consequence of widespread teaching in schools of manaakitanga, the ethic that supports creating *mana* as explained in a recent *Washington Post* opinion piece (Milner and Ngata 2021). The mana concept connects individual and group power; joint and cooperative action increases mana. The people readily understood that limitations on their freedom of movement were necessary to control the disease, while the ability to control its borders also helped. Other islands, such as Britain, did not succeed.

Global climate change, biodiversity loss, and widespread pollution are all public bads that affect the entire planet. Individualism of persons and the sovereignty of states are now hampering a cooperative solution to these large social dilemmas.

This raises important questions: Is relationality not possible at scales larger than Aotearoa / New Zealand? Can the principles of building good relationships among persons be applied to relationships among sovereign states? Roger Fisher, Scott Brown, William Ury, and other scholars at the Harvard Negotiation Project initiated their research with a desire to promote peacemaking between the United States and the Soviet Union to prevent nuclear war. Their advice for negotiation is framed in bilateral terms both for the international negotiations and for their other books, aimed at helping individuals negotiate with other individuals. The advice, however, can be generalized to a national or international level, the next topic.

A Relational State

When leaders support relationships, the interaction of relational subjects of all four levels (personal, micro, meso, and macro) describes both an Indigenous economy and an Indigenous polity. The relational economy can produce good amounts of both common pool and public goods. Among the public goods is the peoplehood identity of the Indigenous nation. One would expect that the political character of a nation built upon relational subjects rather than individuals would be different from states as they are normally conceived.

The peacemaker and his colleagues set out to create peace among warring tribes and created the Haudenosaunee Confederacy. Other confederacies also existed in eastern North America; their confederacy, however, survived the colonial confrontation and still exists at the Six Nations Reserve in Canada. Each of the component tribes also still exists. The Onondaga are still trying to care for their lands even though Onondaga Lake has been severely impacted by industrial waste (Kimmerer 2013, 310–40). The Mohawk are working with neighbors to improve forest management (E. Holmes, Lickers, and Barkley 2002; Lemelin and Lickers 2004).

European political philosophy, led in England by Thomas Hobbes and John Locke, presented their state as a paradox: a government was needed for bringing order to a supposed disorderly state of nature, in which men fought one another. But such a state could also be oppressive. Because of this, the founders of the United States included a Bill of Rights in their new constitution in order to protect individuals against the coercive power of the state. Because of the fear of such a state, judicial processes had to be fair, especially when the state was involved, as in charging a person with a crime.

This paradox exists in the standard model of a state in economic theory. A state is needed to provide public goods, such as a fair judicial system, a way to record ownerships records, a way to provide defense, and so on. Such a state, however, can become oppressive and fail in its task to provide both public goods and common pool goods.

This same problem worries Stephen Cornell and Joseph Kalt (1992a) in their argument that governmental reform is needed in order to have economic development. Cornell and Kalt fear that a government that is not set up correctly will engage in rent seeking, where those in power seek to obtain an unfair share of the nation's wealth. They recommend that tribal governments have separation of powers, especially an independent judiciary.

Porter notes that tribal lawyers trained in the American tradition of litigation also are taught about this paradox. Their education in American law leads them to believe that

strong tribal governments—like all governments—will abuse their authority, victimize their citizens, exploit tribal resources for personal ends, and in
the last analysis, "be destroyed from within." To address this problem, tribal
lawyers conclude that a legal infrastructure must be developed to protect
individual rights. (Porter 1997, 285)

As a result, Porter worries that tribal lawyers, by supporting individualism
and adversarial judicial processes, will seriously damage traditional Indigenous governance systems, based on relational principles. This is an important issue in evaluating cultural match for Indigenous governance.

His article on justice systems uses his own tribe, the Seneca, as an example of the deleterious effects of using adversarial justice on Indigenous governance. The Haudenosaunee Confederacy is a model of a relational state. It
was based on the clan structure of the Iroquois, the clans being an example
of relational subjects. When elements of the Haudenosaunee government
were adopted as part of the American Constitution, the checks and balances of the league were imitated. The basis of the state in the clan relationships of the people was left out, as was the equality of women in the political
process. The resulting constitution was based on the European concept of
man, as individuals who would, if not controlled, act selfishly and in their
own interest. Originally, only male property owners ran the government.
Everyone else was subordinated. The Haudenosaunee Confederacy needs to
be reexamined as an example of a state based on the support of meso- and
macro-relational subjects rather than on the support of selfish individuals.

Elizabeth Tooker (1988) was correct when she insisted that the American Constitution was not like that of the Haudenosaunee. While many of
the features of the Haudenosaunee Confederacy were copied, which Donald A. Grinde (1992), Grinde and Bruce E. Johansen (1991), and others have
pointed to as influencing the Constitution, the fundamental approach of the
confederacy, promoting peace through supporting relationships, was not
carried over to the Constitution. She doubts that the members of the Constitutional Convention would have accepted unanimity as a final rule for
decisions. They had no mechanisms to prevent unreasonable dissent, which
is needed for consensus. She also doubts that having representatives hold
positions based on clan mothers selecting them would have impressed the
attendees in Philadelphia. Grinde and Johansen provide examples of items
shared between the U.S. Constitution and the league, while Tooker insists

that key aspects of the Iroquois League would need to be adopted to show influence. The influence thesis confuses fundamental principles with particular implementation of them. Tooker's admiration of the league makes her insist that certain features were in fact fundamental, and the requirement of consensus is one of those. Since achieving consensus is also needed for a relational subject, Tooker's emphasis on consensus selects a fundamental issue (1988, 315–17). She also points out that league policy is what required consensus; the league did not tell each of its five members (which include the Seneca) what their internal processes should be, although those processes also involved consensus.

Before trying to explain why the influence of the league on the Constitution was a myth, she summarizes her argument.

> The evidence presently available, then, offers little support for the notion that the framers of the Constitution borrowed from the Iroquois ideas respecting the proper form of government, ideas that were, in fact, radically different from those familiar in Western civilization that were subsequently incorporated into the Constitution. (Tooker 1988, 321)

She proceeds to claim that the myth of the influence on the Constitution derives from the settlers' desire to separate themselves from England. They needed new symbols to justify their independence, and like many settlers who colonize other people, they adopted some images from those people, without understanding them.

Most of the relational subjects in an Indigenous economy include non-humans such as animals, plants, rivers, and mountains. The entry of these relational subjects into political processes of governance signifies a large difference from politics as conflict among humans exclusively. Anthropologist Marisol de la Cadena has described how earth beings such as mountains have become important political actors in the Andes as Indigenous peoples have increased their influence. She reported on a demonstration in Cuzco's main square in opposition to a mine in a mountain chain that is dominated by a mountain named Ausangate. She had been invited to the demonstration by her friend Nazario. De la Cadena opposed the mine because she supported the people living in the mountains, who would lose their livelihoods. She explained that her friend responded as follows:

Nazario agreed with me, but said it would be worse: Ausangate would not allow the mine in Sinakara, a mountain over which it presided. Ausangate would get mad, could even kill people. To prevent that killing, the mine should not happen. (de la Cadena 2010, 340)

Her friend was a spiritual leader and might be expected to have this view. But de la Cadena also reports that a local mayor was concerned.

I also talked to Graciano Mandura, the newly elected mayor of Ocongate—the district that houses the complex Coyllur Rit'I-Sinakara-Ausangate. Born like Nazario in Pacchanta, Graciano is a native Quechua speaker who learned Spanish in elementary school, holds a degree in animal husbandry from the University of Cuzco and was working for a local NGO when he decided to run for Mayor. As a candidate, Graciano joined the effort against the mine that threatened the sanctuary and the mountain chain; in our conversation, I asked why he had joined the antimining effort, and he explained that the mine would deter tourism, an activity that was generating income in the region. This was a response I was expecting. But then he added that he knew from experience that the mountains, which he called by their name, demand respect. Otherwise inexplicable accidents happen—it has always been so. Wouldn't it be his responsibility as Mayor to prevent those accidents, whatever their reason? Now, this response—and more specifically its formulation through the logic of a responsible state official—confirmed that there was more than politics as usual in this locality. (de la Cadena 2010, 340)

This mayor recognized the needs of the mountain and acted to keep the mountain happy. That the mountain is alive and sentient is a fact. His view also makes him a leader who supports relationships with nonhumans. By "politics as usual," de la Cadena probably refers to the politics of an individualistic nation-state.

A political system that includes a sentient mountain in its governing system would be unusual in the current time. Combining the sentient beings of the landscape with a people who are organized in a system of relational subjects would need to have a relational state at the highest level of organization. Some examples of such relational states from Indigenous peoples are the Haudenosaunee Confederacy, the Grand Council of the Cree supported by village associations of senior hunters, the Nisga'a Land Committee (which was all the house titleholders of the Nisga'a people), and the Guna of Panama. Each of these come to agreement by consensus; minority voices are always listened to.

A recent book has addressed this issue, presenting a new term, *pluriverse*, to describe an association of different universes, conceived as different local self-governing systems allied within a reconstituted nation-state that supports different kinds of development (Kothari et al. 2019). Another term is *plurinationalism*. Kothari and his co-authors begin the book with a quotation from the Zapatista Army of National Liberation's Fourth Declaration (1966), in which the Zapatistas describe the goal as follows: "The world we want is a world in which many worlds fit."

Relationships with State Bureaucracies

The focus of this chapter is the role of relational leadership in maintaining relationships within an Indigenous economy. The same type of relationship building applies to creating relationships with people outside the Indigenous governance but relevant to Indigenous economy. In each of the five examples presented in chapter 1, Indigenous leaders used their relationship-building skills to forge different types of comanagement arrangements. In four of the cases, the comanagement involved a natural resource agency of the state. The case in Ecuador involved the governance of a province, with the water supply for the capital city, Ambato, depending on the upper Ambato River watershed. Once the outside facilitators in the Tungurahua province started to facilitate building new relationships, the Indigenous peoples dropped their internal divisions and cooperated with the provincial governor and the external facilitators. When the Pikangikum elders wanted to protect their lands against standard forestry practices, they implemented one of their own firm standards: first, get the relationships right. They offered to assist in writing the management plan for their lands with the Ontario Ministry of Natural Resources (OMNR).

Two of the examples demonstrate that solutions involve setting aside the difficult issue of land ownership. Even though the Haida had used unfriendly tactics, both blockades and lawsuits, when the opportunity arose to negotiate, they agreed to comanagement through a protocol agreement that gives them considerable authority over the management of the forest. The leaders of the Tūhoe and Whanganui iwi in New Zealand negotiated with the government in order to establish two comanagement agreements, one for a river and the other for a national park.

Five tribes first formed a coalition to pursue their joint concerns to create the Bears Ears National Monument. They approached the Obama administration and negotiated the details with the Departments of Interior and Agriculture, which contained the agencies that administer the land in the Bears Ears region. Although the agencies retained the final say on management, the five tribes have a recognized advisory committee that allows them to engage in dialogue with the agencies over issues as they arise.

• • •

Each of these examples of action contributes to sustainability and provides an environment for entrepreneurship, examined in the next chapter. Entrepreneurs are the persons who lead in the creation and maintenance of new productive relationships. They can also be disruptive. Once one places relationships as the key analytical category, leaders of such relationships can be called relational entrepreneurs, and the relational system can limit their disruption.

CHAPTER 7

Relational Entrepreneurship

This chapter considers the place of relational entrepreneurship in the growing literature about entrepreneurship in Indigenous societies. Although entrepreneurship is usually considered an individual activity, leaders can engage in creating new ventures within a relational environment. This chapter first describes relational entrepreneurship both in early colonial times and at present in relational societies. It then introduces the public/private structure inherited from settler colonialism. Within that structure, one can find relational entrepreneurs. The chapter then briefly examines some examples of entrepreneurship that use the public/private dichotomy, where hybrid businesses are common in contemporary Indigenous economies. The chapter ends with consideration of relational ethics in a business context.

In much literature on entrepreneurship, the idea of relational entrepreneurship would be an oxymoron because entrepreneurs are individuals. Charles F. Harrington, Carolyn Birmingham, and Daniel Steward (2017, 31) state that the report by the Corporation for Enterprise Development (CFED) and the Northwest Area Foundation (Malkin 2004) "defined *entrepreneurship* as the process by which an individual creates and grows an enterprise." They note that the authors of the report, titled "Native Entrepreneurship: Challenges and Opportunities for Rural Communities," modify the definition as follows:

> Building on this broad definition of entrepreneurship, the report defined *Native entrepreneurship* to include an emphasis on the role of cooperation; value group goals; and the importance of placing material success after emo-

tional, family, or community relationships. (Harrington, Birmingham, and Steward 2017, 31)

This expands the concept of entrepreneurship beyond an individualistic focus. It explicitly includes relationships. It also adds cooperation and group goals. The broader definition does not clearly include creation of a new venture; entrepreneurship can build on existing relationships. The short definition expands on this earlier one offered by Kevin Hindle and Michele Lansdowne (2005):

> We define Indigenous entrepreneurship as the creation, management and development of new ventures by Indigenous people for the benefit of Indigenous people. The organizations thus created can pertain to either the private, public or non-profit sectors. The desired and achieved benefits of venturing can range from the narrow view of economic profit for a single individual to the broad view of multiple, social and economic advantages for entire communities. Outcomes and entitlements derived from Indigenous entrepreneurship may extend to enterprise partners and stakeholders who may be non-Indigenous. (Hindle and Lansdowne 2005, 132)

This broad definition can include relational entrepreneurship, as it identifies payoffs accruing to other than an individual. It fails to note that individualism and relationality conflict.

Harrington and his co-authors summarize the other issues that affect American Indian entrepreneurship, such as concern for the relationship with nature, concern for sustainability, and a need to contribute to other social goals. They also summarize the many obstacles faced by Indian entrepreneurs. A study of Indigenous entrepreneurship needs to take account of these concerns. Among the concerns is that the individualistic focus of standard American business generates skepticism in Indian communities.

To make a definition of entrepreneurship fit in the approach using relationality, the definition should focus on relational goods and on relational subjects, using the previous chapters' definitions of these terms. Drawing on Hindle (2010, 609), this book describes relational entrepreneurship as follows:

> A relational entrepreneurial person or group of persons [relational subjects] undertake the process of evaluating, committing to and achieving, in a given

context, the creation of new social and economic value using new knowledge and new or existing relational goods for the benefit of personal and social relational subjects.

This definition has five parts: the relational subjects, the process, the given context, the new value, and the relational subjects who obtain the new value.

The definition says that *relational subjects* are involved both in directing a new entrepreneurial venture as well as benefiting from it. The point of the definition is to emphasize that such an entrepreneur develops relational goods among the parties in the process of developing the new venture. This would require applying the rules for the creation of good relationships in forming the new organization that will develop new values. As a result of creating better relationships, the persons involved create identity (a sense of group purpose), trust (the ability to trust that each will act for the new purpose and not their own benefit), and equity (the enactment of a fair share of the new values for all persons in the relationship).

The *new values* are another key part of the definition. Normal entrepreneurship focuses on producing monetary values or material values that can be converted into monetary values. This definition broadens the types of value that can be produced. For instance, an enterprise might produce well-being among its customers without translating that fully into money. The workers for the enterprise may experience a sense of empowerment that aids in their work for the enterprise, but that is not translatable into monetary terms. A new tribal college might promote the education of tribal members. A degraded fishery or irrigation system could be reformed to produce increased fish or more available water.

The *given context* for the enterprise can be very significant because the given context can either encourage or impede the new venture. Enterprises that exist within a community context need to fit with the community's values and expectations or operate to change those expectations. Harrington and his co-authors address the initial conditions as deficits by describing access to capital, a lack of education or training in business, patterns of poor health among the potential workers, and obstacles presented by federal and state governments. While such deficits matter, of equal importance is to examine strengths, particularly strong relationships that could support a new venture. New knowledge can be used. Existing relational goods such as identity and trust can be strengthened and turned to achieving new goals.

Finally, the *process* of developing a new venture has many steps. The opportunity has to be evaluated, to see if new ideas or new situations will support the venture. Then the relational entrepreneur needs to commit to the endeavor and carry it out. These activities draw upon the skill of the entrepreneur, which is either a person or a group of people who have joined together to undertake the new activity.

Relational Entrepreneurship in Relational Systems

Relational entrepreneurship is not new in Indigenous societies. While little evidence exists regarding entrepreneurship prior to contact with European markets, the period just after contact often has examples of Indigenous leaders undertaking the new ventures that were possible within the relational systems that existed at contact. The fur trade in North America is one example of relational entrepreneurship. Immediately after contact in Aotearoa, which became New Zealand, Māori entrepreneurs took advantage of new trading opportunities. After the Dutch colonized Bali, members of the noble class switched from politics to business, using the relationships from their system.

Hunting Leaders Among the Cree

The hunting leaders of the boreal forest recognized the opportunities available by harvesting and selling beaver skins and entered into trading relationships with the Hudson's Bay Company on the English side and various French traders on the French colonial frontier. They may have invented the family hunting territory system as a response to the opportunity; they probably modified a previously existing system of family territories. In either case, they engaged in entrepreneurship that fits the definitions given earlier. That the family territory system was relational has been established in chapter 4 with analysis of the Traditional Eeyou Hunting Law.

After the government of Ontario and the Cree negotiated the Paix de Braves (PDB) in 2002, Mélanie Chaplier (2018) undertook to interview the hunting leaders of the community of Nemaska. The hunting territories of these leaders had been severely impacted by the Eastmain-Rubert hydroelectric facility, authorized by the PDB agreement. Its dams and its diversions of water meant they lost access to key land. The hunting leaders, however, gained access to roles as consultants in the environmental studies and as potential contractors with the required projects to provide remedies for the impacts of the dams and other facilities. To succeed within their communities, they had to find ways to provide opportunities to their families through these new activities because hunting on the land was impossible under the reservoirs. Some succeeded and others were less successful. Success was defined by the community in terms of sharing the benefits of the new opportunities. The PDB agreement, however, defined the hunting leaders as landowners in a system of private property, expecting them to treat the profit as their personal income. To do that would be a failure for the new entrepreneur. When a hunting leader acts as an entrepreneur to find another source of income when hunting is less possible, that hunting leader operates in a relational society and becomes a relational entrepreneur who shares the new income among his family, fully informing them while also becoming expert in different activities such as environmental impacts and remedial actions.

Hunting leaders are dealing with the imposition of the hydroelectric dams in an entrepreneurial way, as described by the authors of the special issue of *Anthropologica* introduced by Chaplier and Colin Scott (2018). Consistent with their law, hunting leaders who have failed to follow their obligations to their family have been replaced by others who do comply with the Traditional Eeyou Hunting Law. Chaplier (2018, 69–70) tells the story of "Andrew," who in response to the opportunities offered by the Paix de Braves "started acting like the trapline was his and only his." As a result of his mismanagement, the family selected another member, "John," to take over the role of hunting leader. They went through the official process in the Eeyou Hunting Law and replaced Andrew with John. Other families had similar experiences and found family members who could handle the changes created by the development efforts of the Quebec government.

The Pikangikum elders in their work with the Ontario Ministry of Natural Resources to create the Whitefeather Forest Management Plan are another example of hunting leaders acting as entrepreneurs. The Pikangikum elders recognized that their previous use of beaver furs for income was no longer viable and that other uses of their land would be destroyed by the usual practice of clearcutting the boreal forest. As described in chapter 1, the result has been development of a smaller forest industry using pine that is run by the Pikangikum (Whitefeather Forest Initiative n.d.).

Māori Society Before the Treaty of Waitangi

Paul Tapsell and Christine Woods (2010) provide an interpretation of traditional Māori society in which economic affairs were overseen by male and female elders, the *rangatira*. These elders maintained the Māori relationships among families (whānau) who were associated in subtribes (hapu) who would meet and conduct their affairs on the *marai*, the meeting place of each hapu. Dynamism in the system came from young people, *potoki*, who were individual men and women who sought new knowledge and new ways of doing things. Operating within the supervision of the rangatira, the potoki would engage in new activities that, if successful and contributory to the hapu, would eventually lead to the potoki taking on the roles of rangatira for the next generation of potoki (Tapsell and Woods 2010, 544–46). When the British arrived in the late seventeenth century, many potoki took advantage of the new opportunities for trade and agricultural production. Between 1700 and 1750, this worked well and the traditional leaders were able to keep the existing system in place even as the potoki created new businesses. This success ended, however, when, after the signing of the Treaty of Waitangi with the many Indigenous tribes (hapu), the British proceeded to violate the terms of the treaty and create a system of private property. Through a series of actions that culminated in the creation of a Native Land Court system to facilitate the transfer of land from the Māori to the settlers (Pakeha), the British undercut the powers of the elders, the rangatira, partly by empowering the young Māori entrepreneurs. But these entrepreneurs did not enjoy full support from the colonial government, and other settler entrepreneurs took over the economy while also acquiring Māori property. Tapsell and Woods claim that in the past thirty-five years, the Māori are trying to re-create the older system in the modern era (2010, 546–48). Some of these efforts are clearly relational, as described later, while others apparently are not.

Princes in Bali

Clifford Geertz (1963, 106–20) set out to compare two different towns in Indonesia, one organized as individualistic and the other organized in a relational manner. Tabanan is a relational village of about twelve thousand people on a hillside in the midst of one of the irrigation systems on the mountains of Bali. In 1906 the Dutch changed the structure of the hierarchical relational society by removing the role of a landowning elite from governance, substituting the colonial bureaucracy. The system of dividing the rent to land between the farmer and the landowner also changed, effectively raising the wages of farmworkers. After World War II, as political conditions changed further with independence from Holland, noblemen decided that organizing new businesses would be good. They became entrepreneurs, using the networks in the town and the Balinese seka system of group mobilization to start new enterprises, such as a bus service, ice manufacturing, an export–import enterprise, a tire-recapping factory, hotels, and other businesses based on the growing economy in Bali. When commoners in the town trusted the noble entrepreneur, they were willing to buy shares or lend money to the enterprises, using the interest to support their families (Geertz 1963, 117n23). In spite of the evident success of the many enterprises, Geertz concludes that they face challenges because of the need to "rationalize" their firms to avoid problems arising from the "collectivism" of the seka system and the traditional duties of noblemen to provide public goods and income redistribution. Because of this, he concludes, the mentality of the "professional manager" needs to replace that of the aristocrats (140). He failed to see that he was describing relational entrepreneurs who could succeed in promoting economic growth without becoming "modern" through "rationalization."

The Public/Private Division and Relational Enterprises

Most economic models of contemporary economies assume a distinction between the public and private sectors. The public sector is composed of government, which is responsible for several different functions: enactment of laws that allow the market to operate, provision of public goods, transfers of income from the general revenue of the government to particular people who are left behind by the private sector, and attention to externalities through regulation and taxation. The private sector consists of individuals and the enterprises that individuals create. Corporations created by individual joint investment are also classified as the private sector. Corporations, however, exist under laws that are part of the government's provisions to set up markets.

This public/private distinction is built upon a foundation of individualism. On the public side, the government is structured as a democracy in which individuals vote for the leaders of their choice. On the private side, individuals run their own lives, creating individual proprietorships or joint partnerships if they engage in running a business. Corporations exist in a middle ground, sometimes owned by governments and sometimes owned by individuals; in either case, the government creates the laws that describe how corporations can be created and regulated. They are typically top-down, bureaucratic entities, with shareholders voting their number of shares in electing the boards of directors. Accountability is upward, to the board and shareholders.

The government can allow the private sector to develop many types of corporations and other private businesses. If the government obtains revenue through taxes on businesses, then any entity that is selling things or services will need to obtain a license to do business so that the government can tax it. If there is a tax on labor for the purposes of providing retirement benefits, such as the social security system in the United States, then an individual doing business and employing people, including themselves, must register and pay the tax on wages.

A major alternative created by governments is to license "nonprofit" corporations. This option creates a third sector of organizations that are both nongovernmental and nonindividualistic. In Canada, such corporations are called "societies"; they are allowed to create goods and services without putting the profits into the pockets of shareholders and thus not paying a tax on profits. They still may pay sales or employment taxes. The nonprofit, if it makes an excess of revenue over costs, must put that revenue to a public purpose or reinvest in its own activities. The second word in the name "nonprofit corporation" reveals that the internal governing structure of the entity is structured with a board of directors that is responsible for supervising the corporation; such a board usually hires a chief operating officer. In a for-profit corporation, the board is elected by the shareholders, the people who select the board can vary, and often the board selects its own successors. In other cases, the nonprofit is operating for other stakeholders. The Intertribal Timber Council, for instance, is a nonprofit corporation with a board that is selected by the tribes who are members of the Intertribal Timber Council.

The distinction between public and private sectors was built into the Indian Reorganization Act. Section 17 of the act authorized tribes to create corporations to handle their business affairs. Tribes were offered the same public/private division that had evolved in the United States by this provision in the Indian Reorganization Act. The act also authorized tribes to create legal systems that would generate private corporations chartered by the tribal government through business codes.

Cooperatives are another type of enterprise licensed by governments. A cooperative may be owned by its members and governed by a board elected from the membership, with each member having one vote. The cooperative provides a service shared among the members. Many examples exist in the agricultural sector of the United States, where farmers organize cooperatives both for jointly conducting sales of their products and for finding supplies. Many people are familiar with homeowners' associations, which govern the management of land and structures that are shared among the homeowners. A building full of condominiums needs a governing structure for the care of the roof, for example. The study of cooperatives shows some attention to issues of social capital (Bhuyan and Leistritz 2001; Bhuyan 2007; Nilsson and Hendrikse 2011; Ruben and Heras 2012; Feng, Friis, and Nilsson 2016).

Because people are sociable and can form relational subjects to pursue common goals, relational subjects can develop in a system conceived as a mixture of "public" and "private" activities of individuals. Also, in the public sector, an association of local governments can make agreements that are relational in nature for the purpose of managing a common pool resource such as an underground water supply system, as Ostrom (1990, 103–42) studied in the Los Angeles basin, where the cities had to cooperate to prevent salt water from invading their freshwater underground system if too much water was pumped.

In places conquered by British settlers, the public/private distinction dominates the organization of economies and the states in which they exist. While the public/private distinction is based on individualism governing activities in the private sphere, the flexibility of the possible legal arrangements allows variety in the organization of firms, leaving room for relational entities to come into existence. Indigenous peoples have taken advantage of the opportunity, as illustrated by the following examples.

Living Rhythms in Canada

Without adopting the terminology of relationality used in this book, Wanda A. Wuttunee (2004) reports on many relational entrepreneurs in her book *Living Rhythms: Lessons in Aboriginal Economic Resilience and Vision.* She opens her book with a quotation from the First Nations Development Institute that captures most of what this book argues.

Indigenous economics: the science of dealing with the production, distribution, and consumption of wealth in a naturally holistic, reciprocal manner that respects humankind, fellow species, and the eco-balance of life. (Wuttunee 2004, 3)

She proceeds to refer to a formulation offered by Sherry Salway Black (1994), who described the "Elements of a Development Model" that starts with spirituality, then recognizes the importance of kinship and personal efficacy, and ends with control of assets. In Wuttunee's interpretation, "spirituality" does not clearly state that nonhuman entities have consciousness. Rather, the principle is respect.

A respectful relationship to the land and all living creatures is integrated into the lifestyle of those Aboriginal peoples who are raised with or have regained traditional values. This relationship is characterized by responsibility and thankfulness for all creatures with life in the animate and inanimate worlds, in the sky, deep into the planet and the sun and the moon. (Wuttunee 2004, 13)

She documents this view with quotations from hearings held by the Royal Commission on Aboriginal Peoples. The quotations come close to stating clearly that other beings have consciousness but do not go that far. People testifying to the Royal Commission may well have been aware of universal consciousness but were unwilling to speak about it for fear of being rejected as "too spiritual" or "too romantic."

Elsewhere I summarize traditional economic policy as implementation of "respect," composed of a combination of community, connectedness, seventh-generation thinking, and humility (Trosper 1995). Community includes all beings based on relationships, on all beings having spirit, and on requirements for reciprocity. My article explicitly admits leaving out "sacred or spiritual dimensions" because "to emphasize the sacred aspects in the secular field of economic policy would reduce the plausibility of the underlying argument" (71–72). Canadian Marxist economist Frances Widdowson would not be fooled; she has asserted that "many examples of aboriginal 'knowledge,' in fact, are spiritual beliefs." She quotes authors other than Wuttunee or Trosper but clearly believes that words like *connectedness* have spiritual implications. She notes these are inconsistent with scientific methods and would result in aboriginal people not being able to understand the world, since understanding "cannot emerge in aboriginal communities if it is pretended that ideas contrary to reason are true" (Widdowson 2016, 9, 24). The ferocity of Widdowson's attacks, while unusual in publications, can easily be encountered in discussions about the ideas of relations with nonhumans. All three authors—Salway Black, Wuttunee, and Trosper—are circumspect about their emphasis on spirituality because it seems outside the usual language of objectivity and science.

Wuttunee's book is full of examples of relational entrepreneurship. The Tsuut'ina Nation living on the outskirts of (or now within) Calgary, Alberta, has carefully selected among the many opportunities offered by its location. The aboriginal community of Winnipeg has many separate organizations that work together in numerous ways. These two examples, in Calgary and Winnipeg, demonstrate that relational entrepreneurship works in urban settings. She also provides stories of rural Toquaht and Tla-o-qui-aht First Nations on Vancouver Island, British Columbia, and the Fort McPherson–Gwich'in community in the Northwest Territories. These are examples of communities that have done well developing their own enterprises. Other communities have partnered with non-Aboriginal companies, with success and also with difficulties; relationships between the relational Aboriginal communities and the hierarchical private businesses are not always easy to work out. Wuttunee nonjudgmentally tells their stories and then tries to draw lessons from them. In her conclusion, she uses the four poles taken from Salway Black's development model to illustrate how different communities vary in their implementation of spirituality, kinship, personal efficacy, and control of assets.

Māori Relational Tourism Enterprises and Other Māori Proposals

Some examples that show such characteristics are provided by the tourism sector in Aotearoa / New Zealand. Chellie Spiller, Ljiljana Erakovic, and their co-authors (2011) provide ways to identify the relational goods that the tourism entrepreneurs promote. They describe "five well-beings" that are evidence of relationships generating relational goods.

> Māori values can inform the creation of multi-dimensional relational well-being, and the value embodied in relationships can accrue to become the

value-added propositions of the firm in the marketplace and in the wider world. By creating relational well-being, the businesses in this study demonstrate wealth in terms of its original meaning from the old English word "welth," meaning "to be well." (Spiller, Erakovic, et al. 2011, 154)

The article describes each of five well-beings—spiritual, cultural, social, environmental, and economic—emphasizing relational aspects for each of these well-beings. It recommends focusing on the customers, employees, and community while creating relational goods among each group. One guide reported that in the process of demonstrating care for one of the customers, he offered Māori medicine as treatment. It worked; an elder said the reason for the success was the guide's care for the customer. The medicine was a gift to the customer; other firms also provided unexpected gifts as part of their hosting of customers from elsewhere. They also hosted their customers as visitors and family using Māori principles of hospitality. They offered a cup of tea and greeting well before getting to the issue of payment. One employee said,

> It's just an inbred Māori thing that . . . we give visitors the best of . . . anything. . . . Like the old times visitors would come and they . . . would get out the best of their foods so that those visitors would go away [happy]. That's why we do what we do, and how we do it. (Spiller, Erakovic, et al. 2011, 162)

They expressed concern for the mana of their visitors, and acted to uplift the person's mana through acts of generosity and reciprocity. One of the customers said:

> Everywhere you go, they make you feel so comfortable that it does, it feels natural, and it feels like you're just going to your friend's house for dinner and enjoying a good time with the people of New Zealand. . . . It's like going and hanging out with family more than . . . going on a tour. It's that personable where everybody's having a good time and it's not all uptight and everybody's not sure how to act. (Spiller, Erakovic, et al. 2011, 162)

Another company assisted its visitors in understanding humans' relationships to fish; the entrepreneur had personally placed a prohibition on harvesting large, productive breeders of one of the species he fished. He insisted that his customers not count the number of fish caught, and all the fish would be divided among the guests at the end of the fishing trip. When they processed and ate the fish, the head and bones were given to the local Māori community to use so that none would be wasted. The customers received a lesson in sustainable fishing and were able to feel some of the connection to the land and waters. They were able briefly to feel that they were contributing to environmental well-being as one of the goals of their tourism experience.

Regarding the people involved in the business, one of the enterprises worked hard to assure that the network of people supplying material and experiences to the tourist enterprise felt that they were trusted; they were loyal to the main business, and that business was loyal to them. The enterprise owner showed care for his suppliers and his workers. This network was part of economic as well as social well-being for the enterprise. The relational goods for the network of suppliers were a shared vision and strategy for the activity as well as both loyalty and trust among them.

They also created a nonprofit organization of Māori tourism enterprises that shared the talents of their employees with each other. This nonprofit entity was jointly created by the tourism enterprises and represents another kind of relational subject as an association of relational enterprises.

One of the enterprises was non-Māori owned. The head of that enterprise worked hard to be a member of the local community life; he regarded them as part of his family. Another firm owner said, "Where there's a call, there's a need, then you make yourself available because you know you have that skill or you can contribute." In this way, he fulfilled the duty to "show up" in the community (Spiller, Erakovic, et al. 2011, 162).

The examples from the tourist sector in Māori business illustrate relationality. The entrepreneurs and the Māori scholars of business enterprise, Spiller and her co-authors, are explicit about the importance of relationships and relationality.

Community Enterprises in Chiapas, Mexico, as Examples of Buen Vivir

In early spring 2012, an Italian researcher visited Chiapas, Mexico, in order to meet with local Indigenous community enterprises. She wanted to learn about the relationship of the ideas of buen vivir to Indigenous community enterprises in Chiapas and to see what had helped those enterprises in their growth. The use of a Tseltal term, *lekil kuxlejal*, to describe buen vivir in Chiapas demonstrates that it is debated among local social movements (Giovannini 2015, 73). Using contacts from a local NGO, she interviewed people in thirteen Indigenous community enterprises, five of which were entirely run by women. She supplemented the interviews with written data about the organizations. The enterprises were involved in handicrafts, agriculture, and ecotourism. Some of the organizations were small, with fifteen to twenty members, and three were large, with five hundred or nine hundred members (Giovannini 2015).

The enterprises had entrepreneurial goals that included economic, social, political, cultural, and environmental goals. That the enterprises were relationally constituted is suggested by the following summary of the role of trust and well-being:

> The collective orientation of indigenous culture is expressed by the propensity towards participatory governance models of community enterprises that reinforce participation of community members and strengthen social cohesion. In a context, that social cohesion is constantly threatened by religious and political divisions and by tourist flows that foster competition within communities, this ability is crucial for enhancing social trust. Indeed, these collective organizational practices are directed to the well-being both of the organizations' members and of communities at large. (Giovannini 2015, 79)

Although the enterprises were not willing to disclose detailed financial information out of fear of state intervention, they indicated generally that their economic performance "was generally guaranteeing the sustainability of the organizations" (Giovannini 2015, 81).

Michela Giovannini found that the main enabling factor in Chiapas was their relationship with social movements, particularly the Zapatista movement. Most of the organizations were established after the Zapatista rebellion in 1994, and the organizations that had previously existed were revitalized. They were also enabled by Mexican law, which authorized associations of ejidos and the formation of cooperative "Societies of Social Solidarity." She found that the enterprises generally contributed to three aspects of buen vivir: the actions were taken by people historically marginalized, they conceived well-being in community terms, and they considered the natural environment to have rights. She ended by writing,

In opposition to the neoliberal discourse of assimilation of indigenous people, where traditions and culture are seen as obstacles to development, indigenous social movements assert their right to remain autonomous. These movements follow a "strategy of localization" that is directed to the defense of their territory and culture (Escobar 2001). With firm roots in local communities, these grass-roots enterprises have become instruments for reinforcing the protection of indigenous cultures and territories. (Giovannini 2015, 83)

That Indigenous culture can be an advantage rather than a barrier to community enterprise lines up well with the idea of a "Māori edge" in New Zealand. Relationality in business allows attainment of multiple goals other than purely making a profit. These entities used Mexican laws that allowed cooperatives.

Cooperatives

The cooperative form is another type of corporation that can be used for development of relational firms. The International Co-operative Alliance defines a cooperative as follows:

A co-operative is an autonomous association of persons united voluntarily to meet their common economic, social, and cultural needs and aspirations through a jointly-owned and democratically-controlled enterprise. (Principles Committee 2015)

Democratic control means one person one vote, not one share one vote. The distribution of profits to members is proportional to the use of the products of the cooperative rather than to an ownership share. This definition doesn't clarify that the cooperatives are organized with boards of directors who select the chief operating officer. The plywood worker cooperatives in the Pacific Northwest are organized as corporations, and the workers own shares. Many law firms are high-wage cooperatives among the partners. Workers both earn wages and profit from their shares. Decisions about management and possibly capital investment may be made by majority vote or consensus. Economists model cooperatives as arrangements among individuals that are contracting with each other. These assumptions also motivate legislators in

governments in the United States and Canada to create organizational structures that are recognizable to those governments. Much of the literature on
cooperatives examines entities whose goal mostly is to reduce the cost of
goods purchased, as among many agricultural and consumer cooperatives.
They exist, therefore, within the public/private dichotomy described in the
next section.

Although the legal structure describes a type of structure that works as
a type of normal for-profit enterprise, the general definition quoted earlier
allows those who wish to do so to operate a cooperative more as a relational enterprise than a for-profit enterprise. The extensive survey of Aboriginal cooperatives in Canada provided by Lou Hammond Ketilson and
Ian MacPherson (2001) includes thirteen case studies that show a variety
of success based on the cooperative formula that members obtain benefits
from participation as well as from dividends computed based on their level
of participation when the cooperative provides goods for purchase. Other
cooperatives are credit unions that provide both deposit and loan services to
their communities. Others provide marketing services to members who are
carvers or seamstresses who produce arts and crafts for sale to tourists or
to retail outlets in other communities. A report on the Ikaluktutiak Co-op,
which had existed thirty years, after pointing out that both wages and profit
stay in the community, observed:

> The co-op has also made a positive social impact on the community. As
> noted earlier, the cooperative structure fits well with Inuit culture, and the
> democratic nature of co-operatives allows community members to play a
> significant role in deciding what direction the co-op will take. Other Inuit
> cultural traditions are also reflected in the co-op, such as fishing, hunt-
> ing, and arts and crafts. The co-op runs an arts and crafts operation, sup-
> ports hunters, and is still involved with the commercial fishing operation,
> although to a lesser extent than in years past. (Ketilson and MacPherson
> 2001, 283–84)

The fit between Indigenous cultural traditions and the cooperative structure is reported in many other case studies as well. A worker-owned food
cooperative in Winnipeg is very successful. The consensus decision-making
tradition among its members led them to reject Robert's Rules of Order for
conducting meetings (Tupone 2001, 360). The co-op works with other com-

munity organizations, indicating that meso-level relational organizations exist in Winnipeg (362).

Cooperatives are prevalent in agricultural sectors in many countries. Consumer and worker cooperatives also exist. Jerker Nilsson (2001) explains why many critiques from mainstream economists are not correct; the economists predict cooperative firms will fail in many ways. Nilsson explains that the persistence of cooperatives is often due to their ability to combat market structures such as monopoly and monopsony. A cooperative allows many small producers to integrate vertically and compete with investor-owned firms. Many cooperatives develop "social cohesion of their membership—values of solidarity, trust, fairness, etc. prevail" (Nilsson 2001, 353). Other authors find social capital in cooperatives (Lang and Roessl 2011). Worker cooperatives are successful in many countries, especially Italy and Spain (Pérotin 2013). This all suggests that cooperatives have important relational characteristics; that Indigenous peoples use the cooperative form when it is legally possible is no surprise. This provides an opportunity for the larger relationships involving nature that Indigenous people desire.

Literature That Uses the Public/Private Dichotomy

A substantial portion of the literature on Indigenous entrepreneurship makes recommendations and analysis with an implicit assumption that current reservation economies exist within a system that is structured by the public/private dichotomy discussed previously. Tribal governments are the public sector, citizen entrepreneurs are the private sector, and tribal corporations are somewhere in between. Tribal governments create rules that facilitate economic activity in order to promote development activities constrained by tribal values. The advice to provide cultural match provides room for encouragement of relational entrepreneurship and inclusion of land stewardship (M. Jorgensen 2007).

Tribes own two types of businesses: tribal enterprises, which report directly to a tribal council, and tribal corporations, which are structured with an independent board of directors that in turn reports to the tribal council. The likelihood that a business is profitable if reporting directly to the tribal council is assumed to be less than if the business is operated by an independent board of directors. Much advice for businesses owned by a tribe and reporting to a tribal government is that the relationship should be structured so that day-to-day management does not respond to political pressure. This is one aspect of getting the rules right (Grant and Taylor 2007).

Another part of getting the rules right is to structure tribal law in a way that encourages citizen entrepreneurship. The judicial system is a big part of the recommendation, as businesses need to be able to make and enforce contracts. A great many of the recommendations to support citizen entrepreneurs involve facilitating such entrepreneurship legally. Those recommendations could support laws that authorize firms built on relational principles as well as ones based on individualism (M. Jorgensen 2007; Kennedy et al. 2017; R. J. Miller, Jorgensen, and Stewart 2019).

Another take on the public/private distinction is provided by an emerging literature that describes tribal enterprises and tribal corporations as "neo-tribal capitalism," arguing that the benefits from such businesses entirely accrue to tribal leaders rather than the tribal publics (Rata 1999, 2011; Rose 2014). Samuel W. Rose (2015) points to opposition to the creation of unions on the part of some tribal leaders. Because tribal governments are democratic and respond to their tribal publics, to claim that the workers in these firms have no voice is overstated. In addition, ownership is with the tribe, and many tribes require that the profits from their tribal corporations fund expenditures of the tribal government on community projects; they also distribute substantial sums as per capita payments to tribal members. While these enterprises may act as capitalist enterprises, the profit does not fully belong to tribal leaders, and to call these arrangements "neotribal capitalism" misses these crucial distinctions.

In some cases, however, the fears of Cornell and Kalt that tribal leaders would pursue rent seeking correspond to the charges by Elizabeth Rata that some Indigenous tribes use the special access they have to tribal capital and sovereignty to pursue private goals. The several examples of tribes that set out to disenroll some of the members of the tribe in order to have more wealth for those who remain is an example of obvious rent seeking. The examples of this have generated great attention, especially among Indigenous scholars, because of the inconsistency with Indigenous norms (Wilkins 2017). Not all cases are about money; some are about political power or about disputes among families. The cases David E. Wilkins examines derive from courts deciding in the American way rather than through peacemaking procedures. Wilkins is quite critical of the importation of non-Indigenous norms to decide the cases.

Citizen Entrepreneurship

The private/public model of the role of government in supporting economic activity fits well with recommendations that tribal governments create laws, judicial systems, training programs, and other activities to encourage and support what Stephen Cornell and his co-authors call "citizen entrepreneurship." They encourage tribal governments to develop policies and programs that support efforts by their own citizens to create new businesses. They recognize that such citizen entrepreneurs want to contribute to their community as well as to make some money for themselves. They encourage both individual and family enterprise (Cornell et al. 2007, 214–20).

An emphasis on relationality suggests being careful in the recommendations regarding tribal justice systems. For instance, there is a worry that a tribal court system might be one where a person's chance of success depends on which party may be related to the judge, which is an indication that the judicial system is not fair. This presumes the court system is settling disputes for one party or the other rather than seeking resolution to relationship issues. In a peacemaking judicial system, the peacemaking mediator may be related to the parties, but the mediator does not make the final decision. Of course, in a market society, many people do not expect to regard business problems as relationship issues, and they desire adjudication. A business that is well aware of relationship issues may still need some fairness in a dispute. The recommendation for a commercial code recognizes that situations vary. A commercial code "has to be designed to fit the situation, government and culture of the nation." One approach might be to have one of the nation's courts be in charge of considering business-related cases (M. Jorgensen 2007, 218).

Advice is available from a growing literature on Indigenous entrepreneurship, and much of it recognizes that Indigenous entrepreneurship is different from other kinds. Much advice for managing the financial aspects of a business is the same for any type of business: keep up-to-date accounts, monitor costs and expenses monthly to be sure profits are positive, create an annual budget, set sales prices to cover fixed and variable costs, know the break-even volume of production. Planning an enterprise requires identifying a market and any potential competition in that market. A recent book edited by Robert J. Miller, Miriam Jorgensen, and Daniel Stewart (2019) tends to focus more on standard business advice, while a book by Deanna M. Kennedy et al. (2017) has more material on the inclusion of Indigenous culture in business management.

Kevin Hindle and Michele Lansdowne (2005) sought to define a new paradigm for Indigenous entrepreneurship research based on analysis of forty interviews with opinion leaders in the field. Two years later, in 2007, Hindle and Peter Moroz completed a survey of the literature on Indigenous entrepreneurship, looking for common themes in the published literature, producing an article (Hindle and Moroz 2010). In both articles, the goal was to determine if the field had some unique characteristics that would distinguish it from the general field of research on entrepreneurship. The first article surveyed expert opinion; the second surveyed published material, using the presence of a contribution to the literature as part of the selection mechanism. The second study analyzed sixty-nine papers. In 2015 Léo-Paul Dana published a review of the field that cited some of the articles used by Hindle and Moroz while adding ones published after Hindle's work. With co-authors, he further surveyed the field in the literature review portion of other articles, one of which noted that gender roles in the dominant society include differences in stereotypes regarding relationality (Dana 2015; Ratten and Dana 2017). These literature reviews all confirm that the field of Indigenous entrepreneurship is distinct. They emphasize the importance of relationships. The human aspects of relationships are captured by emphasis on the importance of community and cooperation. The importance of land is also emphasized, which brings in the importance of good relationships with other-than-human beings. Sustainability is a third concern that links to the importance of land and to the importance of perpetuating good relationships.

Hybrid Ventures

An important theme in the entrepreneurship literature is recognition that contemporary Indigenous peoples need to deal with systems of domination, particularly by nation-states. This domination conditions access to markets, particularly for borrowing money, and limits control over policies regarding land use by imposing varieties of private and state property systems upon Indigenous peoples. The consequence is the emergence of "hybrid" firms and "hybrid" economic systems. Such hybridity represents attempts to reconcile the inconsistent norms of two different approaches to entrepreneurship, that of the individual hero of the mainstream literature with the relational hero that exists in the Indigenous entrepreneurial literature. The hybridity runs in the other direction, because the mainstream literature has a few strands that overlap with Indigenous thinking. These other strands are those that are

labeled "stakeholder theory" and "corporate responsibility," as explained by
Chellie Spiller, Edwina Pio, and their co-authors (2011).

The need to accommodate Indigenous viewpoints by business presents
an obvious issue: How can one make a profit selling things or experiences
without fully giving in to market culture with its individualistic focus? Part
of the answer is to distinguish between maximizing profits as a goal and
achieving positive profits as a constraint. This is often stated in this manner: rather than making profits the goal of a firm, the profit requirement is
changed into a constraint. How can a firm pursue other goals without profit
falling into negative territory?

A common approach is to note that civic, business, and governmental
entities are each different but that combinations of these would be "hybrid"
because each type would pursue multiple goals. Rather than focusing on
goals, one could focus on the methods of organization. A "hybrid" venture
would combine relational and contractual methods of organizing people into
a business effort. Rick Colbourne (2018) suggests two types of hybrids, integrated and differentiated. Integrated ventures blend the creation of values.
Integrated ventures are embedded in the community they serve, while differentiated ones are less so. "Differentiated hybrids separate economic value
creation activities from social, cultural and/or environmental value creation
activities" (Colbourne 2018, 113). Integrated ventures stress relationships to
a high degree within their organization. Differentiated ventures separate the
relationships of the venture to their community from the internal organization of the enterprise, which follows standard corporate structure.

The profit from the differentiated enterprise can contribute to community goals, as in the contributions that the Seminole businesses make to the
community. But the profit from the enterprise can also create deep political
divisions, as occurred among the Oneida living in New York State. If the
enterprise uses resource extraction, damage to the land may be too great, as
in a case of oil and gas extraction in Canada (Rose 2015).

Tribal Enterprises: Separating Business and Politics

Cornell and Kalt's Harvard Project on American Indian Economic Development asserts that a separation of business from elected tribal leaders makes
it more likely that an enterprise will be profitable. Informal surveys during
workshops on executive leadership provided an indication that if elected

leaders were involved in the management of enterprises, about 60 percent of them would succeed, while if there was separation of some sort, the chance of success would increase to about 87 percent of the enterprises (Cornell and Kalt 1992b, 32). In 2003–6 I was the principal investigator in a research project that set out to test the assertion for forty forestry enterprises in Canada (Trosper et al. 2008). We collected data for the fifteen enterprises that had not been profitable over a three-year period and compared their characteristics to twenty-five enterprises that were profitable during the same period. Our key variable was separation of the band councils of First Nations governments from the enterprises. Our control variables were whether the band had staggered terms or had been in third-party management, both measures of governance; whether the enterprise was involved in management planning, a measure of information available about the forest and expertise; and whether elders or hereditary chiefs had a formal role. Background probability of success was 56 percent. Separation of politics and business increased the probability of success to 99 percent. The results of our larger study showed that separation of business management from band governance did have a positive effect on profitability. This result is consistent with the general recommendation of Cornell and Kalt and other work of the Harvard project and the summarized recommendations in *Rebuilding Native Nations* (M. Jorgensen 2007).

We also found that a formal role for elders or hereditary chiefs had a negative effect on profitability, reducing the probability of success to only 6 percent. This would not be enough to offset separation; if there was both separation and involvement of elders or hereditary chiefs, the probability of success would still be 87 percent. When we presented these results to a workshop with some of the people from the communities in the larger study, the following was determined:

> Discussion at our workshop indicated that we should examine conditions that provide both a formal role for elders and that indicate situations that can reduce profitability. Profitability could be compromised if the enterprise is operating in an environment with conflicting objectives, resulting from a lack of consensus within the community as to the appropriate compromises among competing values. The lack of consensus could mean that management of the business would be asked to respond to conflicting sets of authorities. The negative role could also be related to a lack of cultural match between the requirements of provincial forest tenures and the views

of elders and hereditary chiefs regarding the balance between extraction and protection of the forest. (Trosper et al. 2008, 236)

This suggests that many enterprises were offending the land because of provincial requirements in forest harvest licenses, and when traditional leaders and elders had influence, harvests were limited or made more expensive to protect the forest.

One of two counterexamples was the Ecolink Joint Venture between the Esk'etemc First Nation and Lignum (Boyd and Trosper 2009). This joint venture did not have separation of business and politics, and it was profitable, contrary to the general pattern in the study. We speculated about the results as follows:

> The Ecolink JV had community support as shown by all nine interviewees expressing support for the idea that community members should have the power to make sound business decisions. We remain puzzled about how the community managed to avoid interfering in business decisions. However, we speculate that the social structure of EFN, made up of two main families, may be a contributing factor. During the research, we noted that one of the main families was operating the EFN's administration and social programs while the other was involved in the businesses. Perhaps an informal arrangement between the families provides a structural feature that is not formally recognized and this accounts for the anomaly that Ecolink is profitable in spite of its lack of strong separation in the business structure. Further research needs to be done to see how community dynamics (i.e. large families) affect the level of support for an economic development initiative. (Boyd and Trosper 2009, 46)

When Jeremy Boyd and I wrote this article, we did not fully understand the importance of good relationships supporting relational entrepreneurship. This story indicates that when relationality is involved, the analysis based on the standard public/private division may not be correct.

Relational Ethics in Business

Recent research has emphasized responsibility and relational ethics. A key process in creating a relational subject is that all participating care for each other. Relational entrepreneurship creates a business that is a relational sub-ject. Because a business develops relations with its workers, its suppliers, and those who purchase its product, a boundary question arises: Are all those affected by the business part of the relational subject created by the business? Within the business as usually defined, the owners, managers, and workers are all clearly participating in the relations, and as a result a duty to care about their concerns becomes part of the role of the entrepreneur as a relational leader. He or she needs to apply the rules of successful relationship building to those within the business. Some of the rules may be difficult, such as inclusion of everybody in decision-making. As Spiller, Erakovic, and their co-authors (2011) explained with regard to the Māori businesses they studied, when a business manager works to improve the mana of his busi-ness, caring for five well-beings of the workers is important. Spiller and her co-authors also found that for the tourism businesses they studied, care for customers was also important. The fishing enterprise extended care to the fish that were the basis of this enterprise, and harvesting practices supported caring for the fish.

In a relational world, all beings are called into being through relationships. This means that each is also called to be stewards of all beings in their rela-tionships. In another article, Spiller, Pio, and their co-authors (2011) elabo-rate on the ways in which the duty to stewardship, *kaitiakitanga*, involves the goal of stewardship: supporting *mauri*, the life energy of all beings. To take care of mauri is also to support *mauri ora*, conscious well-being that results from developing the full potential of relationships (223).

Amy Klemm Verbos and Maria Humphries (2014, 1) present "the rela-tional ethic of the Seven Grandfather Teachings, the ancient ethical values of the Potawatomi and Ojibwe peoples." The teachings come from a sacred story that provides instructions to support seven values: wisdom, love, re-spect, bravery, honesty, humility, and truth. As they explain the values, Ver-bos and Humphries emphasize that "the teachings do not privilege human beings over other aspects of creation" (2–3). They deliberately label the val-ues "relational ethics" because they can trace the values to assumptions that humans are not solitary and have a specific place in creation that must be maintained in order for humans to survive.

To prove the relevance of the seven teachings, Verbos and Humphries cite the work of Sydney Finkelstein, a management consultant and teacher at Dartmouth College who also has a list of seven items, the "seven habits of spectacularly unsuccessful executives." His article (Finkelstein 2004) summarizing the seven habits is based on his book *Why Smart Executives Fail* (2003). The short answer to why they fail is that each of the bad habits illustrates a failure to follow two or more of the seven teachings. Verbos and Humphries use Finkelstein's seven habits as a class exercise: for each of these habits, which of the teachings has been violated? Verbos and Humphries (2015) argue that a relational ethic needs to be added to the Principles of Responsible Management Education (PRME); they provide detailed advice to this UN organization that encourages responsible management.

Jason Paul Mika, Rick Colbourne, and Shamika Almeida (2020) argue that the idea of responsible management should be extended with additional considerations from Indigenous worldviews. Responsible management needs to recognize embeddedness in its community as well as duties to stakeholders and duties to pursue "ethical decision-making and moral excellence" (262). They present a table contrasting Indigenous firms and non-Indigenous firms that are not using responsible management.

When one recognizes the importance of relationships and relational ethics, a result in the environmental field is to ask the question, "What is multispecies justice?" The short answer is that following the principles of good relationship building with other species leads to treating animals, plants, and even purportedly nonliving entities such as mountains or rivers with the respect due to any member of one's valued relationships. In a desire to make this point in the field of environmental politics, Danielle Celermajer and her co-authors (2021) turn to Indigenous philosophies in order to find ideas that support policies that address the environmental disasters that are increasing in frequency and impact. Ecological disasters are not just tragedies; they are examples of injustice. The desire to be just can be mobilized to find ways to address the causes of "natural" disasters. Expanding ideas of justice, however, exceeds "standard notions of that concept" because justice is normally thought to be an issue among humans.

Since entrepreneurship is an activity that brings new things and new values into the world, the impacts of such new entities have to be taken into account. Simply asking "What is relational entrepreneurship?" leads one down a path that ends up with consideration of relational ethics, which in turn leads to a consideration of justice for all beings. Once such caring is recognized, the need to extend it to everything that touches what matters becomes apparent, as Donati and Archer (2015, 263–300) have stressed in the final chapter of their book. They are critical of many practices that have negative effects that the perpetrators are able to ignore. One example is the practice of moving an enterprise from a rich country to a poor country because production costs are less in a country where workers earn low wages and often the governments do not have labor laws to protect the workers. The sweatshops that used to be in New York City are now producing clothing in Bangladesh (293). Their argument about the broad scope of relational ethics lines up well with the entrepreneurial literature by Indigenous scholars. Because entrepreneurial activity involves markets and trade, the worry about connections is a natural concern. Donati and Archer, however, do not extend their relational ethics to consideration of the effects of relations on entities other than humans.

Entrepreneurial Opportunities in Comanagement Relationships

Each of the relationship agreements described in the first chapter provides a framework with opportunities to entrepreneurs. In the pre-treaty Māori system, the elders of each hapu, the rangatira, supervised the young entrepreneurs, the potoki. Dynamism came from the potoki, but guidance and restraint came from the rangatira. Entrepreneurship had limits.

In the Tungurahua case, the water users from the lower watershed agreed to fund projects organized by groups of upstream land users. They agreed to help with fishponds and other projects such as changing the animals grazing the páramos from those that destroyed the plant cover to ones like guinea pigs and alpacas that had hooves with more accommodation to the plants. While an ecosystem services plan would have emphasized individual projects, only groups could apply for development funds.

The Pikangikum elders wanted the Ontario provincial government to issue forest licenses to their own corporation. The nonprofit Whitefeather Forest Community Resource Management Authority (WFCRMA) obtained a Sustainable Forest License. The WFCRMA carries out the terms of the license by hiring Pikangikum entrepreneurs to undertake the harvesting and processing activities. The new timber industry, though small, will be adequate to support many people in the First Nation.

On Haida Gwaii, the reduction in annual harvest that the Haida insist upon preserves the sustainability of the island's economy. Had forest extraction continued at its prior pace, the island's mills would have had to close down, as happened in the rest of British Columbia when all the accessible old growth was harvested. Economic calculation based only on monetary return will always prescribe transforming the value of the old trees to other uses, replacing most of the growing stock with young trees that are not available for a period of time. In addition, substantial clear-cuts would lower the recreation value of the islands. With the Kunst'aa guu–Kunst'aayah Reconciliation Protocol, the annual cut will be reduced and the forest tenure transferred to the Haida Nation. Resolution of trust issues should allow for new entrepreneurial activities within the governing context set up by the protocol.

Legal personhood of the Te Urewera National Park and the Whanganui River was used to create complicated comanagement arrangements for each of them. The board that governs the park has authority over all the concessions in the park. The governance of the river has three different boards with different authorities. The complexity suggests that some commercial activities already existing on the river will continue, but future new businesses will be authorized through the actions of the three governing boards (Sanders 2018, 226–29). The ultimate authority of tikanga Māori depends on how governance works out; Sanders (2018, 230) is optimistic that those values will have a large influence on future decisions and therefore entrepreneurship.

The new Bears Ears National Monument protects the area against extraction of minerals and oil and gas, leaving the surface open to other types of business activities under the supervision of the agencies that are responsible for the land. Entrepreneurs can establish many tourist-oriented businesses to enjoy the beauty of the land and the archaeological sites. These jobs will go to Indians as well as non-Indians in the recreation industry. Oil, gas, and mineral extraction would have profited the mining companies, leaving very little behind except the environmental destruction. With the monument, the land will survive, as it deserves to do, and humans will be able to build lasting relationships with it.

Two Approaches to Economics

The importance of relationality is widely accepted among Indigenous and other scholars describing Indigenous communities. This book explains how the relational viewpoint applies to economic analysis. The result is an approach to economic analysis considerably different from that of mainstream economics. This afterword compares the two approaches. Although any dichotomous comparison risks exaggerating the differences, the differences are great. Some contrasts have been emphasized in previous chapters. Chapter 2 compared the relational persons to individuals. Presentation of the generation of relational goods in chapter 3 compared the approach to that of social capital. The consideration of common pool goods emphasized the dilemmas that exist for individuals making decisions in isolation. Indigenous relational entrepreneurship was distinguished from individual entrepreneurship. This afterword provides an overall summary of the differences.

The differences between the fields of Indigenous and standard economics can be divided into three groups: (1) fundamental principles, (2) consequences for the analysis of structures, and (3) consequences for the analysis of ideas. Distinguishing between fundamental assumptions and other differences that appear to derive from the assumptions can create other problems because some of the derived consequences are treated as assumptions by other analysts. A useful comparison might be to the critiques of mainstream economics offered by Stephen A. Marglin (2008). In *The Dismal Science: How Thinking like an Economist Undermines Community,* Marglin argues that markets undermine community and economists advocate markets without understanding the consequences for community. His arguments are similar to the current book, except that this book emphasizes relationality and the consciousness of all beings in the landscape. Indigenous communities might be similar to Marglin's concept of community in their susceptibility to markets; they may also be similar to strong communities that have resisted market incentives, such as the Amish that impress Marglin. Marglin's main text presents an external critique of economics in which he stresses the errors that derive from "the foundational assumptions of self-interested individualism, rational calculation, the nation-state, and unlimited wants" (265). An appendix summarizes an internal critique of economics that does not challenge those foundational assumptions; the internal critique examines information asymmetries, externalities, public goods, and markets with few buyers or few sellers (293). He concludes his internal critique of economics with an example in which a tropical forest inhabited by Indigenous peoples is in danger of commercial logging. He argues that the economist aware of the internal critique but not accepting the external critique would propose a system of private property rights in the forest, and notes that the Indigenous peoples would object because privatization of land would destroy the community. The Indigenous peoples he was aware of did not like individualism and rejected privatization of the forest (253). This example is a case of common pool goods, a situation Marglin does not examine as a matter of theory. The foundational assumptions identified in this book do overlap with Marglin's, except that this argument asserts the nation-state is a consequence of foundations, not a foundation. The classification into foundations and consequences, thus, is open to critique. Rather than defend such points, this chapter looks to the big picture and tries not to get lost in some of the details.

The Two Row Wampum

The differences in societies were stark in 1492, when both sides of the Atlantic Ocean became aware of the other, although they had been in brief contact before Columbus arrived in the Caribbean. The Americas had very few domesticated animals and few hierarchical states, and persons had considerable autonomy and freedom. Farming methods and domesticated plants were very different. One of the differences, infectious diseases, due to lack of barnyard animals, greatly weakened the peoples of the Americas, a point popularized by Jared Diamond (1997) in *Guns, Germs, and Steel.*

When 90 percent of the people in the Americas died in the sixteenth century, forests took over farms; the result reduced atmospheric carbon dioxide and caused global cooling, contributing to the Little Ice Age (Koch et al. 2019). The dramatic impact of population loss also affected relationships between the Indigenous peoples of the Americas and the invading settlers from Europe.

The differences were clearly recognized when the Haudenosaunee and Dutch sought a peaceful relationship, an agreement now referred to as *kaswentha*, a concept of mutual engagement that created the Two Row Wampum Treaty, given a date of 1613 in Haudenosaunee oral tradition, which has received considerable support in the written record (Parmenter 2013). The Two Row Wampum is a string of beads with two dark-blue or black rows on a white background, symbolizing a sailing ship beside a canoe in a river; the treaty agreed that each ship could proceed with its way of life separate from the other, while sharing the river. The ideas in the Two Row Wampum Treaty were restated in the Royal Proclamation of 1763 and the subsequent Treaty of Niagara in 1764 (Borrows 1997). Jon Parmenter also states that the 1794 Treaty of Canandaigua between the United States and the Haudenosaunee is based on ideas of the Two Row Wampum (Parmenter 2013, 95–98). James Tully (1994) explains how the Royal Proclamation of 1763 provides a framework for negotiating agreements between the two sides regarding land. It provides that land would not be transferred between societies without mutual consent. The Haudenosaunee sought a way to create lasting peace between the two cultures. While the British sought short-term peace in 1763 and 1764, this was disingenuous, as they intended to eventually displace the Indigenous peoples. The same was true of the United States in 1794. George Washington and his colleagues determined that treaties were cheaper than war, especially after a defeat. Although the Canandaigua Treaty offered sharing the land, that was not really the policy (Calloway 2018, 328–45, 442).

This work is an attempt to spell out the economic theory that supports the Indigenous side of the kaswentha, the canoe that goes down the river next to the sailing ship. Both should exist separately but in cooperation as they go down the river. This image is a bilateral world of two worlds, Indigenous and European, although the Indigenous side was a multilateral world of many confederations. History did not proceed as the Indigenous negotiators sought. The settlers' colonialism led to domination by the sailing ship and retreat of the canoe to small enclaves. The European row has grown solid and fat, while the canoe row has broken into pieces, with many of the pieces attaching to the European row. Since the Europeans sought to have their political and economic system dominate, they did not adopt a concept of building equal and fair relationships between different societies.

Finally, the people on what became the dominant side are realizing that relationships can be jointly beneficial. The main reason for this opportunity is that the sailing ship, powered now by coal, oil, and nuclear energy, has wreaked such havoc in ecological systems that restoration is needed. During the decimation of the ecosystems, the relationship was a zero-sum game; what the sailing ship took left next to nothing for the other side. The only point of an agreement was to divide the spoils of environmental degradation; sometimes the people in the canoe were able to obtain a small share, especially when they worked for the companies extracting wood, fish, and minerals. With a degraded system, however, the zero-sum situation changes to non-zero sum. If the parties cooperate, there will be more to divide between the sides. Indigenous peoples, having retained their ideas about how to relate to the nonhumans or more-than-humans on the planet, can assist in the restoration process. The first chapter presented examples of Indigenous peoples continuing to seek working relationships between the two systems, using the concepts of relationality explained in the subsequent chapters to structure the relationships. Perhaps this leadership will allow Indigenous peoples to obtain a better share of what is restored than they obtained when the land was mined and devastated.

Fundamental Assumptions or Principles

Table 6 presents four categories that lay out the differences in fundamental assumptions between Indigenous economics, living well, and standard economics, the source of mainstream development and sustainable development.

Agents

Both systems assume that agents are the causal forces that create economies. The most fundamental difference between Indigenous and standard economics lies in the characteristics of the agents: persons versus individuals. In Indigenous economics, persons are created through relationships both when they are young and as they proceed through life. While the effect of

TABLE 6 Fundamental Assumptions

Assumption categories	Indigenous living well	Mainstream development
Agents	Persons are formed by natural, practical, and social relations	Self-centered individuals have preferences
Extent of consciousness	All components of the world are conscious	Humans have consciousness and spirit; other entities do not
Importance of types of goods	Common pool and local public goods are most important	Private and public goods are most important
Framework for theory	Emergence of properties of emergent entities occurs	Methodological individualism and upward conflation are preferred

relationships on persons and vice versa could be understood in many ways, this text uses the four-part person proposed by Margaret Archer. A person is first an "I," a self with continuity as he or she grows through time; the sense of self continues throughout one's life. Second, a person is a "Me" who has characteristics that are inherited from parents and society's emergent structures as well as created through the effort of the person. Sex, gender, sexual orientation, skin and eye color, and languages spoken are bodily characteristics that are relatively fixed but variable in many ways. These characteristics contribute to "Me" because they are usually evident to other people and serve to classify a person in one or more groups generated by emergent structures. When identity created by a person's characteristics is not evident, as with sexual orientation, they still affect the concept of self. As a person ages, he or she first must come to understand the components of "Me," a concept of self, and decide to undertake to change them into more desired forms. A person conducts an internal conversation that evaluates the meaning of the "Me" characteristics; this internal conversation can be linked to other persons, and in that manner form a variety of associations with those other persons, a set of "We" relationships that provide a person with social identities.

The conversations and many "We" relationships become a key determinant of the actions of the persons. The "We" relationships have emergent characteristics external to the person, such as relational goods, which in turn affect the person's concept of self and the internal conversations a person has. The fourth component, "You," is the roles or positions the person has within the groups that make up the "We" and other roles that are defined by society. A person occupying a role can contribute to the role through her "I," "Me," and "We" characteristics; the role, however, is externally defined and understood. A person becomes an actor by occupying a role.

The individual of standard economics is not a relational person. To the extent that an individual is created by relationships, those occur in childhood through parental influence. The implicit kinship structure is that shared between Anglo-Americans as influenced by Britain: nuclear families. Once an individual grows up, he or she leaves the family and makes an independent living. Their actions in given situations are determined by their preferences, which may be entirely self-regarding but may also include social preferences such as inequality aversion or altruism. These preferences are internal to the individual and determine choices made in interactions with other individuals. In most analysis, the preferences are assumed to be given at the time of entering adulthood, but some economists allow preferences to change as a result of experience (Bowles 2004).

Because mainstream economics is focused on the exchange and production of material things, each individual has an endowment of such things, plus a set of skills that allow production of more things either in combination with other individuals or through solitary action. Of key importance in the endowment is the property a person owns. Some economists narrow their analysis by assuming the preference of an individual is to maximize his wealth in terms of the property rights he owns (Barzel 1997). Other economists recognize that wealth has many dimensions, that an individual may care about other individuals, and that an individual's endowment is more complex than property rights (Bowles 2004).

The Archer model of a person contains the simpler economists' model of an individual. The preferences are part of "I"; the endowments are located in both the "Me" and the "You" components. Since interactions with other individuals are all conducted as exchanges of material things, the economists' model has no "We," a person interacting in a reflexive manner with other persons. Instead, relations with other persons are governed by explicit or implicit contracts. Archer (2000b, 48) argues that the idea of maximizing wealth through decisions determined by preferences treats humans as machines, unable truly to have consciousness and decision-making powers based on reflection on each situation. Bowles, however, claims that equilibrium of games creates social structure, demonstrating that agents do provide causes.

Extent of Consciousness

A fundamental assumption of Indigenous peoples is that humans are not alone in possessing consciousness and being able to think about their reactions to human actions. Many stories used to teach about the nature of reality have animals conversing with each other and arriving at agreements about what to do. While relationality among humans is often emphasized in fields other than economics, particularly by sociologists when they claim that economic affairs are embedded in social affairs, the idea that nonhumans can participate in relations with humans is not acceptable to either mainstream economics or sociology.

Calling the consciousness of more-than-humans to be a "belief" or an "assumption" is unfair to the depth of the knowledge that animals have consciousness. That animals think and consider is a fact. They do not think as humans do; however, they have their own ways of being. The Kluane people of the Northwest Territory in Canada, for instance, insist that the oldest Dall sheep are important for teaching younger sheep how to live; the Kluane oppose killing the oldest rams because that disrupts their society. Biologists working for the territorial government, however, support a big game hunting economy that targets the animals with the largest horns (Nadasdy 2003). Western scientists have established that animals have culture (Brakes et al. 2019; Whiten 2021). With confirmation by other scientists, maybe now the biologists in the wildlife agency will listen to the Kluane on this topic.

Standard economics presumes that the entities of the world other than humans are inert or, if alive, are not capable of decision-making through consciousness and deliberation. Nonrenewable resources are inert and are generally modeled as accumulations of minerals or oil with variable cost of extraction. Renewable resources, being alive, can reproduce and replace those entities that are harvested. Most models of renewable resources assume each is one species, with growth governed by a logistic growth function (Clark 1990; Chichilnisky 1997; Heal 1998). A focus only on the total numbers of animals in a herd, such as the Dall sheep, ignores the structure of the herd. A broader view would use more elaborate models, as in theories of complexity, which some economists recognize. But those models also do not assume animals can respond to the actions of humans; to do so would make prediction very difficult, as it is with human systems (Porpora 2015; Stoffle, Arnold, and Bulletts 2016). A good understanding of how animals respond to humans would be helpful, however.

Importance of Types of Goods

Chapter 5 began with definitions of private, public, common pool, and toll goods. They are distinguished from each other by their excludability and divisibility. Because of their importance for the other-than-humans that live on landscapes, Indigenous peoples have to deal with common pool goods, the ones with divisibility and low levels of excludability. Standard economics focuses only on private goods and public goods (Samuelson 1954). Private goods fit easily into standard economic theory because high excludability and divisibility allow commodification. Public goods are important because standard economics uses governments to set up legal systems that allow enforcement of property rights and contracts. Because individualism creates social dilemmas when confronted with common pool resources, the standard recommendation for economists is to try to convert the common pool resources into either private goods through privatization or public goods through assertion of state property rights. Neither solution is actually feasible because the given characteristics of the goods cannot be changed; the result is that common pool goods become open-access resources and are overexploited (Fitzpatrick 2006). Those who recognize common pool goods are also concerned about relationships among those goods and humans, which leads as a consequence to relational accountability.

Framework for Theory

Theories exist within frameworks. Since this is a work that describes a theory, Indigenous economics, one needs to know that a comparison to standard economic theory is not possible without also comparing the frameworks in which each exists. The differences between relational persons and individuals are an element of framework differences. Both fundamentals intersect with framework issues. One cannot describe Indigenous economic theory with the use of economists' individuals. One cannot also describe Indigenous economic theory with an assumption of inert nature. To explore the differences in frameworks would take much space; not all readers may want to go into the methodological details needed to contrast the frameworks. The important contrast is between methodological individualism, which economists prefer (Archer 2000b), and critical realism, which I use (Trosper 2005; see also Porpora 2015). Connections, as part of relationality, create structures with emergent properties that endure and structure events. To think that events caused by individuals interacting merely cause other events, and to explore correlations among them, gives an incomplete picture. Methodological individualism explicitly denies emergence, claiming that everything needs to be explained by examining the actions of individuals (Barzel 1997, 10).

Emergence occurs when interaction among entities generates a property that none of the entities have. The new property signals a new entity. A simple example is that of a clock. The new entity, the clock, has the property of revealing the time; none of its components have that property. Another example, common in economics, is a corporation, which has many properties its components do not: a name, a logo, a tax ID number for each jurisdiction where taxes are due. That economic theory claims to ignore emergence is puzzling, of course. One of the economists potentially most sympathetic to Indigenous economics, Samuel Bowles, is adamant in his denial of emergence. Norms, rules that people follow even if there is no punishment for not following them, are an emergent property of a cultural system. Bowles (2004, 368), however, insists that norms and other rules are equilibria of games that individuals repetitively solve. When a norm is internalized, it becomes part of a person's preferences and therefore fits into methodological individualism. His emphasis on communities in his final chapter might suggest he does recognize emergence. But he does not recognize relational goods, as shown by his definition of community.

> By community I mean a group of people who interact directly, frequently and in multi-faceted ways. . . . Connection, not affection, is the defining characteristic of a community. (Bowles 2004, 474)

He denies an economy of affection, as Hyden (2006) finds in Africa and as Māori identify (Dell, Staniland, and Nicholson 2018). He goes on to argue that the availability of information on each other creates social capital, "trust, concern for one's associates, and a willingness to live by the norms of one's community and to punish those who do not." Thus, individuals have other-regarding behavior, and if they know their friends also have those values, then they can coordinate.

This book treats cultures as different sets of ideas, as described by Karl Popper (1978) as "world 3." Popper is incorrectly identified by economists with logical positivism, which also denies emergence, even though he eventually claimed to have killed positivism. World 1 is the physical world of entities that do not have sentience. World 2 is the subjective world of the thoughts of the entities who have consciousness. World 3 consists of the products of human minds, which become separated from the persons who originate them and continue to exist. Popper insists that the products of the human mind, while not material, are real and consequently have effects. The products of the human mind do of course exist in human thoughts, but they are also independent of any particular human or set of humans. Ludwig van Beethoven's Ninth Symphony exists independently of each of the performances that present it. The performances may vary in their interpretation of the sequence of notes Beethoven wrote down. The symphony can have real effects each time it is played. Other denizens of world 3 are Albert Einstein's theories of relativity. That energy and matter are linked led to creation of the atomic bombs that killed so many Japanese and also destroyed atolls in the Pacific. Emergence in world 3 refers to the logical relations among ideas. Ideas can be logically consistent with one another, they can contradict one another, or they can simply not be related. Assuming consciousness exists in nonhumans is not consistent with assuming they lack that capacity. Asserting that law comes from the land is not consistent with law originating with a monarch or nation-state.

Consequences for Structure

The following section focuses on the main material ways in which Indigenous economies differ from other economies, particularly the capitalist economies that have grown in the settler societies that arrived from England, France, and Spain to occupy Indigenous land. This section examines differences in social structure, which is the material relations among social positions with respect to social constructs such as capital, resources, and income. Because of the huge variety of social positions, their relations in respect to material matters can vary a great deal, as shown in table 7.

TABLE 7 Consequences for Structure

Categories of structure	Indigenous living well	Mainstream development
Stratification of governance	Polycentric and plurinational; nothing is really private. Full transparency keeps the leaders accountable; relational subjects are overlapping and nested; pluriverse.	One world made up of states, each with a public/private dichotomy that varies, with leaders not being accountable in some states.
Stratification of agents	All persons and species are valuable.	Species, racial, and gender stratification
Leadership	Guiding	Dominating
Land tenure	Conscious beings cannot be owned; things can be owned. Human–land relationships structure land tenure.	All things and beings except humans can be owned. Property relations define land tenure through ownership.
Common pool goods	Common pool resources prosper, as does biodiversity.	Common pool goods are overharvested and tend to disappear.
Exchange	Relationships	Contracts

Stratification of Governance

The ideas of a relational person, on the one hand, and that of the individual, on the other, each lead to different ideas about what should be the fundamental units of analysis in models of economies. Relational persons form relationships through discourse and through agreeing to work together and create relational goods. The resulting relational subjects, as discussed in earlier chapters, rely on such shared relational goods as trust to help them cooperate in various ways.

For analysis based on individuals, larger entities are created through contracts. An employer offers a worker an employment contract. Contracts are not self-enforcing, however; for that reason, a system with contracts needs a government for the enforcement of those contracts. The constitution of the government is treated as a social contract.

For relationality, the units are the relationships that result from persons getting together for many different reasons and supporting each other. The types and structures of relationships can vary across societies; kinship is a fundamental basis for relational groups, but other bases can exist. Kinship relations become one basis for generating relational subjects, the extended families and clans that populate much anthropological work about Indigenous peoples. These groups then generate larger-scale entities such as villages. Among the Iroquois, for instance, a village consists of two halves, or moieties, which take care of each other in particular ways. The role of one side condoling the other after a death is an example. In the Pacific Northwest, persons organize into houses, each with a connection to key territories. The houses assemble at the village level when they hold potlatch feasts, sharing wealth. Governance at the village level results from the titleholders of each house reaching consensus on issues affecting the village. Governance occurs in nested levels. The Haudenosaunee League is one clear example, where villages joined as tribes, and then the tribes joined together, patterned on the moieties of the villages, with two of the five tribes being the "younger brothers," the other two the "elder brothers," and the Onondaga sat in the middle to give its view after the younger brothers and older brothers reached consensus. The arrangements among the five tribes sought to provide "peace, power, and equity" among the different tribes and among the villages that comprised the tribes. The Haudenosaunee attempted to extend their system of peace to the colonists with the original Two Row Wampum Treaty and its successors. This system exists in small scale on the Six Nations Reserve of Grand River in Canada, with the Tuscarora included with the original five.

The individual concept leads to a different structure: individuals comprise a private sphere where relations among the individuals take the form of market exchange. They do their exchanging within markets structured by the laws created by the public sphere, the government. In the simplest model, the units are the individuals in the market and the government that sets the rules for the markets to operate. A village in this model is a collection of individuals who elect a town council to run the town's affairs. For a nation, the towns are assembled into provinces, and the provinces into a national state. Governing powers are distributed among the levels of government. In addition to creating rules, each governmental level provides public goods to the individuals in its jurisdiction. Some public goods are clearly local, others clearly national. The public sector has a nested hierarchy of governing units. The private sector has a set of individual units, focused on the idea of the firm. Individuals assemble themselves into businesses in which the owners provide capital and the workers provide labor, in relationships governed by contracts. In the agricultural sector, landowners rent their land to laborers or hire them as employees. As the Industrial Revolution progressed, network utilities such as railroads, telephones, and electricity introduced the possibility of monopolies providing the networked services. This led to governments attempting to regulate such monopolies to limit their ability to exploit their market power. Such regulation can be weakened if the monopolizing firms capture the regulating entities by using their considerable profits to influence politics and governance.

A good government, also created by contract, is one that provides the rules that allow the private market to create wealth. This idea of good government originated among the thinkers around Locke, who combined the idea of individuals owning property with the idea of a government that provides the rules with the consent of the governed. The Declaration of Independence was written in the spirit of the times and sets the basis for the private/public model of standard economics.

> We hold these truths to be self-evident, that all men are created equal, that they are endowed by their Creator with certain unalienable Rights, that among these are Life, Liberty and the pursuit of Happiness. — That to secure these rights, Governments are instituted among Men, deriving their just powers from the consent of the governed. (National Archives, https://www .archives.gov/founding-docs/declaration-transcript)

The individuals and their government exist in a territory consisting of inert nature managed by the people. In Locke's model, a basis for the development of settler colonialism, individuals and their governments exist on a frontier of land that is not owned as private property. The settlers occupy that land and in doing so they come to own it as property. The reference to the Creator in the Declaration refers to Christianity, which awards dominion over nature to humans. Locke and his fellow theorists assert that ownership belongs to those with a Christian religion who have organized their economy with money, which allows trade in the fruits of the land. His initial concept of acquisition of property asserted that an individual could only hold what he could use, because he would waste extra production. With the presence of money and trade, however, property owners could invest in money, thus not wasting the production above their own needs (Arneil 1996).

This idea of the agrarian economy based on private property, civil government, and money describes the origin of society among the English settlers of North America (Cattelino 2018). The structure remains in economics textbooks to this day. It is evident in Adam Smith's initial construction of the market as well as in the theories of Montesquieu, Jean-Jacques Rousseau, and others, including Friedrich Engels, who relied on the interpretations of the early American anthropologist Lewis Henry Morgan. Jessica R. Cattelino (2018, 275) carefully traces the way in which a false image of Indigenous peoples was used "as a foil for Europeans' use of money and practice of private property." The separation of Indigenous peoples from this "money/property/government complex" is expressed directly in the last of the list of complaints against the king in the Declaration of Independence.

> He has excited domestic insurrections amongst us, and has endeavored to bring on the inhabitants of our frontiers, the merciless Indian Savages, whose known rule of warfare, is an undistinguished destruction of all ages, sexes and conditions.

While the use of the word *savages* indicates deep-seated prejudice against the original peoples of the Americas, the greater polemical issue is which can be described as "savage." Indigenous peoples are willing to build relationships with strange others, including animals, while settlers eliminate what they do not understand.

Stratification of Agents

The combination of individualism and the domination of nature by humans leads to a second major difference in the two systems that confronted each other on the American continent. As explained in chapter 2, the combination of relationality and the consciousness of all other-than-human entities creates a radical level of individual autonomy among all beings. For Indigenous peoples, the Creator's plan involves all beings playing their role in society. Each is valuable because of his or her uniqueness. The system works when all respect the worth of others, an ethic of relationality that must confront a major difficulty: if all are worthy of respect, how can humans justify eating other beings who also have consciousness?

One common answer is consent: a hunter looks for his prey to indicate consent to be killed. The consent is based on knowledge that the body will be treated properly and all steps needed for rebirth of the animals will be followed and has been followed. The deer or moose has a nice forest to live in, the beaver a nice place to build a pond, and the salmon a nice stream or river in which to spawn. By caring for the Earth, humans play their role as custodians. This role involves decisions, however. Among the Tlingit caring for salmon, for instance, Dolly Varden fish must be controlled because they eat young salmon (Langdon 2007). Among the Yurok caring for productive meadows and oak, Douglas fir needs to be controlled with surface fire. Fire must be used in other circumstances and controlled also around settlements to prevent dangerous summer conflagrations (Lewis 1993, 2002; Huntsinger and McCaffrey 1995).

The autonomy of all beings participating in the system must be respected so that they can contribute to the flourishing of relationships. Any resulting stratification follows from the process of living together, with plants definitely serving as food for animals, and animals serving as food for others, up to the top predators. As one of the top predators, humans need to use their powers and responsibilities wisely. The Haudenosaunee Thanksgiving Address recognizes the interdependencies (Kimmerer 2013, 105–17).

This view contrasts to that of humans being given the power to dominate nature and all other species. The assumed inert nature of nonhumans has two separate consequences. First, nature is politically powerless. Some animals can be domesticated, put under human control. Such domestication would not be allowed in a relational society of mutuality. This domination creates speciesism, the idea that species can be ranked in quality from best to least. Humans, being on top, may dominate the rest. Thus, animals can be domesticated and treated as the property of humans. Land, the place where animals live, can also become the property of humans. The idea of Indigenous peoples, that the land owns them, is thoroughly rejected.

Second, the division of powerful humans and powerless nature can be modified to include some humans as closer to nature than to humanity. The racial classification of humans arose in Europe along with the development of the ideas of private property. As Joseph Pugliese (2013, 41) states, based on a review of much literature on the topic, "racism is predicated on speciesism."

Pugliese also connects speciesism and domestication to both Christianity and the idea of property (33–44). Once some humans are assumed to be less worthy than others, even like animals, allowing them to be owned as property is a small step. Similarly, assuming that they have no right to own property and have no ideas that need to be respected are also small steps.

Embedded in the idea of individualism is the idea that some individuals are worthier than others. As Edge (1998) explains, European individualism also assumes that all humans share the same human nature, which includes rationality. People can reason that if everyone is the same, and some do not reach the same conclusions as they do, the others are deficient is some way. This would not be a fair inference if each person is assumed to be different due to being created by different relationships.

The idea that some humans can dominate others was rationalized in the four-stages model of human development that originated in the middle of the eighteenth century as a response to Indigenous critique of European hierarchy. David Graeber and David Wengrow (2021, 48–62) document how the arguments of a Wendat statesman, Kandiaronk, were presented to Europeans by Louis Armond Lahontan as a series of dialogues between himself and Kandiaronk. A similar work, a novel about the Inca, also challenged European inequality in a novel with a female protagonist, the Inca Zilia. The early French economist A. R. J. Turgot responded to the arguments about the superiority of Indigenous America by arguing that the division of labor and technological development evident in Europe was the end result of four stages of societal development. Each society begins as hunters. They then domesticate animals and become shepherds, followed by establishment of farms and agriculture. The fourth stage, commerce, is the best. The four-stages theory influenced Adam Smith and others who developed early social science, as explained also by Ronald Meek (1976). In *Social Science and the Ignoble Savage*, Meek documents how the four-stages theory placed Indigenous thought in the lowest rung, savage and not noble (137–45). The highest stage, commerce, was based on private property, wise government, money, and markets (129). Societies in the New World had both hunting and agriculture; they did not herd animals, as that would be disrespectful. They had trade among themselves but not commerce in the sense of Turgot, Smith, and others.

In summary, for Indigenous economics, all human and nonhuman persons are deserving of respect and join relationships as equals. This includes animals, who are exempt from slavery for that reason. Among humans, men and women are equal. An example is that women controlled agricultural lands among the Iroquois and also selected the chiefs.

For standard economics, following its cultural origins, individuals are sorted into those that matter (such as white men) and those that do not (such as women, Black people, and Indians). Government is responsive to those who matter and can vote. The powerful individuals run things, and the weak can be domesticated (animals) or enslaved (humans). In addition, the humans on top are free to colonize the lands of other people, the original inhabitants. They are also allowed to tell the other people how to run their societies. The assumed differences among individuals, although slavery was outlawed, remain present in economic outcomes, for instance in the relative wages, wealth, and unemployment rates among Indian, Black, and white individuals in the United States. Indigenous peoples have the lowest economic positions in the settler societies of the Americas, Australia, and New Zealand.

Leadership

Leadership differences follow from the other consequences for structure. On the relational side, the role of leaders is to facilitate the good operation of relationships. On the individualist side, leaders are individuals who can assemble other individuals into effective firms. Hierarchy is clear here; certain individuals become the bosses. This is related to the idea of a state that has strong leaders making the state work.

In chapter 5, I detailed how Indigenous leaders are accountable to their people, are peacemakers, nurture their collectives, support all (including nonhumans) in relationships, and socialize the next generation. As explained in chapter 7, when such leaders are entrepreneurs, they organize their firms in a relational manner. They apply relational ethics both to the internal relationships of the firm and to the external impacts of their firm's activities.

In standard economics, chief operating officers in corporations are accountable to their boards of directors, who are selected by the owners of shares in the corporation. Each owner's vote depends on the number of shares he or she owns. The CEO is a decision maker who organizes the workers in the corporation to make the products it sells, market the products, and assure that the price at which the products sell covers the costs of production. Firms that are not corporations are led by the owners of the capital used in the firm; these owners can hire other workers. For both corporations and individually owned firms, the main ethical principle is to make a profit without incurring liabilities that would threaten the wealth of the firm. The liability responsibilities for damages caused by a firm's operation depend on the laws provided by the government that organizes the markets in which they operate. Firms use their wealth to influence government regulation, which then reduces firms' liabilities, allowing their wealth to remain high. Social accountability is very weak.

Land Tenure

Land tenure under Indigenous law differs from land tenure under the law of settler governments. Under Indigenous law, a common principle of Indigenous land tenure is that the community holding the land retains authority over allocation of portions of the land to members of the community for use. Land tenure in Indigenous communities is "usufruct tenure": it depends on use. The rights to exclude other members of the community from use of land under the control of persons, families, or other relational subjects depend on the authority of the community, as mediated by its leaders. Territory is assigned according to the kinds of relationships that work between humans and nonhumans. Territorial structure depends on the needs and desires of all the entities in the area. For agriculture, humans work out what fits. When berries and the products of perennial plants matter, then the plants are aligned with humans in that structure.

We can observe how these principles work out in the few communities that have retained authority to control tenure in their lands, such as the family hunting territories in Canada or in the Indigenous communities in Mexico that operate within a "shell" that allows them to allocate land internally. The laws of settler governments rarely offer a complete shell allowing Indigenous governments to fully control allocation of land within their communities. A reading of the latest edition of *Cohen's Handbook of Federal Indian Law*, for instance, reveals a complicated set of rules that have resulted from laws passed by the U.S. government and interpretation of those laws by the U.S. Supreme Court. Since the end of the nineteenth century, the U.S. Supreme Court has ruled that the U.S. Congress has full authority over Indians, with few restrictions (Newton 2012).

Chapter 4 examined the Eeyou Traditional Hunting Law, which is a contemporary example of usufruct tenure. The chapter also provided a brief summary of the rules in Mexican Indigenous communities. As with the older systems in the Pacific Northwest, holders of usufruct tenure must share a portion of the returns to their land with others in their community. Land areas are defined by the ecological characteristics of the land. Sale is allowed only if the community as a whole agrees, a condition that also was agreed to by the king of England in the Royal Proclamation of 1763.

These systems of land tenure are much different from those that are based on individual private property in the private sector and state-owned property in the public sector of countries that are organized in the way assumed by standard economic theory. Parcels subject to private ownership are laid out on the land with cadastral surveys that create land units of various types determined by the geometric concepts of the surveyors, not by the inherent characteristic of the land. In the United States, land outside the East is set up on a township-and-range system, breaking the land into square sections one mile on a side, as if the land were flat. Since the Earth is curved, the township pattern has to shift as the system moves northward, to accommodate the decrease in area as one moves toward the North Pole. Cities are laid out on a grid as well.

As reviewed in chapter 4, owners of private property control the property and do not have to share the rent that they earn on the property. To say that governments do not restrict the actions of property owners would be incorrect; governments can impose zoning restrictions and other restrictions that in the United States are called the "police power" of government. Other countries also have limitations on the powers of owners. Most importantly, land can be taxed. But in all cases, there is a market in land and ownership that is determined by the ability to purchase land rather than any conditions on the knowledge and skills of the property owner. Of course, the ability of a person to earn income affects his or her qualification to borrow funds for purchasing land, resulting in banks holding mortgages on the land. Being financially capable of purchasing the land dominates; there is no requirement that an owner understand how the land fits into relationships among persons or among other-than-human entities.

Common Pool Goods

To assert that common pool goods are more important than the other three types of goods for Indigenous economics is something that few others have stated about Indigenous worldviews. Type of goods is a recent consideration even in economics, as Ostrom described in her Nobel lecture and in the earlier presidential address to the American Political Science Association (Ostrom 1998, 2010). She credits herself and her husband, Vincent Ostrom, for realizing that common pool goods were typically omitted from the constellation of goods in standard economics, and she cited Paul Samuelson's (1954) work for proof.

The idea of a commons, however, is not new. The overexploitation of a commons was put forth as an argument for enclosing the common fields of England, a literature that was in turn cited by Garrett Hardin (1968) in his famous "tragedy of the commons" article in *Science*. Elinor Ostrom and those working with her in the International Association for the Study of Commons can take credit for thoroughly debunking Hardin's analysis. They have shown the errors of the mainstream solution to the existence of a common pool, converting it into either private or state property. The idea of a group holding the land was not acceptable in the colonies of England. Spain, however, did recognize community ownership of land, a tradition that applied in Mexico, where, as explained in chapter 4, we can still observe Indigenous methods of allocating land in communities.

The emphasis on individualism and refusal to understand the policies needed to solve the dilemmas created by common pool goods led to over-harvest and destruction of a great many common pool goods. Settler governments treated Indigenous territory as open access private goods, letting the settlers grab what they could. The Homestead Act was a case of codifying the process and limiting how much each homesteader could acquire initially. The operation of land markets would later let the small parcels be assembled into economic units. Chapter 5 explained how the dilemmas result from isolating individuals and restricting their ability to communicate or to reach sensible agreements about how to solve the dilemma that leads to excessive harvests.

The effectiveness of a relational economy for fisheries is illustrated by the house system on the Northwest Coast of North America, which is explained in my previous works (Trosper 2002, 2009) and summarized in chapter 5. The relational economy, instead of the distinction between capitalist individuals and worker individuals, has distinctions among relational subjects who are composed of both humans and nonhumans. Two different configurations can be seen along the Pacific Northwest Coast, where salmon and other species, along with the ocean and rivers, constituted the nonhumans. Under the Indigenous system, humans in houses related themselves to each of the salmon runs, which were also conceived as houses. Each run of fish was treated separately and harvest was in the rivers, either at the river mouths or upstream. Humans understood the system to be made up of relational subjects, the houses, which themselves included the salmon in the relationships. There was no overarching state, as governance at the macro level occurred as agreements among the houses.

When the British arrived, they changed the relationships. The colonial government took over the fishery and assigned fishing rights to canneries, which contracted with fishermen. Indigenous peoples continued as fishermen, but the settlers awarded increasing numbers of licenses to themselves. Both humans and salmon were seen as atoms, the humans being individuals and the salmon being nonhuman individuals as well. Capitalists owned the canneries and hired people to operate the fishing vessels. The salmon were the natural resource harvested in the ocean by the fishing boats, with no distinctions among the runs of salmon. What had been separate units of the fisheries each with a relationship to the houses became a homogeneous entity, the fishery, harvested by fishermen and canneries competing with each other. The government issued fishing licenses. When the inevitable consequence of an open-access situation occurred, the decline in the volume of fish available, the government undertook to set regulations to protect the fishery against overharvest. The fisheries biologists empowered by the government to regulate the fishery had two major problems: first, they did not really understand the structure of salmon runs, and second, they were under the control of a government that was responsible to the human individuals that elected it. The decline of the fisheries did not threaten the jobs in the government agency in the way that such declines used to threaten the positions of a house titleholder.

Key to successful organization of the salmon fisheries was an ability to observe and monitor the total value of the fishery. For the individualist system, this total value consisted of the net returns from fishing for each of the individuals. As the individuals were private, their income was also their private information. There was no way to observe the total net return from the fishery. In the Indigenous system, the fishermen in each house, and the house, pooled the net return from the fisheries and then exchanged that return with other houses in the series of potlatch feasts. Those exchanges occurred in public, with people counting the amounts donated and amounts distributed at each feast. The public as a whole, therefore, could observe the annual surplus produced by the fisheries. The titleholders were accountable to keep that return high.

Exchange

The exchange of material goods and services is a fundamental characteristic of all economies because humans always specialize in some way. The two approaches use different ways to organize exchange. Indigenous economics relies on forming relationships and carrying out exchange through the agreement that persons in relationships work out. The agreements depend on shared relational goods that help the members of relationships deal with unanticipated situations.

Mainstream economics assumes that exchange occurs through contracts between the purchasers and sellers, operating in markets. The complexity of the contracts depends on the complexity of the thing being exchanged. The sale of land, for instance, is invariably complex and involves complex contracts: an offer to sell, acceptance of the offer, an actual sale contract, verification that the seller has title to the property, a mortgage agreement with a bank if the purchaser needs to borrow money, and recording the bank as the mortgagee on the new title of the property when the title is filed in the relevant government land title office.

Turning to relational economies, transfer of land from one relationship to another is also complex but is not as well described as the working of contracts in land markets. A community's distribution of land among community members is supervised by the leaders of the community, and transfers between relational subjects are facilitated by the leaders' roles in supporting relationships.

That third-party enforcement by a nation-state can have a profound effect on the outcome of exchanges in a relational compared to a contractual economy is suggested by two experimental studies that compared two different labor markets (Brown, Falk, and Fehr 2004, 2012). One relied on firms and workers forming relationships in which both sides had to be concerned about reputation, in order to maintain agreements from period to period for fifteen periods. Firms would offer a wage and an effort level, but upon accepting the offer, the worker controlled the actual level of effort. In the other market, firms offered a wage and a proposed effort level; the workers decided which offer to accept, and then their effort was committed. A third party enforced the contracts. Their experiments with the two approaches were applied when firms outnumbered workers and when workers outnumbered firms. The resulting agreements in the two markets were quite different. The results showed that surplus production was shared more when there was no third-party enforcement.

In the absence of third-party enforcement, firms and workers established long-term relationships. When firms outnumbered workers, there was excess demand for workers and the workers received two-thirds of the net returns. When workers outnumbered firms in the relational situation, firms had better bargaining positions but could not elicit the effort they wanted without forming long-term relationships. They ended up splitting the surplus available; workers supplied effort to establish reputations in the long-term relationships.

When a third party enforced contracts, workers and firms did not establish relationships that lasted throughout the fifteen periods. When there was an excess supply of labor, firms could offer low wages that would be accepted if they covered the cost of effort. In each period, workers accepted contracts with high work effort, but the offered wages were low and 78 percent of the surplus from production went to the firms. When the situation reversed, with workers fewer than firms, the excess demand for labor led firms to receive only 29 percent of the surplus (Brown, Falk, and Fehr 2012, 895).

The situation without third-party enforcement resembles the situation when titleholders on the Northwest Coast competed with each other for workers to staff their fisheries. Titleholders were generous with workers as well as sharing surplus with each other to avoid overfishing. When the colonial government moved in and supported canneries hiring workers and enforced the contracts, wages fell for workers. As long as there was an excess supply of workers, the cannery owners obtained most of the surplus. In addition, the canneries competed with each other and eventually the fisheries crashed. The colonial governments in both the United States and Canada imposed an economy based on individualism and contracts for the fisheries along the coast, and in both countries the cannery owners made considerable profits for a period of time.

Consequences for Ideas

The differences in culture between Indigenous peoples and the settlers exist in both the fundamental assumptions about the constitution of persons

TABLE 8 Consequences for Ideas

Categories of ideas	Indigenous living well	Mainstream development
Ethics' definition of justice	Multispecies justice	Equality of opportunity among humans
Sustainability	All good relationships maintained	Denial using an oxymoron, sustainable development
Metrics	Subjective indices measuring relational goods and bads	Objective summation of prices and quantities

and the consciousness of the landscape. These key ideas are classified earlier in this chapter as fundamental assumptions, which have consequences for other ideas in the field of ethics, in the concept of sustainability, and in defining metrics for observing economic outcomes. While there are other differences, these three are significant consequences in the area of ideas, as summarized in table 8.

Ethics' Definition of Justice

Indigenous economics expands the subjects of justice to all beings, while standard economics only considers humans. This same expansion applies to business ethics. A relational business considers the impacts of its actions on all beings, while an individualized business, if it considers more than profit, examines the impact on humans either directly or indirectly through positive environmental results.

Celermajer and her co-authors (2021) credit Indigenous philosophies for anticipating, by tens of thousands of years, recent analysis in the fields of political ecology, animal rights, posthuman scholarship, and actor-network theory (121–25). By not acknowledging the prior contributions, "these conceptualisations illustrate the obliteration of Indigenous genealogies of interspecies relationality and their implications for rethinking justice and governance" (124). These approaches do not fully engage with the ideas of the entire world being "animated, agential, knowing, feeling and relational" (125) because they remain tied to dualisms and hierarchy that Indigenous thought ignores. Spiritual matters, in particular, tend to be ignored. They connect this disrespect toward Indigenous thought to colonial practices that are usually ignored by considerations of justice in terms of standard liberal philosophy.

Not only were Indigenous peoples subjected to injustice, so also were most species. The authors, following Indigenous thought, conclude:

> Multispecies justice insists on the need to account for other beings, with their own radically diverse life projects, capacities, phenomenologies, ways of being, functionings, forms of integrity, and relationalities. (Celermajer et al. 2021, 127)

To the extent that standard economics addresses issues of justice, it draws upon ideas of justice that descend from Immanuel Kant, through the recent work of John Rawls (1971, 1993), to elaborate the meaning of justice among humans. In economics, Amartya Sen (1999, 2002) stresses that individuals' access to capabilities needs to be fairly distributed, a position that omits relationality among humans (see also Evans 2002). Bowles and Gintis (1998) have argued that assets need to be fairly distributed, with the idea of assets to include access to education. Nature is ignored in these approaches except for its contributions to human well-being.

Sustainability

Indigenous conceptions of sustainability follow directly from Indigenous conceptions of environmental justice. Virtanen, Siragusa, and Guttorm (2020) introduce a special issue of *Current Opinion in Environmental Sustainability* that provides a variety of views on Indigenous ideas of sustainability, all of which address both relationality and the consciousness of all beings. The result is that the object of sustainability is all of creation.

> Indigenous peoples assert that a just path to a sustainable future must consider all relations, an approach best expressed through Indigenous knowledge systems, legal orders, governance and conceptions of justice. (McGregor, Whitaker, and Sritharan 2020, 36)

Sustainability in standard economics, to the extent it is addressed at all, centers on the idea of sustainable development, as elaborated by the United Nations' Sustainable Development Goals. As long as the word *development* is included in definitions of sustainability, the ideas are oxymorons. Development usually means unconstrained growth as well as the transformation and destruction both of nature and of human relations (Rist 2002). Connecting development to sustainability, as in sustainable development, creates an internally and necessarily contradictory idea. Sustaining relations of all kinds is central to Indigenous ideas of sustainability. This means focusing on strong sustainability as discussed in ecological economics: the maintenance of natural capital rather than transforming natural into man-made capital. Even strong sustainability, however, defines natural capital in inanimate terms.

Metrics

The first chapter gives examples of defining the goal of economic activity in the creation of new and strong relationships. This goal means supporting widespread successful relationships with their generation of relational goods, which include all species and therefore interspecies justice. When local communities define goals for themselves, one should not expect a worldwide consensus on the form of the good life. A comparison of theories should also include a comparison of their systems of measurement, as commensuration has become very important for social thought and systems of power (Espeland and Stevens 1998; Mennicken and Espeland 2019). Michel Callon (1998) and Callon and Fabian Muniesa (2005) stress the importance of calculation in the establishment of markets.

Standard economics assumes universal valuation of increases in material income as earned by individuals, what is known as gross domestic product (GDP) per capita, usually not corrected for estimated depreciation of capital. Many alternatives to GDP have been proposed. Some adjust GDP by counting things differently, such as the Index of Sustainable Economic Welfare, which starts with personal consumer expenditure and then subtracts environmental degradation and depreciation of natural capital while adding public expenditures and services from domestic labor. It also adjusts for income inequality. Others replace GDP, such as the Human Development Index, based on life expectancy, adult literacy and access to education, and GDP per capita. A European climate institute undertook an extensive survey of the many alternatives (Schepelmann, Goossens, and Makipaa 2009). It shows that they all share two characteristics: they are based on attention to individuals' well-being in addition to aggregate statistics, and the indices all can be characterized as different ways to add up factors that affect individuals. Some give heavy weight to environmental conditions. The lists of things to count vary for different indices. They also vary in the method of determining weights for each of the things counted. A market price is the usual weight, but estimates of value to humans are also used, especially for ecosystem services. A great many alternatives to GDP per capita have been proposed.

Metrics to address Indigenous concepts of the value of relationships are different from the metrics considered as alternatives to GDP. They are not measures of individual well-being; they are measures of the quality of relationships among humans and especially between humans and nonhumans. The measures also have major subjective elements. To convert subjective assessments to indices, many studies use one or more descriptive scales that ask respondents to provide an assessment using the scale. Most scales have a list such as very bad, bad, good, very good. One study emphasized that use of an odd number of positions on the scale would lead respondents to pick the middle one more often; having no middle choice made respondents think harder about their assessments (Donatuto, Campbell, and Gregory 2016).

Each of the many Māori concepts for relational goods is a candidate for such treatment. Te Kipa Kepa Brian Morgan (2006) has developed a way to measure mauri through use of a descriptive scale indicating the change in mauri from a baseline using several different types of mauri. Translating *mauri* as well-being, Morgan constructed a mauriOmeter with four categories of well-being: environmental, cultural, social, and economic. Within each category can be subcategories relevant to the particular examples. Using the mauriOmeter for environmental impact analysis requires two steps for each of the categories. First, decide on the relative importance of each of the four categories using a procedure taken from the analytic hierarchy process, which makes pairwise comparisons between the dimensions. Morgan cites a book by Thomas L. Saaty (1980) as the source. After determining the weights, respondents undertake two steps for each of the categories. The first step is to decide on impact as negative, no impact, or positive. Then, within negative, pick −1 or −2; within positive, pick +1 or +2. Many templates are provided at the website mauriometer.org for adding up the subjective estimates of mauri.

Illustrations of applying the mauriOmeter have been published. Morgan, Daniel Sardelic, and Amaria F. Wartini (2012) assess the sustainability of the Three Gorges Project in China and compare the result of assessing mauri to the cost–benefit analysis conducted by the joint venture that built the dam. Both analyses produced positive estimates of the effects of the dam; the Mauri Model Decision Making Framework, which the mauriOmeter uses, could address sustainability better than the cost–benefit results. The method has also been applied to assess the impact of a major oil spill on a coral reef in an important bay. Three recovery actions were evaluated, with full wreck removal producing the best enhancement of mauri but not full recovery to pre-wreck conditions (Morgan and Faui 2014).

Indigenous concerns have also been introduced in the literature on risk management, particularly with special reference to health. Māori have insisted that the government of New Zealand consider the impact of genetically modified organism (GMO) technology from a Māori viewpoint using the ideas of mauri and *whakapapa* (genealogy, ancestry, and resulting relationships). Terre Satterfield and Mere Roberts (2008) explain the ways the government made social accountability required by the Treaty of Waitangi. New Zealand's Environmental Risk Management Authority, in dealing with regulation of GMOs, had to expand its concept of risk to include consideration of Māori concerns. While changes in technical procedures of risk assessment are difficult, Satterfield and Roberts report the Māori made some progress on the GMO issue.

Another example of Indigenous contributions to considerations of health risk is the work of the Swinomish Indian Tribal Community and the Institute for Resources, Environment and Sustainability of the University of British Columbia to develop Indigenous Health Indicators that represent Indigenous concerns about other-than-human beings. Standard health assessments only address physical health impacts to individuals. After an initial project with the Swinomish identified four categories of indicators, consultation with five other Coast Salish communities led to development of health indicators for "community connection, natural resources security, cultural use, education, self-determination and resilience." Listed among the subcategories of the indicators are relational goods such as trust, self-esteem, and identity (Donatuto, Campbell, and Gregory 2016). The indicators were tested in a workshop in which the participants applied them to two different environmental challenges facing the tribe: the need to clean up a beach contaminated by an oil spill and the need to reduce pollution in the community's main fishing river. The researchers presented descriptive scales for each of the subcategories used in the workshop. They also used both swing weighting and pairwise comparisons to have the participants in the workshop reveal their priorities among the indicators. The sixteen workshop participants were willing to learn how to develop weights to demonstrate the importance of each indicator. The workshop and other pilot applications of the Indigenous Health Indicators demonstrated that the health assessment indicators can communicate intangible aspects of health from the point of view of community members.

Working with the Tsleil-Waututh Nation in Canada and two research centers, the Indigenous Health Indicators were combined with environmental indicators to assess the impacts of climate change on Indigenous health. Attention focused on the impacts on shellfish beds, a concern for both the Swinomish Community and the Tsleil-Waututh Nation. Workshops in each community revealed that the Indigenous Health Indicators were successful in communicating the anticipated impacts of climate change according to the participants. Each community had its own assessment, and the two were different. Each community plans to use the results in creating climate adaptation plans (Donatuto et al. 2014).

Metrics that involve adding up the value of things exchanged in markets is easy in comparison to developing qualitative comparisons about the level of effectiveness of relational goods. Because relational goods depend on the reflexivity, discourse, and mutual agreement of relational subjects, the descriptions of the situations to which they apply are unique to each particular community. As a result, making overall assessments such as can be done with the GDP of each nation-state is simply not possible. That observation in comparable terms is difficult doesn't mean the effects are not real and important, however.

Indigenization of Modernity

The purpose of this book has been to explain the logic that supports the relational economies that Indigenous peoples have retained in spite of the dominance that the people of the sailing ships have over the people of the canoe. Indigenous economics is a coherent and feasible alternative to the mainstream system that is facing such crisis. Marshall Sahlins (1999, ix–x) points out that the Inuit of Alaska, the Enga of New Guinea, and many other Indigenous peoples have maintained their cultures and are indigenizing modernity rather than succumbing to it. The introduction to this chapter may have erred in asserting that the beads in the canoe's side have attached to those of the sailing canoe. Rather, the people in the canoe have taken part of the sailor's ship and changed it to accommodate the needs of the canoe. Just as American cuisine is a mishmash of world cuisine, and the United States nonetheless remains a settler colonial state, so can an Indigenous society retain its relational economy while using computers to create a dictionary of the language and provide ways to learn it. Sahlins quotes a study that set out to see how Eskimos had survived; the organizer concluded the study by reporting, "In short, there is a determination on the part of Eskimos to maintain traditional Eskimo culture and at the same time to adopt a pragmatic acceptance of the benefits of modern technology" (J. G. Jorgensen 1990, 6). This determination exists in Indigenous peoples around the world. Although the Zapatistas said it is their goal, the world already has many worlds. The dominant economic system, in spite of little tolerance for diversity and other approaches, is not omnipotent. It should become weaker as its problems multiply and the world continues to heat up. Indigenous peoples are not in denial and can advise others who are looking for alternatives, without dictating solutions to the local problems that are proliferating. Whether the river holding the many rows survives is an open question.

REFERENCES

Alcorn, Janis B., and Victor M. Toledo. 1998. "Resilient Resource Management in Mexico's Forest Ecosystems: The Contribution of Property Rights." In *Linking Social and Ecological Systems: Management Practices and Social Mechanisms for Building Resilience*, edited by Fikret Berkes and Carl Folke, 216–49. Cambridge: Cambridge University Press.

Altmann, Philipp. 2017. "Sumak Kawsay as an Element of Local Decolonization in Ecuador." *Latin American Research Review* 52 (5): 749–59.

Anderson, M. Kat. 2005. *Tending the Wild: Native American Knowledge and the Management of California's Natural Resources*. Berkeley: University of California Press.

Anderson, Terry L. 1992. *Property Rights and Indian Economies*. Lanham, Md.: Rowman & Littlefield.

Anderson, Terry L. 1995. *Sovereign Nations or Reservations? An Economic History of American Indians*. San Francisco, Calif.: Pacific Research Institute for Public Policy.

Anderson, Terry L. 2016. *Unlocking the Wealth of Indian Nations*. Lanham, Md.: Lexington Books.

Anderson, Terry L., Bruce L. Benson, and Thomas Flanagan. 2004. *Self-Determination: The Other Path for Native Americans*. Stanford, Calif.: Stanford University Press.

Anderson, Terry L., and Bryan Leonard. 2016. "Institutions and the Wealth of Indian Nations." In *Unlocking the Wealth of Indian Nations*, edited by Terry L. Anderson, 3–17. Lanham, Md.: Lexington Books.

Apgar, Marina J., Will Allen, Kevin Moore, and James Ataria. 2015. "Understanding Adaptation and Transformation Through Indigenous Practice: The Case of the Guna of Panama." *Ecology and Society* 20 (1): 45.

Archer, Margaret S. 1996. *Culture and Agency: The Place of Culture in Social Theory*. Cambridge: Cambridge University Press.

Archer, Margaret S. 2000a. *Being Human: The Problem of Agency*. Cambridge: Cambridge University Press.

Archer, Margaret S. 2000b. "Homo Economicus, Homo Sociologicus, and Homo Sentiens." In *Rational Choice Theory: Resisting Colonization*, edited by Margaret S. Archer and Jonathon Q. Tritter, 36–56. New York: Routledge.

Archer, Margaret S. 2003. *Structure, Agency, and the Internal Conversation*. Cambridge: Cambridge University Press.

Archer, Margaret S. 2007. *Making Our Way Through the World: Human Reflexivity and Social Mobility*. New York: Cambridge University Press.

Archer, Margaret S. 2012. *The Reflexive Imperative in Late Modernity*. Cambridge: Cambridge University Press.

Arneil, Barbara. 1996. "The Wild Indian's Venison: Locke's Theory of Property and English Colonialism in America." *Political Studies* 44 (1): 60–74.

Arrow, Kenneth J. 1974. *The Limits of Organization*. New York: Norton.

Asch, Michael, John Borrows, and James Tully. 2018. *Resurgence and Reconciliation: Indigenous-Settler Relations and Earth Teachings*. Toronto: University of Toronto Press.

Associated Press. 2019. "San Juan County Formally Switches Sides in Bears Ears Debate." July 17. https://kutv.com/news/local/san-juan-county-formally-switches-sides-in-bears-ears-debate.

Atkins, Paul W. B., David Sloan Wilson, and Steven C. Hayes. 2019. *Prosocial: Using Evolutionary Science to Build Productive, Equitable, and Collaborative Groups*. Oakland, Calif.: Context Press.

Atkinson, Sarah. 2013. "Beyond Components of Well-Being: The Effects of Relational and Situated Assemblage." *Topoi* 32 (2): 137–44.

Awashish, Philip. 2018. "A Brief Introduction to the Eeyou Traditional System of Governance of Hunting Territories (Traditional Eeyou Indoh-Hoh Istchee Governance)." *Anthropologica* 60 (1): 1–4.

Barzel, Yoram. 1997. *Economic Analysis of Property Rights*. 2nd ed. Cambridge: Cambridge University Press.

Bears Ears Inter-Tribal Coalition. 2015. "Proposal to President Barack Obama for the Creation of Bears Ears National Monument." October 15. https://bearsears coalition.org/wp-content/uploads/2015/10/Bears-Ears-Inter-Tribal-Coalition-Pro posal-10-15-15.pdf.

Bergeron, Kristina Maud. 2010. "Global Activism and Changing Identities: Interconnecting the Global and the Local—The Grand Council of the Crees and the Saami Council." In *Indigenous Peoples and Autonomy: Insights for a Global Age*, edited by Mario Blaser, Ravi De Costa, Deborah McGregor, and William D. Coleman, 107–29. Vancouver: University of British Columbia Press.

Berkes, Fikret, Iain J. Davidson-Hunt, et al. 2009. "Institutions for Algonquian Land Use: Change, Continuity and Implications for Sustainable Forest Management." In *Changing the Culture of Forestry in Canada: Building Effective Institutions for Aboriginal Engagement in Sustainable Forest Management*, edited by Marc G.

Stevenson and David C. Natcher, 35–52. Occasional Publications Series 60. Edmonton: CCI Press.

Berkes, Fikret, Terry P. Hughes, et al. 2006. "Globalization, Roving Bandits, and Marine Resources." *Science* 311 (5767): 1557–58.

Bhattacharyya, Jonaki, and Scott Slocombe. 2017. "Animal Agency: Wildlife Management from a Kincentric Perspective." *Ecosphere* 8 (10): 1–17.

Bhuyan, Sanjib. 2007. "The 'People' Factor in Cooperatives: An Analysis of Members' Attitudes and Behavior." *Canadian Journal of Agricultural Economics / Revue Canadienne d'agroeconomie* 55 (3): 275–98.

Bhuyan, Sanjib, and F. Larry Leistritz. 2001. "An Examination of Characteristics and Determinants of Success of Cooperatives in the Non-Agricultural Sectors." *Journal of Cooperatives* 16 (January): 46–62.

Biolsi, Thomas. 1997. "The Anthropological Construction of 'Indians': Haviland Scudder Mekeel and the Search for the Primitive in Lakota Country." In *Indians & Anthropology: Vine Deloria Jr. and the Critique of Anthropology*, edited by Thomas Biolsi and Larry J. Zimmerman, 133–59. Tucson: University of Arizona Press.

Blaser, Mario, Ravi De Costa, Deborah McGregor, and William D. Coleman, eds. 2010. *Indigenous Peoples and Autonomy: Insights for a Global Age*. Vancouver: University of British Columbia Press.

Borrows, John. 1997. "Wampum at Niagara: The Royal Proclamation, Canadian Legal History and Self-Government." In *Aboriginal and Treaty Rights in Canada: Essays on Law, Equity, and Respect for Difference*, edited by Michael Asch, 155–72. Vancouver: University of British Columbia Press.

Bowles, Samuel. 2004. *Microeconomics: Behavior, Institutions, and Evolution*. The Roundtable Series in Behavioral Economics. New York: Russell Sage Foundation; Princeton, N.J.: Princeton University Press.

Bowles, Samuel. 2008. "Policies Designed for Self-Interested Citizens May Undermine 'the Moral Sentiments': Evidence from Economic Experiments." *Science* 320 (5883): 1605–9.

Bowles, Samuel, and Herbert Gintis. 1998. *Recasting Egalitarianism: New Rules for Communities, States, and Markets*. Edited by Erik Olin Wright. Real Utopias Project 3. New York: Verso.

Bowles, Samuel, and Herbert Gintis. 2002. "Social Capital and Community Governance." *Economic Journal* 112 (483): F419–36.

Boyd, Jeremy, and Ronald Trosper. 2009. "The Use of Joint Ventures to Accomplish Aboriginal Economic Development: Two Examples from British Columbia." *International Journal of the Commons* 4 (1): 36–55.

Brakes, Philippa, Sasha R. X. Dall, Lucy M. Aplin, Stuart Bearhop, Emma L. Carroll, Paolo Ciucci, Vicki Fishlock, John K. B. Ford, Ellen C. Garland, and Sally A. Keith. 2019. "Animal Cultures Matter for Conservation." *Science* 363 (6431): 1032–34.

Brown, Martin, Armin Falk, and Ernst Fehr. 2004. "Relational Contracts and the Nature of Market Interactions." *Econometrica* 72 (3): 747–80.

Brown, Martin, Armin Falk, and Ernst Fehr. 2012. "Competition and Relational Contracts: The Role of Unemployment as a Disciplinary Device." *Journal of the European Economic Association* 10 (4): 887–907.

Bryant, Miles T. 1998. "Cross-Cultural Understandings of Leadership: Themes from Native American Interviews." *Educational Management & Administration* 26 (1): 7–20.

Buck, Christopher. 2016. "Deganawida, the Peacemaker." In *American Writers Supplement XXVI*, edited by Jay Parani, 81–100. Farmington Hills, Mich.: Charles Scribner's Sons.

Callon, Michel. 1998. "An Essay on Framing and Overflowing: Economic Externalities Revisited by Sociology." *Sociological Review* 46 (1_suppl): 244–69.

Callon, Michel, and Fabian Muniesa. 2005. "Peripheral Vision: Economic Markets as Calculative Collective Devices." *Organization Studies* 26 (8): 1229–50.

Calloway, Colin G. 2018. *The Indian World of George Washington*. Oxford: Oxford University Press.

Camerer, Colin, and Ernst Fehr. 2004. "Measuring Social Norms and Preferences Using Experimental Games: A Guide for Social Scientists." In *Foundations of Human Sociality: Economic Experiments and Ethnographic Evidence from Fifteen Small-Scale Societies*, edited by Joseph Patrick Henrich, Robert Boyd, Samuel Bowles, Colin Camerer, Ernst Fehr, and Herbert Gintis, 55–95. New York: Oxford University Press.

Cattelino, Jessica R. 2018. "From Locke to Slots: Money and the Politics of Indigeneity." *Comparative Studies in Society and History* 60 (2): 274–307.

Celermajer, Danielle, David Schlosberg, Lauren Rickards, Makere Stewart-Harawira, Mathias Thaler, Petra Tschakert, Blanche Verlie, and Christine Winter. 2021. "Multispecies Justice: Theories, Challenges, and a Research Agenda for Environmental Politics." *Environmental Politics* 30 (1–2): 119–40.

Chaplier, Mélanie. 2018. "Property as Sharing: A Reflection on the Nature of Land Ownership Among the Cree of Eeyou Istchee after the 'Paix Des Braves.'" *Anthropologica* 60 (1): 61–75.

Chaplier, Mélanie, and Colin Scott. 2018. "Introduction: From Beavers to Land: Building on Past Debates to Unpack the Contemporary Entanglements of Algonquian Family Hunting Territories." *Anthropologica* 60 (1): 30–44.

Chichilnisky, Graciela. 1997. "What Is Sustainable Development?" *Land Economics* 73 (4): 467–91.

Christman, John. 1994. *The Myth of Property: Toward an Egalitarian Theory of Ownership*. New York: Oxford University Press.

Cirino, Erica. 2021. "Plastic World or Plastic-Free World?" *YES!*, no. 98 (Summer): 19–28.

Clark, Colin W. 1990. *Mathematical Bioeconomics: The Optimal Management of Renewable Resources*. 2nd ed. New York: John Wiley & Sons.

Clastres, Pierre. 1987. *Society Against the State: Essays in Political Anthropology*. New York: Zone Books.

Colbourne, Rick. 2018. "Indigenous Entrepreneurship and Hybrid Ventures." In *Perspectives & Approaches to Blended Value Entrepreneurship*, edited by A. Corbett and J. Katz, 93–149. Advances in Entrepreneurship, Firm Emergence and Growth 19. Bingley, UK: Emerald Publishing.

Cole, Douglas, and Ira Chaikin. 1990. *An Iron Hand upon the People: The Law Against the Potlatch on the Northwest Coast*. Seattle: University of Washington Press.

Cornell, Stephen, Miriam Jorgensen, Ian Wilson Record, and Joan Timeche. 2007. "Citizen Entrepreneurship: An Underutilized Development Resource." In *Rebuilding Native Nations: Strategies for Governance and Development*, edited by Miriam Jorgensen, 197–222. Tucson: University of Arizona Press.

Cornell, Stephen, and Joseph P. Kalt. 1992a. "Culture and Institutions as Public Goods: American Indian Economic Development as a Problem of Collective Action." In *Property Rights and Indian Economies*, edited by Terry L. Anderson, 215–52. Lanham, Md.: Rowman & Littlefield.

Cornell, Stephen, and Joseph P. Kalt. 1992b. "Reloading the Dice: Improving the Chances for Economic Development on American Indian Reservations." In *What Can Tribes Do? Strategies and Institutions in American Indian Economic Development*, edited by Stephen Cornell and Joseph P. Kalt, 1–59. Los Angeles: American Indian Studies Center, University of California.

Corntassel, Jeffrey. 2003. "Who Is Indigenous? 'Peoplehood' and Ethnonationalist Approaches to Rearticulating Indigenous Identity." *Nationalism and Ethnic Politics* 9 (1): 75–100.

Cox, Michael, Gwen Arnold, and Sergio Villamayor Tomás. 2010. "A Review of Design Principles for Community-Based Natural Resource Management." *Ecology and Society* 15 (4): 38.

Cree Trappers' Association. 2009. "Eeyou Indoh-Hoh Weeshou-Wehwun / Traditional Eeyou Hunting Law." https://www.cerp.gouv.qc.ca/fileadmin/Fichiers_clients /Documents_deposes_a_la_Commission/P-640.pdf.

Cruikshank, Julie. 2005. *Do Glaciers Listen? Local Knowledge, Colonial Encounters, & Social Imagination*. Vancouver: University of British Columbia Press.

Dale, Norman. 1999. "Cross-Cultural Community-Based Planning: Negotiating the Future of Haida Gwaii (British Columbia)." In *The Consensus Building Handbook: A Comprehensive Guide to Reaching Agreement*, edited by Sarah McKearnan and Jennifer Thomas Larmer, 923–50. Thousand Oaks, Calif.: SAGE.

Dana, Léo-Paul. 2015. "Indigenous Entrepreneurship: An Emerging Field of Research." *International Journal of Business and Globalisation* 14 (2): 158–69.

de la Cadena, Marisol. 2010. "Indigenous Cosmopolitics in the Andes: Conceptual Reflections Beyond 'Politics.'" *Cultural Anthropology* 25 (2): 334–70.

Dell, Kiri, Nimbus Staniland, and Amber Nicholson. 2018. "Economy of Mana: Where to Next?" *MAI Journal* 7 (1): 51–65.

Deloria, Vine, Jr. 1997. "Conclusion: Anthros, Indians, and Planetary Reality." In *Indians and Anthropologists: Vine Deloria Jr. and the Critique of Anthropology*, edited by Thomas Bilosi and Larry J. Zimmerman, 209–21. Tucson: University of Arizona Press.

Demsetz, Harold. 1967. "Toward a Theory of Property Rights." *American Economic Review* 57 (2): 347–59.

Diamond, Jared. 1997. *Guns, Germs, and Steel: The Fates of Human Societies*. New York: Norton.

Donald, Leland. 1997. *Aboriginal Slavery on the Northwest Coast of North America*. Berkeley: University of California Press.

Donati, Pierpaolo, and Margaret S. Archer. 2015. *The Relational Subject*. Cambridge: Cambridge University Press.

Donati, Pierpaolo, and Riccardo Prandini. 2007a. "Family and Social Capital: European Contributions." *International Review of Sociology / Revue Internationale de Sociologie* 17 (2): 205–8.

Donati, Pierpaolo, and Riccardo Prandini. 2007b. "The Family in the Light of a New Relational Theory of Primary, Secondary and Generalized Social Capital." *International Review of Sociology / Revue Internationale de Sociologie* 17 (2): 209–23.

Donatuto, Jamie, Larry Campbell, and Robin Gregory. 2016. "Developing Responsive Indicators of Indigenous Community Health." *International Journal of Environmental Research and Public Health* 13 (9): 899.

Donatuto, Jamie, Eric E. Grossman, John Konovsky, Sarah Grossman, and Larry W. Campbell. 2014. "Indigenous Community Health and Climate Change: Integrating Biophysical and Social Science Indicators." *Coastal Management* 42 (4): 355–73.

Driskill, Qwo-Li, Chris Finley, Brian Joseph Gilley, and Scott Lauria Morgensen, eds. 2011. *Queer Indigenous Studies: Critical Interventions in Theory, Politics, and Literature*. Tucson: University of Arizona Press.

Druke, Mary A. 1985. "Iroquois Treaties: Common Forms, Varying Interpretations." In *The History and Culture of Iroquois Diplomacy*, edited by Francis Jennings, 85–98. Syracuse: Syracuse University Press.

Druke, Mary A. 1987. "Linking Arms: The Structure of Iroquois Intertribal Diplomacy." In *Beyond the Covenant Chain: The Iroquois and Their Neighbors in Indian North America, 1600–1800*, edited by Daniel K. Richter and James H. Merrell, 29–39. Syracuse: Syracuse University Press.

Easterlin, Richard. 1974. "Does Economic Growth Improve the Human Lot?" In *Nations and Households in Economic Growth: Essays in Honor of Moses Abramovitz*, edited by Paul A. David and M. W. Reder, 88–125. New York: Academic Press.

Edge, Hoyt L. 1998. "Individuality in a Relational Culture: A Comparative Study." In *Tribal Epistemologies: Essays in the Philosophy of Anthropology*, edited by Helmut Wautischer, 31–39. Aldershot, UK: Ashgate.

Escobar, Arturo. 2001. "Culture Sits in Places: Reflections on Globalism and Subaltern Strategies of Localization." *Political Geography* 20 (2): 139–74.

Espeland, Wendy Nelson, and Mitchell L. Stevens. 1998. "Commensuration as a Social Process." *Annual Review of Sociology* 24 (1): 313–43.

Evans, Peter. 2002. "Collective Capabilities, Culture, and Amartya Sen's Development as Freedom." *Studies in Comparative International Development* 37 (2): 54–60.

Executive Office of the President. 2017a. "Establishment of the Bears Ears National Monument." *Federal Register* 82 (January): 1139–47.

Executive Office of the President. 2017b. "Modifying the Bears Ears National Monument." *Federal Register* 82 (December): 58081–87.

Executive Office of the President. 2021. "Bears Ears National Monument." *Federal Register* 86 (October): 57321–34.

Farella, John R. 1984. *The Main Stalk: A Synthesis of Navajo Philosophy*. Tucson: University of Arizona Press.

Feit, Harvey A. 1988. "Waswanipi Cree Management of Land and Wildlife: Cree Ethno-ecology Revisited." In *Native People, Native Lands: Canadian Indians, Inuit and Metis*, edited by Bruce Alden Cox, 75–91. Ottawa: Carleton University Press.

Feit, Harvey A. 1991. "The Construction of Algonquian Hunting Territories: Private Property as Moral Lesson, Policy Advocacy, and Ethnographic Error." In *Colonial Situations: Essays on the Contextualization of Ethnographic Knowledge*, edited by George W. Stocking Jr., 109–34. History of Anthropology 7. Madison: University of Wisconsin Press.

Feng, Li, Anna Friis, and Jerker Nilsson. 2016. "Social Capital Among Members in Grain Marketing Cooperatives of Different Sizes." *Agribusiness* 32 (1): 113–26.

Fenton, William N. 1998. *The Great Law and the Longhouse: A Political History of the Iroquois Confederacy*. Norman: University of Oklahoma Press.

Ferguson, Jenanne, and Marissa Weaselboy. 2020. "Indigenous Sustainable Relations: Considering Land in Language and Language in Land." *Current Opinion in Environmental Sustainability* 43 (April): 1–7.

Fernández Osco, Marcelo. 2010. "Ayllu: Decolonial Critical Thinking and (an)Other Autonomy." In *Indigenous Peoples and Autonomy: Insights for a Global Age*, edited by Mario Blaser, Ravi De Costa, Deborah McGregor, and William D. Coleman, 27–45. Vancouver: University of British Columbia Press.

Finkelstein, Sydney. 2003. *Why Smart Executives Fail*. New York: Portfolio Books.

Finkelstein, Sydney. 2004. "The Seven Habits of Spectacularly Unsuccessful Executives." *Ivey Business Journal* 68 (3): 1–6.

Finley, Vernon. 2015. Interview with the author, Pablo, Mont., September 14.

Fisher, Roger, and Scott Brown. 1988. *Getting Together: Building Relationships as We Negotiate*. Boston: Houghton Mifflin.

Fiske, Jo-Anne, and Betty Patrick. 2000. *Cis Dideen Kat = When the Plumes Rise: The Way of the Lake Babine Nation*. Vancouver: University of British Columbia Press.

Fitzpatrick, Daniel. 2006. "Evolution and Chaos in Property Rights Systems: The Third World Tragedy of Contested Access." *Yale Law Journal* 115:996–1048.

Franz, Daniel. 2021. "The Subdelegation Doctrine as a Legal Tool for Establishing Tribal Comanagement of Public Lands: Through the Lens of Bears Ears National Monument." *Colorado Natural Resources Energy & Environment Law Review* 32 (1): 1–40.

Galbraith, John Kenneth. 1964. "Economics and the Quality of Life." *Science* 145 (3628): 117–23.

Gaspart, Frederic, and Erika Seki. 2003. "Cooperation, Status Seeking and Competitive Behaviour: Theory and Evidence." *Journal of Economic Behavior Organization* 51 (1): 51–77.

Geertz, Clifford. 1963. *Peddlers and Princes: Social Change and Economic Modernization in Two Indonesian Towns*. Chicago: University of Chicago Press.

Giovannini, Michela. 2015. "Indigenous Community Enterprises in Chiapas: A Vehicle for *Buen Vivir*?" *Community Development Journal* 50 (1): 71–87.

Gisday Wa and Delgam Uukw. 1992. *The Spirit in the Land: Statements of the Gitksan and Wet'suwet'en Hereditary Chiefs in the Supreme Court of British Columbia, 1987–1990*. Gabriola, B.C.: Reflections.

Goldberg, Carole E. 1997. "Overextended Borrowing: Tribal Peacemaking Applied in Non-Indian Disputes." *Washington Law Review* 72:1003–19.

Gone, Joseph P. 2006. "Mental Health, Wellness, and the Quest for an Authentic American Indian Identity." In *Mental Health Care for Urban Indians: Clinical Insights from Native Practitioners*, edited by Tawa M. Witko, 55–80. Washington, D.C.: American Psychological Association.

Gordon, H. Scott. 1954. "The Economic Theory of a Common-Property Resource: The Fishery." *Journal of Political Economy* 62 (2): 124–42.

Gould, Rachelle K., Māhealani Pai, Barbara Muraca, and Kai MA Chan. 2019. "He 'ike 'ana Ia i Ka Pono (It Is a Recognizing of the Right Thing): How One Indigenous Worldview Informs Relational Values and Social Values." *Sustainability Science* 14 (5): 1213–32.

Gowdy, John M. 2000. "Terms and Concepts in Ecological Economics." *Wildlife Society Bulletin* 28 (1): 26–33.

Graeber, David, and David Wengrow. 2021. *The Dawn of Everything: A New History of Humanity*. New York: Farrar, Straus and Giroux.

Granovetter, Mark. 1985. "Economic Action and Social Structure: The Problem of Embeddedness." *American Journal of Sociology* 91 (3): 481–510.

Grant, Kenneth, and Jonathan Taylor. 2007. "Managing the Boundary Between Business and Politics: Strategies for Improving the Chances for Success in Tribally Owned Enterprises." In *Rebuilding Native Nations: Strategies for Governance and Development*, edited by Miriam Jorgensen, 175–96. Tucson: University of Arizona Press.

Greenwald, Emily. 2002. *Reconfiguring the Reservation: The Nez Perces, Jicarilla Apaches, and the Dawes Act*. Albuquerque: University of New Mexico Press.

Grinde, Donald A. 1992. "Iroquois Political Theory and the Roots of American Democracy." In *Exiled in the Land of the Free: Democracy, Indian Nations, and the U.S. Constitution*, edited by Oren Lyons, John Mohawk, Vine Deloria Jr., Laurence Hauptman, Howard Berman, Donald Grinde, Curtis Berkey, and Robert Venables, 227–80. Santa Fe, N.Mex.: Clear Light Publishers.

Grinde, Donald A., and Bruce E. Johansen. 1991. *Exemplar of Liberty: Native America and the Evolution of Democracy*. 3rd ed. Native American Politics Series 3. Los Angeles: American Indian Studies Center, University of California, Los Angeles.

Gudynas, Eduardo. 2011. "Buen Vivir: Today's Tomorrow." *Development* 54 (4): 441–47.

Guiso, Luigi, Paola Sapienza, and Luigi Zingales. 2011. "Civic Capital as the Missing Link." In *Social Economics Handbook*, edited by Jess Benhabib, Alberto Bisin, and Matthew O. Jackson, 1:417–80. London: Elsevier.

Hardin, Garrett. 1968. "The Tragedy of the Commons." *Science* 162 (3859): 1243–48.

Harrington, Charles F., Carolyn Birmingham, and Daniel Steward. 2017. "American Indian Entrepreneurship." In *American Indian Business: Principles and Practices*, edited by Deanna M. Kennedy, Charles F. Harrington, Amy Klemm Verbos, Daniel Steward, Joseph Scott Gladstone, and Gavin Clarkson, 27–45. Seattle: University of Washington Press.

Harris, Douglas C. 2001. *Fish, Law, and Colonialism: The Legal Capture of Salmon in British Columbia*. Toronto: University of Toronto Press.

Heal, Geoffrey. 1998. *Valuing the Future: Economic Theory and Sustainability*. Economics for a Sustainable Earth Series. New York: Columbia University Press.

Henare, Manuka. 2001. "Tapu, Mana, Mauri, Hau, Wairua: A Maori Philosophy of Vitalism and Cosmos." In *Indigenous Traditions and Ecology: The Interbeing of Cosmology and Community*, edited by John A. Grim, 197–221. Cambridge, Mass.: Harvard University Press.

Hewitt, John Napoleon Brinton. 1920. "A Constitutional League of Peace in the Stone Age of America: The League of the Iroquois and Its Constitution." In *Annual Report of the Board of Regents of the Smithsonian, 1918*, 527–45. Washington, D.C.: U.S. Government Printing Office.

Higgs, Robert. 1996. "Legally Induced Technical Regress in the Washington Salmon Fishery." In *Empirical Studies in Institutional Change*, edited by Lee H. Alston, Douglass C. North, and Thrainn Eggertsson, 247–79. Cambridge: Cambridge University Press.

Hindle, Kevin. 2010. "How Community Context Affects Entrepreneurial Process: A Diagnostic Framework." *Entrepreneurship and Regional Development* 22 (7–8): 599–647.

Hindle, Kevin, and Michele Lansdowne. 2005. "Brave Spirits on New Paths: Toward a Globally Relevant Paradigm of Indigenous Entrepreneurship Research." *Journal of Small Business and Entrepreneurship* 18 (2): 131–42.

Hindle, Kevin, and Peter Moroz. 2010. "Indigenous Entrepreneurship as a Research Field: Developing a Definitional Framework from the Emerging Canon." *International Entrepreneurship and Management Journal* 6 (4): 357–85.

Holm, Tom, J. Diane Pearson, and Ben Chavis. 2003. "Peoplehood: A Model for the Extension of Sovereignty in American Indian Studies." *Wicazo Sa Review* 18 (1): 7–24.

Holmes, Elizabeth, Henry Lickers, and Brian Barkley. 2002. "A Critical Assessment of Ten Years of On-the-Ground Sustainable Forestry in Eastern Ontario's Settled Landscape." *Forestry Chronicle* 78 (5): 643–47.

Holmes, Miles C. C., and Wanta Jampijinpa. 2013. "Law for Country: The Structure of Warlpiri Ecological Knowledge and Its Application to Natural Resource Management and Ecosystem Stewardship." *Ecology and Society* 18 (3): 19.

Hotte, Ngaio, Stephen Wyatt, and Robert Kozak. 2018. "Influences on Trust During Collaborative Forest Governance: A Case Study from Haida Gwaii." *Canadian Journal of Forest Research* 49 (4): 361–74.

Huffman, Terry. 2001. "Resistance Theory and the Transculturation Hypothesis as Explanations of College Attrition and Persistence Among Culturally Traditional American Indian Students." *Journal of American Indian Education* 40 (3): 1–23.

Huffman, Terry. 2008. *American Indian Higher Educational Experiences: Cultural Visions and Personal Journeys.* New York: Peter Lang.

Huffman, Terry. 2013. "Native American Educators' Perceptions on Cultural Identity and Tribal Cultural Education: An Application of Transculturation Theory." *Journal of American Indian Education* 52 (3): 21–40.

Huntsinger, Lynn, and Sarah McCaffrey. 1995. "A Forest for the Trees: Forest Management and the Yurok Environment, 1850 to 1994." *American Indian Culture and Research Journal* 19 (4): 155–92.

Hurt, R. Douglas. 1987. *Indian Agriculture in America: Prehistory to the Present.* Lawrence: University Press of Kansas.

Hyden, Goran. 2006. *African Politics in Comparative Perspective.* Cambridge: Cambridge University Press.

Ishizawa, Jorge. 2006. "Cosmovisions and Environmental Governance: The Case of In Situ Conservation of Native Cultivated Plants and Their Wild Relatives in Peru." In *Bridging Scales and Knowledge Systems: Concepts and Applications in Ecosystem Assessment,* edited by Walter V. Reid, Fikret Berkes, Thomas Wilbanks, and Doris Capistrano, 207–24. Washington, D.C.: Island Press.

Jacobs, Sue-Ellen, Wesley Thomas, and Sabine Lang. 1997. *Two-Spirit People: Native American Gender Identity, Sexuality, and Spirituality.* Urbana: University of Illinois Press.

Jennings, Francis. 1976. *The Invasion of America: Indians, Colonialism, and the Cant of Conquest.* New York: Norton.

Jorgensen, Joseph G. 1990. *Oil Age Eskimos.* Berkeley: University of California Press.

Jorgensen, Miriam, ed. 2007. *Rebuilding Native Nations: Strategies for Governance and Development.* Tucson: University of Arizona Press.

Kauffman, Craig M., and Pamela L. Martin. 2014. "Scaling Up Buen Vivir: Globalizing Local Environmental Governance from Ecuador." *Global Environmental Politics* 14 (1): 40–58.

Kauffman, Craig M., and Pamela L. Martin. 2018. "Constructing Rights of Nature Norms in the US, Ecuador, and New Zealand." *Global Environmental Politics* 18 (4): 43–62.

Kealiikanakaoleohaililani, Kekuhi, and Christian P. Giardina. 2016. "Embracing the Sacred: An Indigenous Framework for Tomorrow's Sustainability Science." *Sustainability Science* 11 (1): 57–67.

Kelly, Dara. 2017. "Feed the People and You Will Never Go Hungry: Illuminating Coast Salish Economy of Affection." PhD diss., University of Auckland.

Kennedy, Deanna M., Charles F. Harrington, Amy Klemm Verbos, Daniel Stewart, Joseph Scott Gladstone, and Gavin Clarkson. 2017. *American Indian Business: Principles and Practices.* Seattle: University of Washington Press.

Kenny, Carolyn, and Tina Ngaroimata Fraser. 2012. *Living Indigenous Leadership: Native Narratives on Building Strong Communities.* Vancouver: University of British Columbia Press.

Ketilson, Lou Hammond, and Ian MacPherson. 2001. *Aboriginal Co-operatives in Canada: Current Situation and Potential for Growth.* Centre for the Study of Co-operatives, University of Saskatchewan. https://usaskstudies.coop/documents /books,-booklets,-proceedings/aboriginal-co-ops.pdf.

Kimmerer, Robin Wall. 2013. *Braiding Sweetgrass: Indigenous Wisdom, Scientific Knowledge, and the Teachings of Plants.* Minneapolis, Minn.: Milkweed.

Koch, Alexander, Chris Brierley, Mark M. Maslin, and Simon L. Lewis. 2019. "Earth System Impacts of the European Arrival and Great Dying in the Americas After 1492." *Quaternary Science Reviews* 207 (1): 13–36.

Kothari, Ashish, Ariel Salleh, Arturo Escobar, Federico Demaria, and Alberto Acosta. 2019. *Pluriverse: A Post-development Dictionary.* New Delhi: Tulika Books.

Krakoff, Sarah. 2018. "Public Lands, Conservation, and the Possibility of Justice." *Harvard Civil Rights-Civil Liberties Law Review* 53 (1): 213–58.

Laastad, Synneva Geithus. 2019. "Nature as a Subject of Rights? National Discourses on Ecuador's Constitutional Rights of Nature." *Forum for Development Studies* 47 (3): 401–25.

Lang, Richard, and Dietmar Roessl. 2011. "The Role of Social Capital in the Development of Community-Based Co-operatives." In *New Developments in the Theory of Networks: Contributions to Management Science,* edited by Mika Tuunanen, Josef Windsperger, Gérard Cliquet, and George Hendrikse, 353–70. Heidelberg: Physica.

Langdon, Stephen J. 2007. "Sustaining a Relationship: Inquiry into the Emergence of a Logic of Engagement with Salmon Among the Southern Tlingits." In *Native Americans and the Environment: Perspectives on the Ecological Indian,* edited by Michael E. Harkin and David Rich Lewis, 233–73. Lincoln: University of Nebraska Press.

Lansing, J. Stephen. 2007. *Priests and Programmers: Technologies of Power in the Engineered Landscape of Bali.* Princeton, N.J.: Princeton University Press.

Latour, Bruno. 2004. *Politics of Nature: How to Bring the Sciences into Democracy.* Cambridge, Mass.: Harvard University Press.

Leeds, Stacy L. 2006. "Moving Toward Exclusive Tribal Autonomy over Lands and Natural Resources." *Natural Resources Journal* 46 (2): 439–61.

Lemelin, Raynald Harvey, and F. Henry Lickers. 2004. "Implementing Capacity-Building, Respect, Equity, and Empowerment (CREE) in the Social Sciences." In *Parks and Protected Areas Research in Ontario, 2004: Proceedings of the Parks and Research Forum of Ontario Annual General Meeting, May 4–6, 2004,* edited by Christina K. Rehbein et al., 251–62. Waterloo, Ont.: Parks Research Forum of Ontario.

Lewis, Henry T. 1993. "Patterns of Indian Burning in California: Ecology and Ethnohistory." In *Before the Wilderness: Environmental Management by Native Californians,* edited by Thomas C. Blackburn and Kat Anderson, 55–116. Menlo Park, Calif.: Ballena Press.

Lewis, Henry T. 2002. "An Anthropological Critique." In *Forgotten Fires: Native Americans and the Transient Wilderness,* edited by Henry T. Lewis and M. Kat Anderson, 17–36. Norman: University of Oklahoma Press.

Libecap, Gary D. 1989. *Contracting for Property Rights.* Cambridge: Cambridge University Press.

Malkin, Jennifer. 2004. "Native Entrepreneurship: Challenges and Opportunities for Rural Communities." With Brian Dabson, Kim Pate, and Amy Mathews. CFED and Northwest Area Foundation, December. https://community-wealth.org/sites/clone.community-wealth.org/files/downloads/report-malkin-et-al.pdf.

Marglin, Stephen A. 2008. *The Dismal Science: How Thinking like an Economist Undermines Community.* Cambridge, Mass.: Harvard University Press.

Marshall Thomas, Elizabeth. 1994. *The Tribe of Tiger: Cats and Their Culture.* New York: Simon & Schuster.

Martin, Pamela L. 2011. "Global Governance from the Amazon: Leaving Oil Underground in Yasuni National Park, Ecuador." *Global Environmental Politics* 11 (4): 22–42.

McGregor, Deborah. 2014. "Lessons for Collaboration Involving Traditional Knowledge and Environmental Governance in Ontario, Canada." *AlterNative: An International Journal of Indigenous Peoples* 10 (4): 340–53.

McGregor, Deborah, Steven Whitaker, and Mahisha Sritharan. 2020. "Indigenous Environmental Justice and Sustainability." *Current Opinion in Environmental Sustainability* 43 (April): 35–40.

Meek, Ronald L. 1976. *Social Science and the Ignoble Savage.* Cambridge: Cambridge University Press.

Mennicken, Andrea, and Wendy Nelson Espeland. 2019. "What's New with Numbers? Sociological Approaches to the Study of Quantification." *Annual Review of Sociology* 45: 223–45.

Mika, Jason Paul, Rick Colbourne, and Shamika Almeida. 2020. "Responsible Management: An Indigenous Perspective." In *Research Handbook of Responsible Management,* edited by edited by Oliver Laasch, Roy Suddaby, R. E. Freeman, and Dima Jamali, 260–76. Northampton, Mass.: Edward Elgar.

Miller, Andrew M., and Iain Davidson-Hunt. 2013. "Agency and Resilience: Teachings of Pikangikum First Nation Elders, Northwestern Ontario." *Ecology and Society* 18 (3): 9.

Miller, Robert J., Miriam Jorgensen, and Daniel Stewart, eds. 2019. *Creating Private Sector Economies in Native America: Sustainable Development Through Entrepreneurship*. Cambridge: Cambridge University Press.

Mills, Antonia. 1994. *Eagle Down Is Our Law: Witsuwit'en Law, Feasts, and Land Claims*. Vancouver: University of British Columbia Press.

Milner, Matthew, and Richard Ngata. 2021. "The Indigenous Custom Behind New Zealand's Strong Covid-19 Response." *Washington Post*, March 11.

Milnor, John. 1995. "A Nobel Prize for John Nash." *Mathematical Intelligencer* 17 (3): 11–17.

Morantz, Toby. 1986. "Historical Perspectives on Family Hunting Territories in Eastern James Bay." *Anthropologica* 28 (1/2): 64–91.

Morantz, Toby. 2018. "Foreword: Remembering the Algonquian Family Hunting Territory Debate." *Anthropologica* 60 (1): 10–20.

Morgan, Te Kipa Kepa Brian. 2006. "Decision-Support Tools and the Indigenous Paradigm." *Proceedings of the Institution of Civil Engineers: Engineering Sustainability* 159:169–77.

Morgan, Te Kipa Kepa Brian, and Tumanako Ngawhika Faui. 2014. "Decision Support Systems and Promoting Socially Just Environmental Management." *Proceedings, 11th International Conference on Hydroinformatics* 449. https://academicworks.cuny.edu/cc_conf_hic/449/.

Morgan, Te Kipa Kepa Brian, Daniel N. Sardelic, and Amaria F. Waretini. 2012. "The Three Gorges Project: How Sustainable?" *Journal of Hydrology* 460:1–12.

Morgensen, Scott Lauria. 2011. *Spaces Between Us: Queer Settler Colonialism and Indigenous Decolonization*. Minneapolis: University of Minnesota Press.

Muir, William M. 1996. "Group Selection for Adaptation to Multiple-Hen Cages: Selection Program and Direct Responses." *Poultry Science* 75 (4): 447–58.

Nadasdy, Paul. 2003. *Hunters and Bureaucrats: Power, Knowledge, and Aboriginal-State Relations in the Southwest Yukon*. Vancouver: University of British Columbia Press.

Nadasdy, Paul. 2007. "The Gift in the Animal: The Ontology of Hunting and Human-Animal Sociality." *American Ethnologist* 34 (1): 25–43.

Nash, John F. 1950. "Equilibrium Points in N-Person Games." *Proceedings of the National Academy of Sciences* 36 (1): 48–49.

Necefer, Len, and Taylor Luneau. 2018. "Conflict and Cooperation Between Tribes, Climbers, and the Outdoor Industry in Large Landscape Conservation in the Bears Ears National Monument." Department of American Indian Studies, University of Arizona. Manuscript in author's possession.

Newton, Nell Jessup, ed. 2012. *Cohen's Handbook of Federal Indian Law*. San Francisco: LexisNexis.

Nielsen, Marianne O., and James W. Zion, eds. 2005. *Navajo Nation Peacemaking: Living Traditional Justice*. Tucson: University of Arizona Press.

Nilsson, Jerker. 2001. "Organisational Principles for Co-operative Firms." *Scandinavian Journal of Management* 17 (3): 329–56.

Nilsson, Jerker, and George Hendrikse. 2011. "*Gemeinschaft* and *Gesellschaft* in Co-operatives." In *New Developments in the Theory of Networks: Contributions to Management Science,* edited by Mika Tuunanen, Josef Windsperger, Gérard Cliquet, and George Hendrikse, 339–52. Contributions to Management Science. Heidelberg: Physica.

Nisga'a Lisims Government. 1998. "Constitution of the Nisga'a Nation." http://www.nisgaanation.ca/legislation/constitution-nisgaa-nation.

O'Nell, Theresa DeLeane. 1996. *Disciplined Hearts: History, Identity, and Depression in an American Indian Community.* Berkeley: University of California Press.

Ontario Ministry of Natural Resources. 2009. "2012–2022 Forest Management Plan for the Whitefeather Forest." https://nrip.mnr.gov.on.ca/s/published-submission?language=en_US&recordId=a0z3g000000CdVaAAK.

Ostrom, Elinor. 1990. *Governing the Commons: The Evolution of Institutions for Collective Action.* New York: Cambridge University Press.

Ostrom, Elinor. 1998. "A Behavioral Approach to the Rational Choice Theory of Collective Action: Presidential Address, American Political Science Association, 1997." *American Political Science Review* 92 (1): 1–22.

Ostrom, Elinor. 2005. *Understanding Institutional Diversity.* Princeton, N.J.: Princeton University Press.

Ostrom, Elinor. 2010. "Beyond Markets and States: Polycentric Governance of Complex Economic Systems." *American Economic Review* 100 (3): 641–72.

Otis, D. S. 1973. *The Dawes Act and the Allotment of Indian Land.* Norman: University of Oklahoma Press.

Parmenter, Jon. 2013. "The Meaning of *Kaswentha* and the Two Row Wampum Belt in Haudenosaunee (Iroquois) History: Can Indigenous Oral Tradition Be Reconciled with the Documentary Record?" *Journal of Early American History* 3 (1): 82–109.

Parrotta, John, and Ronald L. Trosper, eds. 2012. *Traditional Forest Knowledge: Sustaining Communities, Ecosystems and Biocultural Diversity.* Dordrecht: Springer.

Penner, J. E. 1997. *The Idea of Property in Law.* Oxford: Clarendon.

Pérotin, Virginie. 2013. "Worker Cooperatives: Good, Sustainable Jobs in the Community." *Journal of Entrepreneurial and Organizational Diversity* 2 (2): 34–47.

Pierotti, Raymond. 2010. *Indigenous Knowledge, Ecology and Evolutionary Biology.* London: Routledge.

Pikangikum First Nation and Ontario Ministry of Natural Resources (PFN and OMNR). 2006. *Keeping the Land: A Land Use Strategy for the Whitefeather Forest and Adjacent Areas.* Red Lake, Ont.: Ontario Ministry of Natural Resources. https://www.whitefeatherforest.ca/wp-content/uploads/2008/06/land-use-strategy.pdf.

Popper, Karl. 1978. "Three Worlds: The Tanner Lecture on Human Values, Delivered at the University of Michigan, April 7, 1978." https://www.thee-online.com/Documents/Popper-3Worlds.pdf.

Porpora, Douglas V. 2015. *Reconstructing Sociology: The Critical Realist Approach.* Cambridge: Cambridge University Press.

Porter, Robert B. 1997. "Strengthening Tribal Sovereignty Through Peacemaking: How the Anglo-American Legal Tradition Destroys Indigenous Societies." *Columbia Human Rights Law Review* 28:235–305.

Pretty, Jules. 2003. "Social Capital and the Collective Management of Resources." *Science* 302 (5652): 1912–14.

Pretty, Jules, Bill Adams, Fikret Berkes, S. Ferreira De Athayde, Nigel Dudley, Eugene Hunn, Luisa Maffi, Kay Milton, David Rapport, and Paul Robbins. 2009. "The Intersections of Biological Diversity and Cultural Diversity: Towards Integration." *Conservation and Society* 7 (2): 100–112.

Pretty, Jules, and Hugh Ward. 2001. "Social Capital and the Environment." *World Development* 29 (2): 209–27.

Principles Committee. 2015. "Guidance Notes to the Co-operative Principles." International Co-operative Alliance. https://www.ica.coop/sites/default/files/publication-files/ica-guidance-notes-en-310629900.pdf.

Pugliese, Joseph. 2013. "Biopolitical Caesurae of State Violence." In *State Violence and the Execution of Law: Biopolitical Caesurae of Torture, Black Sites, Drone*, edited by Joseph Pugliese, 33–55. New York: Routledge.

Putnam, Robert D. 1993. *Making Democracy Work: Civic Traditions in Modern Italy*. Princeton, N.J.: Princeton University Press.

Rata, Elizabeth. 1999. "The Theory of Neotribal Capitalism." *Review (Fernand Braudel Center)* 22 (3): 231–88.

Rata, Elizabeth. 2011. "Encircling the Commons: Neotribal Capitalism in New Zealand Since 2000." *Anthropological Theory* 11 (3): 327–53.

Ratten, Vanessa, and Léo-Paul Dana. 2017. "Gendered Perspective of Indigenous Entrepreneurship." *Small Enterprise Research* 24 (1): 62–72.

Rawls, John. 1971. *A Theory of Justice*. Cambridge, Mass.: Harvard University Press.

Rawls, John. 1993. *Political Liberalism*. New York: Colombia University Press.

Rigsby, Bruce. 2014. "A Survey of Property Theory and Tenure Types." In *Customary Marine Tenure in Australia*, edited by Nicolas Peterson and Bruce Rigsby, 37–77. Sydney: Sydney University Press.

Rist, Gilbert. 1997. *The History of Development: From Western Origins to Global Faith*. New York: Zed Books.

Rist, Gilbert. 2002. *The History of Development: From Western Origins to Global Faith*. Rev. ed. New York: Zed Books.

Robbins, Lionel. 1952. *An Essay on the Nature and Significance of Economic Science*. 2nd ed. London: Macmillan.

Roscoe, Will. 1988. *Living the Spirit: A Gay American Indian Anthology*. New York: St. Martin's.

Roscoe, Will. 1998. *Changing Ones: Third and Fourth Genders in Native North America*. New York: St. Martin's.

Rose, Samuel W. 2015. "Two Thematic Manifestations of Neotribal Capitalism in the United States." *Anthropological Theory* 15 (2): 218–38.

Rott, Nathan. 2021. "Deb Haaland Confirmed as 1st Native American Interior Secretary." NPR, March 15. https://www.npr.org/2021/03/15/977558590/deb-haaland-confirmed-as-first-native-american-interior-secretary.

Ruben, Ruerd, and Jorge Heras. 2012. "Social Capital, Governance and Performance of Ethiopian Coffee Cooperatives." *Annals of Public and Cooperative Economics* 83 (4): 463–84.

Ruple, John C. 2019. "The Trump Administration and Lessons Not Learned from Prior National Monument Modifications." *Harvard Environmental Law Review* 43:1–76.

Saaty, Thomas L. 1980. *The Analytic Hierarchy Process: Planning, Priority Setting, Resource Allocation*. New York: McGraw-Hill.

Sahlins, Marshall. 1976. *Culture and Practical Reason*. Chicago: University of Chicago Press.

Sahlins, Marshall. 1996. "The Sadness of Sweetness: The Native Anthropology of Western Cosmology." *Current Anthropology* 37 (3): 395–428.

Sahlins, Marshall. 1999. "What Is Anthropological Enlightenment? Some Lessons of the Twentieth Century." *Annual Review of Anthropology* 28 (1): i–xxiii.

Salmón, Enrique. 2000. "Kincentric Ecology: Indigenous Perceptions of the Human-Nature Relationship." *Ecological Applications* 10 (5): 1327–32.

Salway Black, Sherry. 1994. "Redefining Success in Community Development: A New Approach for Determining and Measuring the Impact of Development." Richard Schramm Paper on Community Development. Lincoln Filene Centre, Tufts University, Medford, Mass.

Samuelson, Paul A. 1954. "The Pure Theory of Public Expenditure." *Review of Economics and Statistics* 36 (4): 387–89.

Sandefur, Gary, and Philip J. Deloria. 2018. "Indigenous Leadership." *Daedalus* 147 (2): 124–35.

Sanders, Katherine. 2018. "'Beyond Human Ownership'? Property, Power and Legal Personality for Nature in Aotearoa New Zealand." *Journal of Environmental Law* 30 (2): 207–34.

Sato, Hajime. 2018. "The Emergence of 'Modern' Ownership Rights Rather than Property Rights." *Journal of Economic Issues* 52 (3): 676–93.

Satterfield, Terre, and Mere Roberts. 2008. "Incommensurate Risks and the Regulator's Dilemma: Considering Culture in the Governance of Genetically Modified Organisms." *New Genetics and Society* 27 (3): 201–16.

Schepelmann, Philipp, Yanne Goossens, and Arttu Makipaa, eds. 2009. *Towards Sustainable Development: Alternatives to GDP for Measuring Progress*. Wuppertal Special 42. Berlin: Wuppertal Institut for Klima, Umwelt, Energie.

Scott, Colin. 1986. "Hunting Territories, Hunting Bosses and Communal Production Among Coastal James Bay Cree." *Anthropologica* 28 (1/2): 163–73.

Scott, Colin. 2018. "Family Territories, Community Territories: Balancing Rights and Responsibilities Through Time." *Anthropologica* 60 (1): 90–105.

Scott, James C. 2009. *The Art of Not Being Governed: An Anarchist History of Upland Southeast Asia*. New Haven, Conn.: Yale University Press.

Sen, Amartya. 1999. *Development as Freedom*. New York: Anchor Books.

Sen, Amartya. 2002. "Response to Commentaries." *Studies in Comparative International Development* 37 (2): 78–86.

Shearer, Janene, Paddy Peters, and Iain J. Davidson-Hunt. 2009. "Co-producing a Whitefeather Forest Cultural Landscape Monitoring Framework." In *Changing the Culture of Forestry in Canada: Building Effective Institutions for Aboriginal Engagement in Sustainable Forest Management*, edited by Marc G. Stevenson and David C. Natcher, 63–84. Occasional Publications Series 60. Edmonton: CCI Press.

Shoemaker, Jessica A. 2019. "The Challenges of American Indian Land Tenure and the Vastness of Entrepreneurial Potential." In *Creating Private Sector Economies in Native America*, edited by Robert J. Miller, Miriam Jorgensen, and Daniel Stewart, 67–81. Cambridge: Cambridge University Press.

Simard, Suzanne W. 2009. "The Foundational Role of Mycorrhizal Networks in Self-Organization of Interior Douglas-Fir Forests." *Forest Ecology and Management* 258:S95–107.

Simard, Suzanne W. 2018. "Mycorrhizal Networks Facilitate Tree Communication, Learning, and Memory." In *Memory and Learning in Plants*, edited by František Baluška, Monica Gagliano, and Guenther Witzany, 191–213. Chalm, Switzerland: Springer.

Simpson, Leanne Betasamosake. 2017. *As We Have Always Done: Indigenous Freedom Through Radical Resistance*. Minneapolis: University of Minnesota Press.

Spiller, Chellie, Ljiljana Erakovic, Manuka Henare, and Edwina Pio. 2011. "Relational Well-Being and Wealth: Maori Businesses and an Ethic of Care." *Journal of Business Ethics* 98 (1): 153–69.

Spiller, Chellie, Edwina Pio, Lijijana Erakovic, and Manuka Henare. 2011. "Wise Up: Creating Organizational Wisdom Through an Ethic of *Kaitiakitanga*." *Journal of Business Ethics* 104 (2): 223–35.

Starr, Douglas. 2019. "The Confession." *Science* 364 (6445): 1022–26.

Stevens, Taylor. 2019. "'I'm Sure It's a Culture Shock for Most of You': Navajos Take the Majority on the San Juan County Commission." *Salt Lake City Tribune*, January 7.

Stoffle, Richard W., Richard Arnold, and Angelita Bulletts. 2016. "Talking with Nature: Southern Paiute Epistemology and the Double Hermeneutic with a Living Planet." In *Collaborative Heritage Management*, edited by Gemma Tully and Mal Ridges, 75–99. Piscataway, N.J.: Gorgia Press.

Stoffle, Richard W., Rebecca Toupal, and Nieves Zedeño. 2003. "Landscape, Nature, and Culture: A Diachronic Model of Human-Nature Adaptations." In *Nature Across Cultures*, edited by Helaine Selin, 97–114. Dordrecht: Kluwer.

Susskind, Lawrence, Sarah McKearnan, and Jennifer Thomas-Larmer, eds. 1999. *The Consensus Building Handbook: A Comprehensive Guide to Reaching Agreement*. Thousand Oaks, Calif.: SAGE.

Tabellini, Guido. 2010. "Culture and Institutions: Economic Development in the Regions of Europe." *Journal of the European Economic Association* 8 (4): 677–716.

Tanner, Adrian. 1979. *Bringing Home the Animals: Religious Ideology and Mode of Production of Mistassini Cree Hunters*. London: Hurst.

Tanner, Adrian. 2009. "From Fur to Fir: In Consideration of a Cree Family Territory System of Environmental Stewardship." In *Changing the Culture of Forestry in Canada: Building Effective Institutions for Aboriginal Engagement in Sustainable Forest Management*, edited by Marc G. Stevenson and David C. Natcher, 53–62. Occasional Publications Series 60. Edmonton: CCI Press.

Tapsell, Paul, and Christine Woods. 2010. "Social Entrepreneurship and Innovation: Self-Organization in an Indigenous Context." *Entrepreneurship and Regional Development* 22 (6): 535–56.

Tauli-Corpuz, Victoria. 2007. "How the UN Declaration on the Rights of Indigenous Peoples Got Adopted." In *UN Declaration on the Rights of Indigenous Peoples*, by Tebtebba Foundation, 1–34. https://www.tebtebba.org/index.php/resources -menu/publications-menu/books/109-un-declaration-of-the-rights-of-indig enous-peoples/file.

Tennant, Paul. 1990. *Aboriginal Peoples and Politics: The Indian Land Question in British Columbia, 1849–1989*. Vancouver: University of British Columbia Press.

Tikina, Anna V., John L. Innes, Ronald L. Trosper, and Bruce C. Larson. 2010. "Aboriginal Peoples and Forest Certification: A Review of the Canadian Situation." *Ecology and Society* 15 (3).

Toledo, Victor M., B. Ortiz-Espejel, P. Moguel, and M. D. J. Ordonez. 2003. "The Multiple Use of Tropical Forests by Indigenous Peoples in Mexico: A Case of Adaptive Management." *Conservation Ecology* 7 (3): 9.

Tooker, Elisabeth. 1988. "The United States Constitution and the Iroquois League." *Ethnohistory* 35 (4): 305–36.

Trewavas, Tony. 2016. "Plant Intelligence: An Overview." *Bioscience* 66 (7): 542–51.

Triandis, Harry C. 2018. *Individualism and Collectivism*. London: Routledge.

Triandis, Harry C., Robert Bontempo, Marcelo J. Villareal, Masaaki Asai, and Nydia Lucca. 1988. "Individualism and Collectivism: Cross-Cultural Perspectives on Self-Ingroup Relationships." *Journal of Personality and Social Psychology* 54 (2): 323–38.

Triandis, Harry C., and Michele J. Gelfand. 1998. "Converging Measurement of Horizontal and Vertical Individualism and Collectivism." *Journal of Personality and Social Psychology* 74 (1): 118–28.

Trigger, Bruce G. 1969. *The Huron: Farmers of the North*. New York: Holt, Rinehart and Winston.

Trigger, Bruce G. 1990. "Maintaining Economic Equality in Opposition to Complexity: An Iroquoian Case Study." In *The Evolution of Political Systems: Sociopolitics in Small-Scale Sedentary Societies*, edited by Steadman Upham, 119–45. Cambridge: Cambridge University Press.

Trosper, Ronald L. 1976. "Native American Boundary Maintenance: The Flathead Indian Reservation, Montana, 1880–1970." *Ethnicity* 3 (4): 256–74.

Trosper, Ronald L. 1995. "Traditional American Indian Economic Policy." *American Indian Culture and Research Journal* 19 (1): 65–95.

Trosper, Ronald L. 2002. "Northwest Coast Indigenous Institutions That Supported Resilience and Sustainability." *Ecological Economics* 41 (2): 329–44.

Trosper, Ronald L. 2005. "Emergence Unites Ecology and Society." *Ecology and Society* 10 (1): 14.

Trosper, Ronald L. 2009. *Resilience, Reciprocity and Ecological Economics: Sustainability on the Northwest Coast.* New York: Routledge.

Trosper, Ronald L. 2019a. "Caring, Not Competing: The Meaning and Relevance of Indigenous Economic Theory." *Native Science Report*, March. http://nativescience report.org/2019/03/caring-not-competing.

Trosper, Ronald L. 2019b. "Place of the Falling Waters: How the Salish and Kootenai Tribes Dealt with Settler Colonialism to Acquire and Name Sèliš Ksanka Qlispè Dam." In *Reclaiming Indigenous Governance: Reflections and Insights from Australia, Canada, New Zealand, and the United States,* edited by William Nikolakis, Stephen Cornell, and Harry W. Nelson, 193–227. Tucson: University of Arizona Press.

Trosper, Ronald L., Harry Nelson, George Hoberg, Peggy Smith, and William Nikolakis. 2008. "Institutional Determinants of Profitable Commercial Forestry Enterprises Among First Nations in Canada." *Canadian Journal of Forest Research* 38 (2): 226–38.

Tully, James. 1994. "Aboriginal Property and Western Theory: Recovering a Middle Ground." *Social Philosophy and Policy* 11 (2): 153–80.

Tupone, Juliano. 2001. "Neechi Foods Co-operative Limited." In *Aboriginal Co-operatives in Canada: Current Situation and Potential for Growth,* by Lou Hammond Ketilson and Ian MacPherson, 358–62. University of Saskatchewan: Centre for the Study of Co-operatives. https://www.ica.coop/sites/default/files/publi cation-files/ica-guidance-notes-en-310629900.pdf.

Turner, Nancy J. 2005. *The Earth's Blanket: Traditional Teachings for Sustainable Living.* Vancouver, B.C.: Douglas & McIntyre.

Uhlaner, Carole Jean. 1989. "'Relational Goods' and Participation: Incorporating Sociability into a Theory of Rational Action." *Public Choice* 62 (3): 253–85.

Umeek (E. Richard Atleo). 2004. *Tsawalk: A Nuu-chah-nulth Worldview.* Vancouver: University of British Columbia Press.

United Nations General Assembly. 2007. "United Nations Declaration on the Rights of Indigenous Peoples." https://www.un.org/development/desa/indigenouspeoples /declaration-on-the-rights-of-indigenous-peoples.html.

Vásquez-Fernández, Andrea M., and Cash Ahenakew pii tai poo taa. 2020. "Resurgence of Relationality: Reflections on Decolonizing and Indigenizing 'Sustainable Development.'" *Current Opinion in Environmental Sustainability* 43 (April): 65–70.

Vendryes, Thomas. 2014. "Peasants Against Private Property Rights: A Review of the Literature." *Journal of Economic Surveys* 28 (5): 971–95.

Verbos, Amy Klemm, and Maria Humphries. 2014. "A Native American Relational Ethic: An Indigenous Perspective on Teaching Human Responsibility." *Journal of Business Ethics* 123 (1): 1–9.

Verbos, Amy Klemm, and Maria Humphries. 2015. "Amplifying a Relational Ethic: A Contribution to PRME Praxis." *Business and Society Review* 120 (1): 23–56.

Villalba, Unai. 2013. "*Buen Vivir* vs Development: A Paradigm Shift in the Andes?" *Third World Quarterly* 34 (8): 1427–42.

Virtanen, Pirjo Kristiina, Laura Siragusa, and Hanna Guttorm. 2020. "Introduction: Toward More Inclusive Definitions of Sustainability." *Current Opinion in Environmental Sustainability* 43 (April): 77–82.

Walens, Stanley. 1981. *Feasting with Cannibals: An Essay on Kwakiutl Cosmology.* Princeton, N.J.: Princeton University Press.

Wallace, Anthony F. C. 1970. *The Death and Rebirth of the Seneca.* New York: Alfred A. Knopf.

White, Sarah C. 2017. "Relational Well-Being: Re-centering the Politics of Happiness, Policy and the Self." *Policy & Politics* 45 (2): 121–36.

Whitefeather Forest Initiative. n.d. "Enterprise." Accessed November 12, 2021. https://www.whitefeatherforest.ca/enterprise/.

Whiten, Andrew. 2021. "The Burgeoning Reach of Animal Culture." *Science* 372 (6537): eabe6514.

Whyte, Kyle P., Nicholas J. Reo, Deborah McGregor, M. A. Peggy Smith, James F. Jenkins, and Kathleen A. Rubio. 2017. "Seven Indigenous Principles for Successful Cooperation in Great Lakes Conservation Initiatives." In *Biodiversity, Conservation and Environmental Management in the Great Lakes Basin*, 182–94. New York: Routledge.

Widdowson, Frances. 2016. "'Indigenizing the University' and Political Science: Exploring the Implications for the Discipline." Paper presented at the Annual Meeting of the Canadian Political Science Association, University of Calgary, May 31–June 2. https://cpsa-acsp.ca/documents/conference/2016/Widdowson.pdf.

Wilkins, David E. 2017. *Dismembered: Native Disenrollment and the Battle for Human Rights.* Seattle: University of Washington Press.

Williams, Robert A., Jr. 1997. *Linking Arms Together: American Indian Treaty Visions of Law and Peace, 1600–1800.* New York: Oxford University Press.

Wilson, David Sloan, and Edward O. Wilson. 2007. "Rethinking the Theoretical Foundation of Sociobiology." *Quarterly Review of Biology* 82 (4): 327–48.

Wilson, Shawn. 2008. *Research Is Ceremony: Indigenous Research Methods.* Black Point, N.S.: Fernwood.

Winthrop, Robert H. 2014. "The Strange Case of Cultural Services: Limits of the Ecosystem Services Paradigm." *Ecological Economics* 108 (December): 208–14.

Wood, Paul M. 2000. *Biodiversity and Democracy: Rethinking Nature and Society.* Vancouver: University of British Columbia Press.

Wuttunee, Wanda A. 2004. *Living Rhythms: Lessons in Aboriginal Economic Resilience and Vision*. McGill-Queen's Native and Northern Series 37. Montreal: McGill-Queen's University Press.

Yachnin, Jennifer. 2021. "Antiquities Fight Could Land Utah Monuments in Supreme Court." E&E News, October 12. https://www.eenews.net/articles/antiquities-fight-could-land-utah-monuments-in-supreme-court/.

Zapatista Army of National Liberation. 1966. "Fourth Declaration of the Lacadon Jungle." https://schoolsforchiapas.org/wp-content/uploads/2014/03/Fourth-Declaration-of-the-Lacandona-Jungle-.pdf.

INDEX

Note: Page numbers followed by *t* indicates tables.

ABOUT THE AUTHOR

Ronald L. Trosper, professor at the University of Arizona, has published in American Indian studies, ecological economics, economics, policy studies, forestry, and anthropology. His PhD in economics is from Harvard University. He is also the author of *Resilience, Reciprocity and Ecological Economics: Northwest Coast Sustainability*. He is a member of the Confederated Salish and Kootenai Tribes of the Flathead Indian Reservation, Montana.